Veteran and
Edwardian Motor Cars

DAVID SCOTT-MONCRIEFF

B. T. BATSFORD LTD LONDON

Dedicated by
gracious permission to
His Late Majesty King Feisal
of Iraq

First Published 1955
Second Impression 1956
Paperback edition 1961

Revised Edition © David Scott-Moncrieff, 1961

PRINTED AND BOUND IN THE NETHERLANDS BY
THE HOOIBERG PRINTING COMPANY, EPE, FOR THE PUBLISHERS
B. T. BATSFORD LTD
4 FITZHARDINGE STREET, PORTMAN SQUARE, LONDON W. I

Preface

THIS has been a difficult book to write; the great problem was not what to put in, but what to leave out. So, if the reader finds that data about his favourite Vilbrequin-Manivelle (23·8 h.p., 1906) has been omitted, together with an account of the Bedworthy Magna speed trials (August, 1907), I trust he will forgive me. There wasn't anything like room for it all. There are other omissions of quite well-known cars, simply because the documentation does not exist in this country, and I thought that the reader would rather have authenticated facts about less important cars than flannel padding on the better known ones.

I have had great help from two Americans, John ("Demon") Leathers and Arthur Rippey, and also from many friends on the continent of Europe. In fact, without them this book could never have been written. I am deeply indebted to Walter O. MacIlvain of Connecticut for permission to raid his vast store of knowledge for much of the "Winton story"; also to the one and only "Austie" Clark without whom the book would never have gone to press in time. I am also most grateful to my friend Ken Purdy for his help with the proofs.

At home, among many others, Anthony Heal gave me invaluable data about Sunbeams, as did Raymond Playfoot about Singers. Arthur Jeddere-Fisher more than kindly took time off from packing his *batterie de cuisine* and cookery books, necessary for his appointment as Chief Justice in the Cannibal Islands, to write down for me little-known facts about Lagonda. The Victoria and Albert Museum spent an astronomical number of man-hours on helping me with research for the chapter on motoring clothing. I virtually established squatter's rights in the V.C.C. of G.B. library and in the files room of *The Autocar*; and that great historian, John Pollitt, was a tremendous help. Thanks are due also to certain manufacturers' Public Relations Officers, who supplied much-needed data.

It has been very difficult striking a balance between obscure and fascinating details presented for virtually the first time, and better known facts, without which the story would have had no backbone. Whether I have been successful is for the reader to judge.

Autumn, 1955   DAVID SCOTT-MONCRIEFF

Acknowledgment

THE Author and the Publishers are indebted to the following for permission to reproduce the Plates, and the drawings which appear on the pages listed after their names:

The Editor of *The Autocar*, pages 36, 92 and 94; Mr. James Barron, Plates 17 and 23; Mr. W. J. Brunell, Plate 36; the Daimler Co. Ltd., Plate 54; Daimler-Benz A.G., Plates 12 and 40; pages 26, 49, 66 and 184; F.I.A.T. (England) Ltd., Plate 20; Mr. C. W. P. Hampton, Plate 37; Mr. Peter Helck and Brown Brothers, New York, for Plate 31; Long Island Automotive Museum, Southampton, New York, Plate 30; Monde et Caméra, Paris, Plates 27, 41 and 47; Mr. George A. Oliver, pages 116, 194 and 208; Radio Times Hulton Picture Library, Plates 1–7, 10, 13–15, 18, 19, 21, 22, 24–26, 28, 29, 32–35, 38, 39, 42, 43, 46, 48–53, 55 and 56; Mr. Arthur G. Rippey, Denver, Colorado, Plate 45; Mr. Walter Risley, Park Ridge, Illinois, page 191; Rolls-Royce Ltd., Plate 11; Rootes Motors Ltd., Plate 16; the Rover Co. Ltd., pages 81, 124 and 141; the Smithsonian Institution, Washington, Plate 44; the Standard Motor Co. Ltd., Plate 8; Vauxhall Motors Ltd., Plate 9; pages 155 and 156.

Contents

List of Illustrations

THE PLATES

Between pages 48 and 49

DRAWINGS IN THE TEXT

The photograph on the cover of this book, showing Mr. P. C. Waring's 1904 Renault Park Phaeton, was taken by Mr. J. B. Mason of Fact Photography

1

Steam Ancestors

WE are taught that Cugnot's steam tractor (1769) was the first to move under its own power. There is, however, a strong possibility that a Jesuit priest, Father Verbeest, accredited to the Court of Chien Lung, Emperor of China, constructed one nearly a century earlier. One of the methods by which the Jesuits attempted to, and very nearly succeeded in, converting the Emperor was by the production of ingenious mechanical contrivances. Many of these can, or could until very recently, be seen in the old Winter Palace at Pekin. But, alas, this steam car is not among them. I have been promised, however, on my next visit to Rome, an introduction to the Vatican librarian, so I may be able to find more concrete details.

Cugnot's steam tractor worked, even with its inefficient power plant, for one reason: it had quite a sensible power/weight ratio, a ratio which was to be on the wane for the best part of a century. The steering and weight distribution were both unsatisfactory, and Cugnot built a second tricycle in 1770. This did not steer much better, for obvious reasons, as we can see, for this historic machine has been preserved. Steam was raised in a copper fire-tube boiler, with two fire tubes, with the boiler descending as a kind of jacket round the furnace. Low-pressure steam thus generated was admitted to two single-acting cylinders. The piston rod crossheads were attached to oscillating arms that pushed round a pawl, integral with the one fifty-inch driving wheel, a quarter of a revolution to each stroke of the piston.

In England James Watt planned, in conjunction with Doctor Robinson, a steam road vehicle, but the firm of Boulton and Watt were far too busy building pumping engines for mines for the project to get beyond the drawing-board. Sadler in Oxford was experimenting simultaneously with Cugnot, but when Boulton and Watt advised him that he would be infringing their patents, he let the matter drop. For two decades after Cugnot's steam tricycle had actually worked, little was done in England except for models made by Murdoch, Watt and Symington, which appear to have run, especially Murdoch's. We all know the story of how, as early as 1784, his model steam carriage, going well after dark, frightened the vicar of Redruth out of his wits. But to my mind this miniature veh-

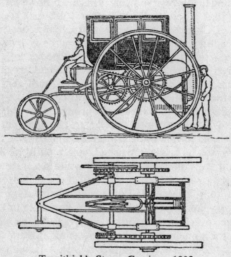

Trevithick's Steam Carriage, 1802

icle is, apart from its mirth-provoking qualities, of extreme historical importance. By means of a connecting rod from a rocking beam to a cranked axle between the wheels, it was the first wheeled vehicle to be power-driven by reciprocating action. And besides this, for Murdoch was an employee of Boulton and Watt, it was so successful that it caused the jealous Watt to keep Murdoch so hard at work on other engines that the development of motoring was held up in Great Britain for over a dozen years.

Meanwhile, in the recently revolted colony of America, one Oliver Evans obtained licences to operate steam road wagons in Pennsylvania in 1787. What is more, this resourceful man is reputed to have made a steam-driven D.U.K.W.! If this catches the eye of any American reader who can give me more details, or still better, drawings, I shall be deeply grateful.

Unfortunately, we have not space to cover the experiments that took place in a number of countries between 1770 and 1820, but mention must be made of Trevithick's steam car in

David Gordon's Steam Carriage, 1824

1802. It had an excellent power/weight ratio, a horizontal boiler, a fine tall stack to give the furnace draught, and was driven by a crank operating on to the road wheels through a train of interchangeable gears, thus anticipating by nearly a century Monsieur (*"c'est brutal mais ça marche"*) Levassor. Trevithick drove his steam car to London and used it for some time. Most surprisingly, no one, at least no one with money, was interested. Trevithick, therefore, seeing no profit, scrapped his car, sold the engine to drive a mill, and turned his attention to trams and railways.

1822 was the *annus mirabilis,* steam cars and coaches coming fairly tumbling out, to rattle merrily along the fine hard roads constructed by Telford and Macadam. Among the earliest were the carriage of Julius Griffiths, which condensed its exhaust steam through air-cooled tubes, and those of Brunton, Henry Peto, Nasmyth, Burton and Mill, Summers and Ogle

13

and others. But the two earliest to settle down into regular service were those of James and Goldsworthy Gurney. There was also a character called Gordon who actually built a huge and cumbrous coach in 1824, with mechanical feet to walk along! These were most ingeniously operated to imitate the human act of walking by two three-throw cranks, one set of cranks having a lesser throw than the other. To be fair to Gordon, Gurney's first carriage also had walking feet, retractable like a modern undercarriage, to help start it under load. This particular motor-car had an ignominious end: it was driven to Wales and ended its days converted into a tram! Gurney's water-tube boilers were fired with a mixture of coke and charcoal (foreshadowing those nightmare producer-gas plants from which we suffered during the late war), and a 'separator' made an attempt to supply dry steam to the cylinders.

Soon after 1832 there were ten or more companies operating steam coaches on regular routes, some running as far afield as Holyhead. By this time the steam car proper was in a temporary decline and the industry was concentrating on public passenger-carrying vehicles. In 1833 both Hancock, and Macerone and Squire came out with practical working hackney coaches, and Sir Charles Dance was running a regular Gloucester–Chelten-ham service with a short-wheelbase Burney "drag" pulling a four-wheeled, long-wheelbase omnibus just like a modern artic-ulated vehicle. Dr. Church built a monstrous Rococo coach which from its pictures does not look as if it would work, but apparently it did. Patents, too, were being filed thick and fast in America, but I can find no records of any steamers being actually built and run at this time, but that does not preclude their existence.

The Macerone and Squire was a satisfactory performer, put-ting up *average* speeds of fifteen or sixteen miles an hour and rattling over the cobbles at well over twenty, nine up as well as driver and fireman. Contemporary records call it "this simple and efficient machine", which, I think, just about des-cribes it. It had a vertical firetube boiler, and was probably the first vehicle ever to run with a steam pressure as high as 150 lb. per square inch. Unfortunately Macerone was not as good a

business man as he was an engineer, and he was ruined by un-
scrupulous associates.

Although operating only in London, Hancock's ten steam
motorbuses were not only practical, but incorporated many new
ideas. Most of the others had the engines, and often the boilers,
mounted rigid with the axle. Not so Hancock's: they were
mounted above the springs and the movement was taken up
by a chain drive, and thus the unsprung weight was lessened
by the best part of a ton! It must also be remembered that
at that time Stephenson had not yet revolutionised the steam
engine by directing a blast of exhaust steam up the chimney,
thus creating a forced draught. Hancock got his forced draught
from a rotary fan driven off the engine. But, personally,
I think his neatest gadget was his firebars. These were cast
with a rack on the under side. When the set of firebars in use
got clinkered up, a pinion worked by a handle caused the rack
to traverse and fresh bars were brought into place. The
clinkered bars moved into the open air, cooled down, and so
the clinker was easily knocked off and the bars were ready
in their turn to be slid back under the furnace. The chain grate
was thus anticipated by over half a century. The boiler was a
most unusual arrangement of square water and steam boxes
interconnected, with the flames playing on five sides. This
curious design certainly provided a very large area of heating
surface and seems to have worked very well. Even Hancock's
wheels were an improvement on the orthodox coach wheel,
having metal hubs which were very similar to the field-gun
wheels used in the 1914-18 war. And not content with this,
Hancock had his furnace magazine-fed! The vertical two-cyl-
clinkered bars moved into the open air, cooled down, and so
that it could be kept clean, and for, I believe, the first time in
the history of the steam carriage a clutch was fitted, so that the
engine could be run, with the carriage remaining stationary, to
pump water or blow up the furnace with the fan. About this
time a Mr. Roberts of Manchester patented the differential
gear, much as we know it today, to relieve the strain on driving
wheels when cornering. But the Marquis de Chasseloup Laubat
claims its invention in France half a dozen years earlier.

15

Motoring before 1840 was thus making good progress: differential gears, dry steam, condensers, and in France an axle with each wheel on a separate pivot instead of a swivelling undercarriage. We can safely say that the steam car was in a state of development which it took the petrol car from about 1884 to 1901 to catch up.

1840 was about the peak period of the steam coach. Let us examine the reasons why our steam coaches, over half a century ahead of any other country and after getting away to such a flying start, declined and were abandoned. First of all, as far as the gentry went (and they held the bulk of the country's money), the liberal free-thinking era of the second half of the eightenth century was over, and a reactionary mood had succeeded it. So those who could have had private steam carriages built for them did not, and that is why the steam car as opposed to steam coach faded out.

But not only were the gentry opposed or apathetic to road locomotion; the workers were bitterly against any form of machinery, for they believed that the industrial revolution would lead to mass unemployment. With the construction of fine new roads, tolls -- as was perfectly reasonable -- were charged for their use to offset heavy initial cost. Most unfairly, however, they discriminated grossly against steam coaches. The classic example of this is the Liverpool-Prescot road, where a toll of £2 8s. was levied on a steam coach as against 4s. on a fully loaded coach and four!

These discriminating levies, beginning as early as the 1820s, knocked nail after nail into the coffin of the steam carriage. But the steamers carried on, getting technically better and better till the infamous Road Locomotives Act, better known as the Red Flag Act, drove them off the roads.

Let us a take a look at some of these later steam coaches. From 1840 onwards few steam coaches or carriages were built. Hancock's efficient service ran in London up to about 1846, when it ceased to pay, and he himself had some years previously gone in for railway work. Hill and Anderson and a few others ran country services, but they too petered out in the 'forties. The last to operate was one of the latest comers, the Scott-

Russell carriages. These were much more like steam carriages than the great cumbrous coaches, and of a most efficient design with very little unsprung weight. They were run on services both in London and Scotland. I believe they ceased to pay their way in the south long before they did in Scotland. But the explosion of a boiler in Glasgow with considerable injury and loss of life administered the *coup-de-grâce*, and they, the last public-service road vehicles, were out of business by 1857.

After the last steam coach had ceased to carry paying passengers, history turns one more of its improbable cartwheels. People began to build steam cars again! The more ridiculous the law that is passed, the greater the urge to break it, and the 'sixties saw a whole pride or covey of steam cars clandestinely taking the road in defiance of the Red Flag Act. In 1861 both Rickett and Garrett produced heavy steam tricycles. These more or less light reproductions of the contemporary railway engines, tiller-steered by one wheel for'ard and with the fireman on a platform hung out aft. Here the resemblance ends, for while Rickett's carried seven or eight passengers and a fireman, the Garrett was a sporting two-seater with the fireman on the platform. In the following year Yarrow and Hilditch put one or more on the road, and in 1868 the author of that rare and valuable book, *Notes on Motor Carriages* (1896), John Henry Knight, began to run one himself. Other makers in this period included Tangye and J. W. Boulton. Knight tells us that he drove his car for several hundred miles. One of his worst troubles seems to have been with the steering, and he had two accidents, one due to the car running away down a hill, the other caused by a pin working loose in the steering.

The 1870s brought out yet more makers, Catley and Ayres, J. L. Todd, Charles Randolph, Inshaw and Blackburn: this last-named making probably the greatest single advance in the history of the steam car. Besides this, in 1873 Loftus Perkins exhibited at the International Exhibition at South Kensington a "steam drag" that, apart from its use of a compound engine (1¾ in. × 3¼ in. × 4½ in.), and steam pressure as high as 450 lb. per square inch, had nothing to commend it. The engine and boiler were mounted unsprung on the single front wheel and the whole cumbrous contrivance had not the same performance as Gurney's "steam drags" of nearly half a century earlier. In 1874 a Mr. Mackenzie built a steam brougham (two cylinders, $3\frac{3}{4}$ in. $\times$ $4\frac{1}{2}$ in.) with a drop-tube boiler working at 135 lb. per square inch pressure. It was chain-driven, with a two-speed gear box, and ran well. Meanwhile in America, we are told, Lee and Larned built a self-propelled steam fire engine in 1863. John A. Reid built a steam wagon in the same year and operated it on the prairies. In 1867 Frank Curtis of Newburyport, Massachusetts, built and ran a steam buggy. In France too things were stirring. In 1873 the firm of Léon Bollée went in for the manufacture of steam carriages for private use and soon they had on the road a steam victoria capable of twenty-five miles an hour, chain-driven and with each of the two front wheels having its pivot set slightly at an angle, giving the wheels a "dish".

Charles Randolph's steam carriage of 1872 is interesting because of its external appearance. Were it not for its short funnel it would pass for an electric brougham of forty years later. But the man who, to my mind, makes history is Mr. Blackburn. Many text-books claim that Serpollet invented the flash boiler or at least was the first to adapt it to motoring. This is quite untrue. Monsieur Serpollet's first steam tricycle, coal-fired, was not on the road till 1887, and ten years earlier, 1877, a steam dogcart *with flash boiler* had not only been patented but was actually built and running. This was ten years ahead of the others, but Blackburn's liquid fuel burning under forced draught over a surface carburettor was a quarter of a century ahead. But somehow he fell foul of the law and was prohibited from using his car. About the same time a similar fate befell Sir Thomas Parkyns, whose steam tricycle had been built for him by Bateman of Greenwich.

1880 saw the firm of Bollée at Le Mans building steam coaches and omnibuses. There was nothing particularly novel about these, but they were a sound and practical job. On the caléche a two-cylinder engine was mounted under a "bonnet" right for'ard outside the wheelbase, which was only 7 ft. 4 in.

(4½ in. less than an Austin A.40). Power was transmitted back by a propeller shaft to a countershaft with differential, and the final drive was by chain. The boiler was a vertical water-tube "field" type, about 30 in. in diameter, hung out aft of the back axle, with a sort of light pavilion for the stoker. There does not appear to have been any attempt at condensation, with the result that although we get the very reasonable coal-consumption figure of 3·6 lb. per mile at 18 m.p.h., the water consumption was a minimum of sixty gallons an hour.

The 'eighties of the last century saw the beginning of the renaissance of road travel. No other countries were handicapped by the ridiculous Red Flag Act. In 1884 Gottlieb Daimler produced the internal combustion engine, and the Marquis de Dion (who only died a few years ago) financed M. Bouton in a manufactory for steam wagonettes. We are not concerned in this chapter with the birth-pangs of the petrol-driven car except to say that its rapid growth helped on the demand for steam cars. Third in the field after Bollée and de Dion was Serpollet in 1887. M. Serpollet may really be called the Bugatti of his day, and his passion for perfection, even if it meant complex and extremely delicate machinery, contrasts vividly with the rugged blacksmith's work of Bollée and de Dion, and the ceaseless quest for the foolproof by the Americans who came into the field a dozen years later. Serpollet's first tricycles were not dissimilar to the early motor tricycles in appearance; except for the firebox and boiler hung out behind the rear axle. Whether in imitation of the internal combustion pioneers or whether on his own is not certain, but Serpollet, for the first time for half a century, produced a steam vehicle with a reasonable power/weight ratio. The water tank and, after his second tricycle, the fuel magazine were under the seat. The two-cylinder engine was mounted horizontally under the driver's feet, cranked directly on to a shaft with differential, which in turn drove the back wheels by chain. Steering was by handlebars extended from the forks of the front wheel like a present-day push-bike. There is a beautiful economy about M. Serpollet's designing.

But, of course, the thing that put Serpollet head and shoulders above all others was his use of the "flash" boiler. His first one was made of lap-welded iron pipe slightly flattened to give an internal width of about ⅛ in. Water was injected at one end of this coil over a small coke furnace, and emerged at the other as dry steam with a pressure of 300 lb. per square inch. As even the earliest model withstood test up to 1500 lb. per square inch, the risk of a burst boiler was negligible. His later models used copper tube bound with piano wire and these were tested up to even higher pressures. It was efficient, too, yielding 1 brake horse power to 108 square inches of grate surface. The feed pump was given a few strokes before starting and there-after was engine-driven. There was no steam valve between engine and boiler, but there was a variable by-pass between the injector pump and the boiler. This drew off water and returned it to the reservoir, thus regulating the volume of water pumped into the boiler. Possibly the most important point about this type of boiler is that, with reasonably clean water, the velocity through the spiral "flash" tube is so great that internal incrustation is nil. The earliest Serpollet carried enough coke for 35 miles and enough water for 12.

In the nineties Bollée, de Dion and Serpollet were all building steamers. Scotte, in France, and Weidknecht, in Germany, were each building steam wagonettes and omnibuses. In England the long-forgotten firm of Clarkson and Capel of Richmond were building the most attractive little steam victoria, that seems, on paper anyhow, to have been technically far in advance of its contemporaries. I doubt whether there is one of these in existence, which is the greatest pity, for it had many attractive features well ahead of its day. In America too, White, Stanley, and many other firms were experimenting but were not yet in production. In France, even in the early nineties, steam vans, some built in England, were in regular postal service, giving excellent results.

The first-ever motoring event was organised by the newspaper, *Le Petit Journal*, in 1894. The Marquis de Dion got second prize, driving one of his own steamers, Serpollet was third, and a Scotte wagonette sixth. In 1895 a Bollée steam coach was last in the Paris-Bordeaux and back race, taking 90 hours against the winner's 49! One cannot help wondering how many of those 90 hours were spent taking water! In this country the "Red Flag" proviso had been rescinded by the "Highways and Locomotives (Amendment)" Act of 1878. This, in turn, was followed by the "Locomotives on Highways" Act of November 1896, giving motor vehicles liberty up to twelve miles an hour. So, in spite of restrictive laws, motoring went on continually in this country from the turn of the eighteenth century to 1896, the date most people think it started.

Randolph's Steam Carriage, 1872

2

Some Petrol Pioneers

INTERNAL combustion engines were first built in seventeenth century. But the motive power was gunpowder, and metallurgy had not advanced very far. It is believed that although these stationary engines actually worked, anyhow for a number of revolutions, there was soon a marked shortage of inventors of the devices.

It was not until coal gas was substituted for gunpowder as an explosive fuel, in the middle of the nineteenth century, that we get any real progress.

These gas engines were the direct forebears of the early motor-car, for when Gottlieb Daimler was building gas engines he already had the horseless carriage in mind. And indeed if he had not done so well with small, portable stationary petrol engines, he would not have been able to develop his prototype cars.

The pioneer of gas engines in France, Etienne Lenoir, also experimented with liquid fuels which were vaporised, fed into the working cylinder and exploded by an electric spark. He is reputed to have built a horseless carriage as early as May 1862, which ran several times over the six-mile journey between Paris and Joinville-le-Pont. If this is so, he anticipated Siegfried Markus by some years. But, in any case, it would be difficult to establish a claim to the first petrol driven car, as there does not seem to be any record of the fuel used. Petrol was originally a trade name for what had been known as benzine; it was registered by a firm of importers, Carless, Capel and Leonard in the early years of the twentieth century.[1] Benzine, by the way, is nothing to do with Karl Benz. It was called after a professor of chemistry at the Berlin University, who first

[1] The first known use of the word "petrol," in its present meaning, is to be found in a letter written by Eugen Langen in September 1876.

isolated it in Germany. It had been isolated already a few years earlier in England, during the first few decades of the nineteenth century. It had, in fact, been isolated and determined for almost half a century before it was put to any practical use as a motive power.

To return to Lenoir. Even if it is doubtful what fuel was used in this car, it seems quite certain that in the eighteen-sixties he built a few four-stroke, electrically ignited petrol engines for boats. He was involved in the famous patent case when Otto sued a number of French engine builders for infringement of his so-called "Otto-cycle" or "four-stroke" patents. The Frenchmen claimed that Otto's patent had been anticipated by that of Alphonse Beau de Rochos of 1862 and won their case.

Quite early on, Daimler went to Paris to look at Lenoir's work. The late Professor Siebertz, a personal friend of Daimler's, told me that the Swabian engineer was not at all impressed with what he saw, and decided to work along his own lines.

However, one thing is quite certain, and it is that Etienne Lenoir was the father of the internal combustion engine in France, even if Panhard-Levassor and Peugeot both built under the German Daimler patents. Lenoir died, in comparative poverty, about the same time as Gottlieb Daimler, in 1900.

The next claimant is Siegfried Markus, a brilliant but somewhat dilettante Jewish scientist and inventor, working in Vienna in the 1860s and 'seventies. He built four cars.[1] And what strengthens his claim enormously is the fact that one of the Markus cars, built considerably before both Daimler and Benz, not only exists in the Vienna Museum but can still be driven under its own power.

The general consensus of opinion is, however, that Markus forfeits his claim, for like Hiram Maxim and his steam aeroplane, as soon as he had satisfied himself that it worked, he immediately lost all interest in it. Markus's patents, it will be remembered, were produced by Henry Ford in rebuttal of

[1] The first one was broken up and forgotten; one is in the Vienna Museum, and the other two are rumoured to have gone to America and Holland.

23

Selden's claim that he patented the motor-car *totus porcus*, and that all manufacturers must pay him a licence fee. St John Nixon, a fine German scholar, has done a great deal of research on all the contemporary documents about Siegfried Markus.

About the same time as Markus, Ravel, a Frenchman, also has something of a claim to have made a car go on benzine, but although he was building steam cars for upwards of forty years till his death in 1908, they were not propelled by internal combustion engines. He was certainly the pioneer of steam cars with benzine-fired boilers.

The first vehicle in England to be propelled by actual combustion was Edward Butler's tricycle, of which the drawings were exhibited at the Stanley Cycle Show of 1884, and at the Inventions Exhibition in 1885.

Butler had obviously gone to great lengths to avoid infringing the four-cycle patents and produced a very odd double-acting engine with rotary valves and magneto ignition. Apparently both the latter had to be abandoned before it worked properly. It took the form of a tricycle with one wheel aft. The double-acting cylinders were water-cooled. The carburettor was well ahead of its day, for not only was the fuel sprayed through a jet, but the air was filtered before admission.

It is said that Butler's backers withdrew before his tricycle had a fair trial on the road, and, handicapped financially, he was unable to finish building his improved version till 1889. Working with him was Charles T. Crowden, who in 1896 went as works manager to Lawson's Great Horseless Carriage Company and, about the turn of the century, set up on his own, building the Crowden car at Leamington. He does not seem to have benefited from Butler's forward thinking about carburation, for the 10 h.p. Crowden of 1902 had a surface carburettor.

Butler never really got into production, but continued to experiment with rotary valves, which he fitted to Bollées, built by Humber under licence.

In 1892, Messrs. Roots and Venables built proprietary

motor engines. There are conflicting descriptions of these, both as a crude two-stroke and as a four-stroke. One was exhibited attached to a tricycle made by the firm of Coventry Machinists. At that time the only buyers of this engine, which weighed 90 lb. and turned at 600 r.p.m., were French manufactures who bought one each to take home and see if anything could be learned from them. In 1895 Roots and Venables built a two-seater tricar. A firm called Bremer at Walthamstow built and, it is believed, marketed a car in 1894, but I am unable to obtain any details.

Contemporary with these came what is generally accepted as the first British-built motor-car. John Henry Knight of Farnham had been building steam-driven road vehicles, and he had also done a great deal of pioneer work on stationary oil engines. By early 1895 he married the two, and produced a very practical little car, weighing 1075 lb. and developing just under 1 h.p. at 500 r.p.m.. It was water-cooled, and belt-driven through a countershaft. It would run up to 8 or 9 m.p.h., with a cruising speed of 7½ m.p.h. At the Crystal Palace Show of 1896, it was exhibited, and gave demonstration runs alongside de Dion, Panhard, Peugeot and the others, being billed as the only British-built car propelled by internal combustion.

Although they do not strictly come under the heading of petrol pioneers, I think mention must be made of Walter Bersey and Ratcliffe Ward. The latter was operating an electric single-decker bus, powered by accumulators, as early as 1888. Bersey, who was barely twenty years old at the time, designed Ward's second electric bus which, in 1890, was licensed to ply for hire between Charing Cross and Victoria. In 1893 he designed a Post Office van and in 1894 he built an electric four-seater motor car, which had him in constant trouble with the police for exceeding 3 m.p.h., for not having a man walking in front, for having only one driver and all the usual nonsense. They do not seem to have minded about the buses. Bersey was the moving spirit behind the electric taxicabs and those elegant broughams which were so much a feature of Edwardian life.

As we have seen, several people built motor-cars that ran

prior to Daimler or Benz, but as these two were the first to put the automobile on a practical footing and go into production, it is generally held that they are the true originators.

It is remarkable that they worked in towns no great distance from each other yet neither of them knew that the other was engaged in work of a similar nature.

Benz "Mylord-Coupé", 1901

The life of Karl Benz runs on a curious parallel with that of George Stephenson. While Daimler was born of comfortable small town bourgeoisie, the parents of Karl Benz were very poor and humble. Like Stephenson, Benz came up the hard way, meeting many reverses. The similarity does not end here, for the fathers of both men met their deaths, directly and indirectly, through steam-engine accidents when the boys were very young.

The mother of Karl Benz went out to work (she was a superb cook) to pay her son's way through school and university. At the latter he came under the influence of one of the lecturers, Professor Redtenbacher, an early experimentalist with the internal combustion engine.

After working for Johan Schweizer and then Benckiser brothers, the bridge-builders, Karl Benz got married and in 1872 had set up, in a very small way, on his own, building two-stroke gas engines, in Mannheim. When the first engine was complete and running, Benz was so broke that he and Frau Benz had not the price of a meal. However, backers were found, and the gas-engine business went well. These were supplemented by a similar stationary engine running on petrol. Benz had long wished to employ this to drive a carriage, but the backers said that he must keep to stationary engines. So it was not till 1885 that Benz actually had a car running. But it was Frau Benz who did the first long run ever accomplished by car.

The first Benz cars developed about ¾ h.p. at 250-300 r.p.m., were water-cooled, had surface carburettors and coil ignition and were chain-driven with two-speed belts on a countershaft. The cars themselves were designed as such, not like Daimler's earliest efforts, which were nothing more than an engine put into a normal horse carriage with the shafts removed. The early Benz cars also had a differential gear. The two or three ever built had three wheels, but after that the cars always had four.

Having built his motor-car, belt-driven with one horizontal cylinder under the seat, Benz firmly refused to make any radical changes. An immense number were sold, and in France Emile Roger assembled them under the name Roger-Benz. This was all very well for the first fifteen years or so, but about 1901 the buying public began to turn away from the reliable but paralysingly slow Benz cars, which even then had a remarkably antiquated appearance.

In 1899 the firm had been turned into a limited company, and in 1903 they engaged a French designer and racing driver, Marius Barbaroux, to design an up-to-date car. This was called the Benz-Parsifal. These cars were not a success and Barbaroux, who found Benz very difficult to get on with, did not stay long. But he laid the foundations of the forward-engined Benz cars. The original type of Benz was still being made as late as 1908, and Karl Benz was still using one for several years after that.

Gottlieb Daimler was a Swabian. The Swabians are the Aberdonians of Germany: thrifty, hard-working, and not easily parted from their money, they are the butt of a thousand and one jokes. Keen on mechanics from a very early age, the boy was apprenticed to Reythel, a gunsmith. The pair of pistols which he made as his "masterpiece" exist and are beautiful work. In 1853 he went to work for the Werkzeug Maschinenfabrik near Strasbourg. Later he worked for Armstrong-Whitworth in England, also in Belgium and France, and then at Renblingen, where he met Wilhelm Maybach, his lifelong friend and collaborator.

In 1872 Daimler and Maybach went to build gas engines for Otto and Langen at Deutz. The earliest of these engines ignited its charge not electrically but by opening, momentarily, a slide valve to expose it to the flame. It can well be seen that this method was hardly conducive to "high revs".

Daimler and Otto did not get on well and the firm treated him rather shabbily, so, after ten years work for Otto and Langen, Daimler and the faithful Maybach withdrew. They set up on their own at 13, Taubeheimstrasse in Cannstatt.

Here they built small, relatively fast-turning (up to 900 r.p.m.) stationary engines, running on petrol and ignited by Daimler and Maybach's patent 'hot tube'. In 1885 they built a motorcycle. This was a crude device, but it ran. No further development was carried out on motor-cycles, and Daimler turned his attention to motor-boats. It was not motor-cars that brought commercial success to Daimler, but small stationary engines. These "portable power packs" were sold for a variety of purposes, driving every kind of machinery from printing presses to fire pumps, anywhere that gas or water power was not available. The German Admiralty gave him an order for boat engines.

Motor-cars were not exactly an afterthought; for twenty years or more he had dreamed of self-propelled traction. But this as yet undeveloped side of the business had to take second place to the profitable stationary and marine engines for which there was so much demand. Daimler did not, like Benz, envisage a complete motor-car, but a motorising attachment which could be fitted to a normal horse carriage. Only when he saw how unsatisfactory this was did he turn his attention to designing the whole thing. This motorised carriage was completed and running in 1886. During the next couple of years he built a motor-trolley running on rails, and in conjunction with a Leipzig bookseller called Wölffert, a motorised, but not very dirigible airship. When the time came for trying this, it was found that Wölffert was too big and heavy for the airship to lift, so a lightweight and courageous spectator, whose name unfortunately has not been preserved, entirely impromptu was the pilot for the first flight.

In 1886 Daimler appointed an old friend, Sarazin, a Belgian living in Paris, to handle the Daimler patents. He died and his widow, like most Frenchwomen, was extremely capable; she so impressed Gottlieb Daimler that he allowed her to carry on in her late husband's place. Quite soon she married Emile Levassor, who began research work for fitting Daimler engines into a motor-car chassis. Madame Sarazin's Daimler patent rights counted under French Law as part of her dowry, and became her husband's property.

So, parallel with Daimler's early cars of 1890–95, Panhard Levassor were developing Daimler-engined vehicles, as were Peugeot. Gottlieb Daimler had worn himself out with hard work. He suffered from a weak heart, which was the reason why he never drove himself, and during the period of 1895 to 1900 he was rather a sick man. We shall never know how much of the development of the Cannstatt Daimlers of that period was due to him and how much to Maybach, for they virtually pooled their ideas. It is sad to record that he died in 1900 and did not see the full blossoming of his many years of gruelling pioneer work in the Mercedes of the following year.

I think that perhaps F. W. Lanchester just scrapes into this chapter, as he was, as far as England goes, a pioneer. He built an experimental 5 h.p. air-cooled car of most original design in 1895. Like both Daimler and Benz, he had done earlier work on gas engines.

3

Victorian Prelude, 1895-1900

THERE are a number of definitions of what is rather loosely termed the "Edwardian" period of motoring. Strictly speaking, it should, I suppose, open in 1901 and close with a snap in 1910. But, by general consent, the term has been extended to cover motor-cars built up to the end of the year in 1916. Then we have also the "Veteran" period, impinging up to 1904. For the purposes of this book I propose to ignore this distinction and treat it as a consecutive story starting in 1901. But what happened in the six years before this is so inextricably bound up with our story that appreciable space must be devoted to the Victorian era.

Prior to 1896 there had been in England no less than four "Locomotive" Acts: one of 1861, another of 1865, another in 1878, and a portion of the Local Government Act of 1888. "Locomotive" was held to mean, in law, any vehicle propelled by any power except animal. Let us suppose for a moment that a motorist before the Act of 1896 wished to comply strictly with the law. These are the conditions he must observe:

(1) At least three men shall be employed to drive such a locomotive. Also a man must walk in front – the earlier Acts decreed that he should carry a red flag.
(2) Observe a 3-m.p.h. speed limit.
(3) Pay £10 licence fee for each county in which he drove.
(4) Refrain from crossing bridges unless they bore a notice permitting it.

There were further regulations on these lines, some of which had been swept away by the 1878 Act, while the 1896 Act was much more reasonable and raised the speed limit from 4 m.p.h. to 12 m.p.h.

In 1895, as a natural result of the earlier "Locomotive"

30

Acts, there was no British motor industry at all. The French and Germans were already turning out cars and motor-cycles in quite respectable numbers. In America the Duryea Brothers and Haynes-Apperson had set up as manufacturers, but were not yet in production.

In England a few wealthy enthusiasts, like Sir David Salomons and the Honourable Evelyn Ellis, had imported European cars. A few firms also, notably F. R. Simms in London and L'Hollier Gascoigne in Birmingham, were beginning to import for resale. And there was Harry John Lawson. A lot of very hard things have been said, probably with justification, about H. J. Lawson, but there is no doubt that he was one of the earliest pioneers of the British motor industry.

He was probably no less scrupulous than any of the other remarkable characters who used other people's money to amass vast fortunes for themselves in the City of London at the turn of the nineteenth century. On the credit side, those who worked for him said that he was both fair and generous. He was certainly not a greedy man who loved money for its own sake.

Lawson was already a rich man; he had launched a number of extremely successful bicycle and tyre companies, Rudge among them, by the time the Act of 1896 was envisaged. He was nothing if not a man of vision who saw, very clearly, the incalculably vast future of horseless carriages. He proposed no less than a complete monopoly of motor manufacturing in England!

This is how he went about it. In 1895 he registered and formed the British Motor Syndicate (capital £150,000) with Charles McRobie Turrell, who subsequently went into business building cars on his own, as secretary. He then bought up the Daimler patent rights for England from F. R. Simms, formed the Daimler Motor Company (capital £100,000) and took the option on an enormous disused cotton mill in Coventry.

It says a lot, I think, for Lawson, that he got capital for all these schemes when, by law, a motor-car still had to have three drivers and a man walking in front!

The British Motor Syndicate then proceeded to buy up the British rights of every existing patent. They bought up all the

31

past, present and future patents of Count de Dion – for £20,000. They bought up the patents of Bollée, father and son, at Le Mans. Then they made a bad mistake. Lawson, largely influenced by his co-director Rucker, paid E. J. Pennington, a very plausible gentleman of Chicago, £100,000 for his patents relating to motor-cars, and such reputable engineering firms as Humber, Coulthard, Robey of Lincoln and Fowler of Leeds all took out licences from the British Motor Syndicate to build cars under Pennington patents.

The British Motor Syndicate, whose business was primarily buying motor-car patents and leasing them out, paid a dividend of 30 per cent and their pound shares stood at forty shillings. The following year they brought an action against the Hon. C. S. Rolls who did not dispute it and paid them a royalty of £15 to use his Peugeot car, which infringed their patents.

Still before the 1896 Act, Lawson floated another company: the Great Horseless Carriage Company, capital £750,000! However, while strong financially, these vast companies were weak in engineering knowledge and they did not succeed in producing motor-cars in any quantity, and such few as they did build ran very badly and broke down constantly! If they had kept to the relatively well-tried designs they had bought from France and Germany, they would have done better, but as it was the engineers tried to improve and modify them with disastrous results.

So much for the beginning of the industry. Now for some other aspects. In 1895 Sir David Salomons organised a Motor Car Show on the Agricultural Show ground at Tunbridge Wells. There cannot have been more than half a dozen cars in England at the time. Two of these and a Daimler-engined fire engine arrived, and French manufacturers sent over two more vehicles to swell the exhibits to nearly half a dozen.

The next show was organised by H. J. Lawson in May 1896 at the Imperial Institute in South Kensington. At least six makes were represented. The Prince of Wales with a crowd of fashionable people came to a private view, and the show was very successful. W. C. Bersey stole the show with his elegant electric brougham. The visitors were tremendously

32

impressed by its smooth, absolutely silent, effortless progress. They did not realise what a very short distance it would travel before its batteries needed recharging.

In 1895 "The Self-Propelled Traffic Association" was formed under the presidency of Sir David Salomons. A few months later Lawson, with Simms and Harrington Moore, formed "The Motor Car Club", a disguised trading organisation with headquarters on the second floor at 40, Holborn Viaduct. The uniform was of the naval variety and could not have been worn with propriety by the skipper of a steam yacht of less than two thousand tons.

While all this was going on in England, production was growing in France and the Panhard order book was full for months ahead. And while in England we still had a 4-m.p.h. speed limit, the French were staging full-scale motor races. In June 1895 the Paris–Bordeaux race of 732 miles was won by Monsieur Levassor on a Panhard two-cylinder at an average speed of 15 m.p.h. H. J. Lawson immediately bought the winning car at a very stiff price.

In 1896 several major races had been run in France before, on November 14th, the "Locomotives on Highways Act, 1896" at last legalised motoring in England. Lawson again bought the winners of the French races. The Motor Car Club decided to celebrate their newfound freedom with "a procession to Brighton". Léon and Camille Bollée brought over three racing tricars. Gottlieb Daimler, although a sick man, also came. Monsieur Mayade, works manager at Panhard, who a year or two later was to be the first fatal casualty in a motor race, came over to drive one of Lawson's Panhards.

There were thirty-three entrants. Quite a large proportion of them arrived, but there is a strong suspicion that most of the electric vehicles did some of the journey by train. Then there is the mystery of the two Duryeas which arrived at the finish. They were not entered in the event, nor were they at the start in London, and there does not seem to be any record of them having been observed en route. I have always heard it said that they were sent down by train the night before. The Bollée Brothers frightened everyone out of their wits by driving their racing tri-cars at incredible speeds of around 30 m.p.h., dodging in and out of horse-drawn traffic without slackening speed. On top of this the racing Bollées had a peculiar exhaust note like a quick-firing machine gun, which was both loud and penetrating. Léon arrived first in three hours forty minutes, Camille was second in four hours. The next car, a Panhard, took over five hours for the 52 miles. The "Paris–Marseilles" Panhard, always known as "new number 5" and, at that time, reputedly the fastest car in the world, broke down on the way, and arrived very late. The event was very badly organised, and no two reports of it agree.

At the time of the "London–Brighton", buyers were offering £200–£300 premium for immediate delivery of a production Panhard-Levassor. As a result of the demand, virtually the whole bicycle industry in France started to build motor vehicles of some sort in 1897.

In England, Lawson had his monopoly, but as the works were badly managed, and the engineers did not have the necessary knowledge, little progress was made. In the Spring the Great Horseless Carriage Company, which was doing badly, was re-formed as the Motor Manufacturing Company to make M.M.C. Cars. Now that motoring in Great Britain was "free" a number of foreign cars and motor bicycles and tricycles were imported.

In France, as elsewhere, the motor-car was the toy of a wealthy minority, so in January, 1897, motor races were organised at Nice, where the rich congregated in the winter sunshine. There were a number of other races in France that year, which showed the four-wheel petrol car in a poor light, for invariably the tiny Bollée tricars went a lot faster. Frequently the petrol-driven four-wheelers were beaten by steamers which were sometimes faster and usually more reliable.

The French cars were improving technically, and a few racing cars were beginning to use pneumatic tyres. The majority of cars had hot-tube ignition. This technique consisted of a platinum tube with one end attached to the combustion chamber and the other heated by an external burner. The system had been in use some years and improvements had been made so that the burner did not blow out so often. The event of the year was that a number of cars went over from tiller to wheel steering. There had been several deaths due to the combination of momentary inattention and a road shock powerful enough to wrench the tiller from the driver's hand.

We hear, for the first time in 1897, a name that was to dominate motor racing for a decade, Emile Mors. Both Belgium and Switzerland held their first motor races in the following year, 1898.

At the end of the year Count de Chasseloup Laubat and a young Belgian, Camille Jenatzy, were contending for the world's speed record. Both were driving electric Jeantaud cars. Eventually, it was by this time early 1899, Jenatzy streamlined his Jeantaud, "La Jamais Contente", into a cigar-shape and achieved 65·75 m.p.h. over the flying kilometre.

New names were appearing in France in 1899. De Dietrich and Rochet Schneider were big steel manufacturers newly entering the apparent Eldorado of motor building, and Delahaye, makers of agricultural machinery, were getting well into production. These, and others, competed against long-established Panhard, Peugeot and Bollée.

Technically, Panhard were leading the world, making cars as powerful as 24 h.p. and building the first vertical four-cylinder engine. From the point of view of ignition it was an interesting period. Electrical ignition was far superior to hot tubes, especially because the timing of the spark could be varied, but it was, as yet, hopelessly unreliable. So a number of cars of 1899 were fitted with both!

Automatic inlet valves, opened by the downstroke of the piston, were almost universal.

Emile Mors, rather like Bugatti in the 1920s, specialised in producing racing cars for amateur drivers. He also organised small races for new drivers – "les petits coureurs qui poussent". Until the legislation of 1900 there was nothing to prevent anyone having a motor race in France, providing no authorities forbade him at first.

The first race of 1900, called the "Course du Catalogue", divided the cars according to their catalogue prices, an excellent

35

idea that, no doubt, someone will one day rediscover. Although there was no racing in this country, the Automobile Club organised a 1000-mile trial, including some very steep hills, which aroused nation-wide interest.

In England Lawson was not finding it as easy as he had hoped to enforce his monopoly: agile brains were beginning to find loopholes.

One of those who supported the Lawson monopoly was S. F. Edge, who put an 8-h.p. Napier engine in "old number 8", one of the racing Panhards originally bought by Lawson. From this was born the original Napier, a 9-h.p. car which was made in 1900 and acquitted itself extremely well in the 1000-mile reliability trial run by the Automobile Club of Great

The 4 h.p. Peugeot which competed in the
Paris–Marseilles Race of 1896

Britain. In the same year Napier produced a 16-h.p. four-cylinder car that was undoubtedly the most practical and up-to-date car in England.

The negotiations between that eccentric but eminently successful newspaperman, James Gordon Bennett, and the Automobile Club de France were now complete and the first Gordon Bennett race was run, Versailles to Lyon. The rules put it, broadly, on a national basis. Each country was to nominate, through its automobile club, a team of three cars, every component, including tyres, being made in that country. England had nothing to enter, although Napier was preparing a car for the following year. France, Belgium and Germany entered teams, and Alexander Winton, who finished fifth, represented America. Charron, champion racing cyclist, already a veteran of several years' racing, won it. Girardot, as always in his racing life, was second, and that jovial bearded bear, Chevalier de Knyff, was third. All of them were driving Panhards.

Lawson and the Marquis de Dion were no longer on speaking terms. The Frenchman had every reason to feel aggrieved, as Lawson had treated him badly. But H. O. Duncan, who was working for Lawson, managed to negotiate a reconciliation, as he had done with Bollée at Le Mans, brought about by the vast quantities of engines ordered by Lawson. De Dion's price was steep, no less than an independent agency to sell his own products throughout the British Empire. This was the thin end of the wedge that rapidly broke up the Lawson monopoly.

In spite of the exhibition at the 1900 Crystal Palace show of the "Raft-Victoria", Pennington was getting into very deep water indeed. The £100,000 which he had received for the English rights of his patents had been dissipated. He liked to deck himself and his wife out like Christmas trees with costly jewellery and he lived at a great rate, supporting an immense staff. In 1900 he became bankrupt and he departed to America, where he bluffed himself into another vast fortune out of airships and armoured cars!

By the end of 1900, S. F. Edge, now the up-and-coming man in the motor world, held at his offices at 14, Regent Street, London, not only the de Dion and Napier sole agencies, but also that of Gladiator, and several others as well. Each imported motor vehicle had to pay a royalty to Lawson's British Motor Syndicate. Over the next couple of years costly litigation proved to Lawson that it would be quite impossible to continue his stranglehold on the swelling tide of the new industry. The climax came when Lawson, as owner of the Maybach float-feed carburettor patent for England, sued Charles Friswell for royalty on a Peugeot car fitted with one. Royalty was claimed on the whole car, not just the carburettor. Mr. Justice Farwell gave the verdict and costs against Lawson. This was the final nail in the coffin of the Lawson monopoly, and the British Motor Syndicate went into liquidation. A number of its minor but enforceable patents were bought by Edge, which brought him in a very useful income for many years. The end of the story of the Lawson monopoly is that in 1907 Napier bought the whole thing, lock, stock and barrel, including de Dion, Daimler, Maybach and hundreds of other patents for £1000.

Another of Lawson's schemes in the motor world was the flotation of "The London Steam Omnibus Company" with a capital of nearly half a million pounds. The whole scheme was brilliantly and practically conceived. It was proposed to build the chassis to a de Dion design which had been operating most efficiently for many years in France. Straker, who later built the Straker-Squire, and was a power omnibus expert, gave, as a consultant, the weekly cost of running a steam bus, including everything, as £12 4s. 3d., against for a horse bus, £15 8s. 4d. This includes £1 a week for a stoker which presumably would have been saved on steam buses running on liquid fuel as were those running under "Lifu" patents. The steam buses would cover a far greater mileage in the day, and it seemed that Lawson's bold scheme of one penny fare "from anywhere to anywhere" would pay handsome dividends. Contemporary accounts seem to agree that there was only one thing wrong with this carefully thought-out scheme – it was ten years ahead of its time. This killed it stone dead.

In America, the manufacturers were getting into their stride and, in 1900, they built over 4000 cars, mostly of the "gas-buggy" type, with the engine under the seat. Car racing, however, was proving a popular sport, and the first race on Long Island was run that year. Petrol in England cost sixpence a gallon and less in America.

And so we come to the end of the early years – of Victorian motoring, one might say; and we are free to begin our story in 1901, the year the popular Prince of Wales (who had from its earliest moment, pronounced his blessing on motoring) ascended the throne.

Motoring was already free from the original "Locomotives on Highways Act". The shackles of patent monopoly were being broken. The engineers in England who had so stubbornly fumbled in the dark instead of following the lead of the French, had now acquired a basis of technical knowledge. With the turn of the century many of the obstacles to the beginning of motoring had been removed.

4

The Experimental Years, 1901-1904

1901

THIS was a thoroughly exciting year. Manufacturers, who had hitherto concentrated on constructing their motor-cars as stoutly as possible, now found that, by fitting bigger engines, they could make them go very fast indeed. The largest cars built in 1900 had been of about 24 h.p. In 1901, however, 40-, 50-, 60- and even 70-h.p. cars were produced.

In the competition world at the beginning of 1901, Panhard and Mors were the most succesful makes, with Peugeot, De Dietrich, and Daimler well behind. But from relative newcomers, Darracq in France, Napier in England, and Dürkopp in Germany, great things were expected. There were also rumours that Maybach and Gottlieb Daimler, on his deathbed, had designed a new and advanced model at Cannstatt, and that the Austrian banker Jellinek, who lived at Nice, had bought the whole works production for a year ahead on condition that it was called after his pretty daughter, Mercedes. Details of this new Daimler there were none, for even then a new model built by Daimler A.G. was kept secret until the moment came when they saw fit to release it.

Here we will have to digress a little to clear up a curious point. Although the Mercedes cars did not appear till January 1901, there are earlier records in lists of the competitors in various events, of a "Mercedes" car whose driver concealed his identity under the *nom-de-guerre* "Mercedes". This was in fact a Daimler car, or cars, driven by Consul Jellinek.

The practice of racing under an assumed name was sometimes adopted in the first decade of motor racing. There seem to have been two reasons. One, the desire, in what seems to us an incredibly class-conscious age, to emphasise the amateur status of the competing gentleman chauffeur, and the other the possible necessity of concealing his activities from wealthy and influential relatives, who disapproved of motor racing. They could show their disapproval in two ways; either by cutting off an allowance, or, as is said to have been done in the case of Fritz von Opel with his Darracq a year or so later, by bribing the mechanics to see that the car did not get to the starting line. It also happened to a Jewish friend of mine, whose strictly orthodox family had his car "arranged" so that he could not race on a day when their religion said that he should not.

There is little doubt that the appearance of the 35-h.p. Mercedes at Nice in the spring of 1901 influenced the design of motor-cars of the future more profoundly even than did the Henry-designed Peugeot twelve years later. Admittedly it was developed from that high and rather dangerous car, the Phoenix model Daimler of 1899. The Phoenix design was intelligent fumbling in the dark, whereas the 35-h.p. Mercedes was definitely the shape of things to come. It had a four-cylinder engine mounted in the front of the chassis with mechanically operated inlet valves and magneto (low-tension) ignition. It had wheel steering, brakes on both transmission and wheels, the latter internal-expanding, a four-speed gearbox with gate change, pneumatic tyres, and a steel channel chassis frame extended beyond the radiator. It also had the new Mercedes patent helical steel spring clutch. Above all it had the first honeycomb radiator with integral water tank. The latter caused great confusion in the British technical press. The French press translated "Bienenwaben" quite correctly as "Nid des Abeilles", but the English papers imagined that "Nid des Abeilles" meant Beehive. As nobody had ever seen a honeycomb radiator before, considerable explanation was required.

Of course, by modern standards, the Mercedes was crude and noisy. Engine speed was controlled by varying the lift of the inlet valves which made driving it a difficult operation. But the fact remains that it was far in advance of anything that had been seen, and it also went very fast indeed. Speed was what counted with the wealthy buyers in 1901. The fastest cars of 1900 had a maximum speed of not much more

41

than 45 m.p.h.

By the middle of 1901 Fournier was driving his 60-h.p. Mors over 687 miles from Paris to Berlin at an *average* running time, including tyre troubles, of over 44 m.p.h.

Another even more revolutionary car appeared in 1901: the Lanchester. From an engineering point of view, it was a masterpiece, but it made no pretentions to great speed; otherwise, although unconventional, it might have been as slavishly copied as was the Mercedes. In point of fact, this car, which had been running in prototype form since 1897, had already appeared in 1899, but F. W. Lanchester did not offer the car for sale until two years later when he had redesigned it considerably.

The two-cylinder horizontally opposed engine was placed amidships and canted backwards. The valve gear was like nothing before or since, for there was only one port to each cylinder, through which both inlet and exhaust gases passed. I have always imagined that the very distinctive noise, a sort of gentle flutter-flutter, made by early Lanchesters was caused by this system. But unorthodox as this arrangement was, it was amazingly efficient. In 1901, metallurgical knowledge of steel for valves, acting in high temperatures, was not very far advanced. After 1000 miles one could count oneself lucky if one only had to grind one's valves. It was quite probable that they would all have to be replaced. The curious Lanchester valve gear lasted many times this mileage.

Then there was the Lanchester flywheel magneto. The permanent magnets were integrated with one of the flywheels and revolved round a fixed armature. The Lanchester contact breaker and sparking plugs were also miracles of unorthodox ingenuity. The lubrication was fully automatic, and transmission was by epicyclic gears to a worm drive in the back axle. Both features were years ahead of their time. The tiller steering was so very efficient and free from road shock that Lanchesters retained it for many years after all other cars had gone over to wheel steering. The same may be said of the Lanchester wick carburettor which was a standard fitting until the time of the Kaiser war.

42

The spectacular debut of the Mercedes cars at the Nice Week in March 1901 has passed into history, and their tryout at the Pau races in February has been mercifully forgotten. Mercedes cars have always been unfortunate at Pau. The 1901 cars stripped their gears and behaved in a thoroughly reprehensible manner, thus establishing a tradition that was to last through the years, right up to the present day. The race was a Panhard victory for Maurice Farman and Girardot, "The Eternal Second", who, like Lancia some five or six years later, was always robbed of victory by some stroke of bad luck.

But the Mercedes cars were ready and right for Nice Week and swept the board in almost every event. Jellinek found that his pre-purchase of a year's output was already oversold to his wealthy friends, and orders were given to increase production. An Alsatian racing cyclist, Charles Lehmann, persuaded Jellinek to give him the Parisian agency for sales and service. Charles, who was an extremely astute man, managed virtually to corner the market for the next two years at least, and made a fortune in the process.

Mercedes were not successful in their races that year. This cannot have worried them unduly; their order book was so full that any further successes would only have brought embarrassment.

This did little, however, to decrease the tremendous interest in the Paris-Bordeaux race, which was run concurrently with the Gordon Bennett race. Not only was the band of enthusiastic motorists growing daily, but from the public point of view, now that cars were getting so much faster, a race was becoming a most exciting spectacle.

Henri Fournier won the Paris-Bordeaux race with a 60-h.p. Mors followed by five Panhard "forties", so of course France won the Gordon Bennett trophy. A 12-h.p. Panhard driven by Giraud won the light-car class, in which Baras, the Darracq ace, distinguished himself by finishing second with his engine tied on to the chassis with rope, as the engine bearers had snapped off! 8-h.p. Renaults took the first four places in the voiturette class, the winning car being driven by Louis Renault.

43

There was considerable alarm in France over the Paris-Berlin race. The memory of the Germans overrunning and occupying the country in 1871 was only too fresh on the minds of people of middle age and over, who did not hesitate to prophesy disaster of every kind. So much so indeed that, before the race, Monsieur Serpollet drove over the course to inspect it and to reassure the public. He was able to report that the Germans were going to unbelievable trouble to make everything pleasant and that the real enemy would be the dust. In both these predictions he was entirely correct.

"Controls" were established in towns of any magnitude which could not be bypassed. From the inward control where the cars were halted and their times taken, each racing car was preceded by a cyclist whom he was forbidden, under pain of disqualification, to pass, as far as the outward control. The cyclist carried a card stating the time of the racer's arrival at the inward control, which he handed to the officials at the outward control who then started the racer again, taking his his time of departure. In the villages they did not have controls. It was left to the local policeman to see that the villagers stayed indoors while the cars raced through. They did. At that time familiarity had not yet bred the recklessness which led to so many terrible accidents two years later.

At the frontier each competitor was handed a card saying "Soyez les bienvenus en Allemagne", one of the many pleasant gestures made by the Germans who had arranged a royal welcome for the drivers of all nationalities. If any of these cards are in existence today, they would be much-prized collectors' pieces. The banqueting was sumptuous and Jarrott, driving in a big race for the first time, relates that although he did not speak a word of German, he was overwhelmed with kindness. Fournier won again on his Mors, and of course Girardot was second. Giraud in his 12-h.p. Panhard again won the light-car class and Louis Renault again won the Voiturette class on a single-cylinder 8-h.p. car at the really astonishing speed of 36·9 m.p.h. He was actually a little faster than Giraud, and faster than all but the first six of the monster "heavy cars".

Perhaps 1901, more than any other year in the history of motoring, supports the truism, "This year's racing car is next year's touring car". The lessons learned in the 1901 racing kept the designers, many of whom were also the drivers, very busy at their drawing boards. Now that cars were faster, streamlining was beginning to become important. Dapper little Fernand Charron, who was always thinking ahead, had started it with his Panhard, and Serpollet had fitted his racing steamer with a body like an upturned boat. There were to be more attempts along these lines the following year, after which the idea of steamlining seems to have been dropped for a decade. Another development during the year, coupled with the foregoing, was the increase of rake in the steering mechanism from the vertical position. This had really started in 1899. I think Charron's Panhard was the first, but by 1901 the rake from the vertical was becoming pronounced. America, it seems, had only just taken to wheel steering; a few cars, notably the Auburn, being so fitted. In 1901, the first shaft-driven car, the Autocar, was sold in America. However, if the Americans were rather behind technically, their production methods were far from slow, for in the year 1900 7000 cars were built in the U.S.A. And in both Europe and America that year an enormous number of new rms started to build motor-cars, including practically every bicycle maker in both continents.

1902

This year, manufacturers were quite prepared to try anything new. And not only manufacturers. The financier Lawson was still attempting large coups and the cosmopolitan Dr. Lehwess born in Germany, educated in France, and a naturalised Briton, proposed to drive his immense yellow Panhard berline "Passe-Partout" round the world! About ten feet high, this immense machine, specially built at a cost of over £3000, was mounted on a 25 h.p. chassis with pneumatic tyres. They left London with a great flourish in April 1902. By September they were well and truly bogged down near Nijni Novgorod. Dr. Lehwess, who, by this time, had had enough of Russian roads, gave up.

The following year, Charles Friswell, the big London motor dealer, who held the Peugeot distributorship, went out to the dreary little village near Nijni, where "Passe Partout" had been abandoned. Here he bribed the moujiks to dig it up, for it was now three feet under the snow as well as stuck in a bog. The Panhard, apparently little the worse for this treatment, was sent back to London by rail, where it was exhibited both at Friswell's garage and the Motor Show at the Agricultural Hall.

The Americans were also trying hard. They were concentrating on producing great quantites of rather old-fashioned "gas buggies". Ransome E. Olds alone built 2000 "Merry Oldsmobiles". Thomas B. Jeffery, one of the contenders for the title of first American to use wheel steering, built 1500 of the "Rambler", the ancestor of the present-day Nash. Production figures of this order were rare in the extreme in Europe. Though quantity of production was more advanced than design, there were a number of brilliant innovations. For example, the "Silent Northern", built by J. D. Maxwell and C. B. King in partnership, had three-point suspension, with the gearbox, clutch and engine all in one unit, and running boards.

In Europe the sporting year began in a welter of political intrigue. The French Minister of the Interior had banned racing on the public roads during 1902. The French Minister of Agriculture had a vast annual surplus of agriculturally produced alcohol to contend with. So, with true Gallic subtlety, one was played off against the other. The ban was removed on the condition that the Circuit du Nord race was to be run on alcohol fuel only, instead of petrol, in an attempt to popularise the use of the former.

The Automobile Club of Nice, emboldened by their tremendously successful Motor Weeks of previous years decided to run a 500-mile race to Abazzia in Italy in conjunction with the 1902 Week. The course was to pass through Austria and Switzerland, so political arrangements with those countries were necessary. The course was changed a dozen times or more to meet with exigencies as they arose, but on the eve of the race the Italian Minister of the Interior turned a political somersault and forbade the whole race.

The first race to be run under the new 1000-kilogram weight limit for the big-car class was the Circuit du Nord. It seems to have proved that cars ran adequately on alcohol, though not nearly as well as on petrol. In spite of this, the race and its attendant publicity had not the slightest effect on alcohol fuel sales. The steam cars in this race behaved particularly badly on the fuel. There was only one accident in the race which was won by Maurice Farman on a Panhard. Charles Jarrott hit the Chief of Police with his 40-h.p. Panhard and sent him flying. This official does not seem to have been much hurt and "took it all very philosophically".

To me, the most attractive of all the great city-to-city races has always been the "Paris–Vienna". Mostly because the Vienna of 1902 must have been a most heavenly destination, but also because of the route and the colourful personalities of the drivers. The race was very nearly cancelled because of the difficulty of obtaining permission from the various authorities concerned. Then, just as all necessary arrangements had been made with the French, Swiss and Austrian governments, the French Government was defeated, and, after the ensuing election, the race had to be legalised again with the new government.

Unfortunately there is not space here to describe the whole dramatic race which was so full of incident, but I will recount two which are no more than typical of the whole fabulous adventure. Captain Genty, a soldier, better known today under his racing name of "De La Touloubre", was going down a very steep hill in Austria, his Clément well under control. Above the noise of the wind and the governed engine, he heard shouts for help. Looking back he saw an unfortunate motor-cylist, whose brakes had failed, rapidly catching him up. As the runaway machine drew level with the Clément, Genty reached out, grabbed the motor-cyclist by the coat collar, and with a super-human effort dragged him to safety on board the car.

Then there is the immortal story of Jarrott sawing up the furniture at dead of night in an hotel, and smuggling out table legs inside his trousers to effect temporary repairs to the fractured chassis of his Panhard.

The Gordon Bennett race was run concurrently with the Paris–Vienna as far as Innsbruck. On the last stage before Innsbruck there were only two survivors of the official teams, in fact quite a few of the original 200-odd entrants had dropped out. The Chevalier de Knyff was leading S. F. Edge when the sleeve of the differential casing of his Panhard broke, leaving Edge, who had had tyre trouble with his Napier, to limp into Innsbruck the technical winner of the Gordon Bennett trophy. This meant that the Gordon Bennett race would have to be held, in 1903, somewhere in the British Isles.

When I was a boy, it was still often debated whether or not Count Eliot Zborowski won the Paris–Vienna race. Although he made fastest time in the big-car class, there was a difference of opinion about a timing technicality, and the officials awarded first place to Henri Farman on a 70-h.p. Panhard. The Panhard and Mors cars were now at their zenith, but Mercedes were creeping up. Zborowski might, perhaps should, have won, and another brilliant amateur, Baron de Forest, also driving a 40-h.p. Mercedes, would have finished in the first three if his petrol tank had not split wide open a few miles outside Vienna.

But the most astonishing performance in this fascinating race was put up by Marcel Renault, who drove his little 16-h.p. four-cylinder Renault from Paris to Vienna faster than the winning "heavy car", a 70-h.p. Panhard. Renault's average speed was 38·9 m.p.h. and Farman's was 38·4 m.p.h.

For such a small country, Belgium produced quite a large proportion of the very early drivers, including Baron Pierre de Crawhez, Baron Jean de Crawhez and that delightful character, Baron de Caters, who raced for over a decade, just because he enjoyed racing, hardly ever winning anything. And of course, among the less-moneyed drivers, a quiet, gentle creature with a red beard called Camille Jenatzy, who drove extremely fast and well any curious vehicle with which no one else would be bothered.

So it came as no surprise when the Belgian Motor Club

1 Lord Dudley's four-cylinder chain-driven Panhard at a meet of the Worcestershire Foxhounds at Elmley Lovett in 1901

2 The famous London to Brighton Run, 14th November 1896: an Arnold Benz and a Panhard outside the Hotel Metropole, Brighton, on the following day

3 Tunbridge Wells Exhibition, 1895: Sir David Salomons (right) on his Peugeot

4   J. A. Koosen and a friend in an 1895 Lutzmann

5   Hon. C. S. Rolls on his 4-h.p. Léon Bollée tri-car, 1897

6   1902 Panhard et Levassor: Sir Harry Preston at the wheel and, beside him, Doctor W. G. Grace

7   1898 Panhard et Levassor 8-h.p. four-cylinder: Hon. C. S. Rolls at the wheel

8, 9 First of their *marques*, 1903: *above* 6-h.p. Standard and *below* 5-h.p. Vauxhall

10 1905 Tourist Trophy Race in the Isle of Man: Percy Northey cornering the Rolls-Royce in which he finished second at 33.7 m.p.h.

11 1904 Royce two-cylinder car, outside the Manchester works

12 60-h.p. Mercedes-Simplex, 1903

13 18-h.p. Mercedes landaulette, 1905

14 Dicer: Madame Du Gast in the 30-h.p. De Dietrich which she drove
in the Paris–Madrid race of 1903

15 Dresser: descending from her Richard Brasier, 1906

staged a full-dress event, the Circuit des Ardennes. It was won by Jarrott on a 70-h.p. Panhard with Gabriel second on a 60-h.p. Mors. The American millionaire, W. K. Vanderbilt, was third on similar Mors.

The light-car class was won at nearly 50 m.p.h. by one of the curious opposed-piston Gobron-Brilliés.

I do not know if I am alone in finding a fascination in what happens to famous racing cars after they vanish from the limelight, but I have been lucky enough to trace what happened to some of the 1902 racing cars.

George Heath sold his 40-h.p. Panhard to another American called Bishop, who shipped it back to U.S.A., where he had it converted to a touring car. Fournier's car was kept by its owner, Captain Laycock, for whom Fournier was driving. Jellinek paid £2000 for Maurice Farman's Panhard for the Mercedes works to inspect more closely. When they had learned all they wanted to know, they resold it for £1600. Henri Far-

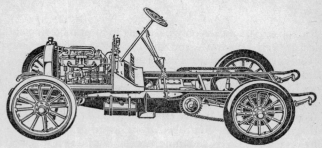

Veteran chassis: the 1902, chain-driven Mercedes-Simplex
with a four-cylinder engine

man's car was bought by Stephen Ribes, who was connected with oil refining. Charron, as fine a salesman as he was driver, took £3000 off a Monsieur Maigret for his. Girardot's car, which probably also belonged to Charron, went to Baron Henri de Rothschild at an undisclosed but undoubtedly high figure. A 40-h.p. Panhard, belonging to Leys, which he drove into 17th place in the Paris-Berlin race, was bought by Lord Carnavon.

I mention these figures, admittedly at the top end of the scale, because, since the "discovery" of speed in 1901, the motoring public had become very sharply divided. One could either have a little single cylinder, probably solid-tyred, "teuf-teuf", which took you along reasonably reliably and cheaply at about 15 m.p.h., dropping to a walking pace on hills, or if one was sufficiently wealthy to pay £2000 – £3000 for, shall we say, an ex-Paris-Berlin racing car, one could expect it to cost a further £700 or £800 a year to run. Although maintenance was laborious it was not expensive, for one probably kept a skilled engineer at a wage of £2 a week, who did nothing but maintain the car. However, one would have to face a tyre bill of about £400 per annum and although petrol was cheap one could expect only 8 to 12 miles to the gallon. Oil consumption was also very heavy.

By 1902, motoring, except in the humblest and most old-fashioned way, had become a very, very rich man's hobby.

1903

I suppose 1903 means only one thing to most motoring enthusiasts, "Paris–Madrid", and the end of the most glamorous events ever held: the trans-continental motor races between the capital cities of Europe. But there is a great deal more to this year than that, and it is of considerable historic importance. The vertical multi-cylinder forward engine had definitely arrived. Admittedly, it was crude and rough, plagued with lubrication troubles, controlled by a governor, and very noisy by reason of its outside timing wheels. But there it was, and the death warrant of the old slow-turning horizontal engine mounted under the seat was written plainly for all to see. On account of their reliability and economy, these relatively light but paralysingly slow voiturettes gave many more year's service to the impecunious than did the new type of 1903 car.

Almost all of the new cars of 1903 had started, or were starting, as copies of the 1901 Mercedes. Quite a lot of them, however, were not yet fitted with mechanically operated inlet valves. Ignition was generally by trembler coil, wipe contact and accumulator. The latter had not progressed very far along the road to the comparative state of perfection of today, and it was a constant source of trouble, nor was there any means of recharging it carried in the car. Many people became so disgusted with their accumulators that they preferred the rather extravagant procedure of using a dry battery for a given number of hours, then throwing it away and replacing it with a new one. Some of the makers of the more expensive cars adopted the low-tension ignition, with which the make and break occurred actually inside the cylinder, manufactured by Robert Bosch. Transmission was still mostly by chain.

Had I been a wealthy buyer in 1903, I think I would have bought a steam car for normal touring. Admittedly they were costly, but they had all the speed and more acceleration than anything built, except an out-and-out racing car. On top of this they were absolutely silent, and, in the hands of a man trained to their proper maintenance, much more reliable than many multi-cylinder cars of 1903. Most heavy lorries and tankers for delivering petrol were powered by steam.

In England, police traps were on the increase, and societies to protect motorists from persecution were formed. A section of the population, including a number of otherwise reasonably sane Members of Parliament, whipped themselves up into a dementia of anti-motor phobia. One even said in the House that Mors cars were so-called because Mors meant death, and that chauffeurs believed they had a right to kill anyone or anything that got in their way. History does not relate whether the English papers reporting this speech were ever shown to that pioneer motorist and manufacturer, Monsieur Mors.

It was in this atmosphere that the Motor Cars Act of 1903 was passed, replacing the "Locomotives in Highways" Act of 1896, which in turn had replaced the "Locomotives on Highways (Amendment)" Act of 1878. Considering all the hysterical talk, it was a very reasonable and moderate Act. For example, a section of the House wished to empower a policeman to take into custody and hold any driver whom he believed to be committing an offence. The Act stated that he could only do this if the driver refused to give him his name and address. Much of this Act remains today. A most important point was that all motor owners must register their cars with their local county councils, and carry numbers allotted to them by those councils. Neither of these had been required before. Some of the wording was extremely ambiguous and, for years afterwards, the London County Council was holding vexatious test cases against unfortunate motorists to establish obscure points of the law of registration.

Another important provision of the Act was that the speed limit was raised for the whole country to 20 m.p.h. It was also stated that, in future, and this holds good today, there must be two police witnesses for any speeding offence.

In the Spring, one of those gay, wealthy amateurs who had made the early days of motor racing so colourful, was killed. Eliot Zborowski who, like the other dandies of this time, wore long, stiffly starched shirt cuffs. One of his cuff links caught in the hand throttle on the steering wheel, as he was turning a corner in the La Turbie hill-climb, and opened it wide. (The engine was governed and there was no foot accelerator.) S. C. H. Davis told me the rather curious fact that when Lou Zborowski, his son, was killed, also on a Mercedes, twenty-two years later, he was wearing his father's cuff links. I do not think it is generally known that it was Eliot Zborowski who suggested originally that a different colour should be allotted to each nation competing in the *grandes épreuves*.

As a result of Eliot Zborowski's death, the Minister of the Interior panicked and stopped the rest of the Nice Motor Week, which infuriated a number of manufacturers who had spent thousands of pounds on preparing cars for this meeting, where winning any event meant a flood of orders.

However, the following month, Monsieur Combes had calmed down sufficiently to allow the Paris–Madrid race to start from Versailles. There was no attempt whatever at spectator control. An analysis of the terrible number of accidents is more than interesting. Nearly all of them seem to have been caused by dogs or spectators getting on the course. Louis Renault, first to arrive at Bordeaux, admits to running over no less than four dogs. Even a peasant in a donkey-cart drove on to the course, in such a manner that Georges Richard could do nothing but hit it fair and square. A few of the accidents were due to inexperience on the part of some of the three hundred-odd competitors who had never driven in a race of any magnitude before. The race was "won" by Gabriel at an average speed of 60 m.p.h., a wonderful feat on a heavy unwieldy Mors with a top speed of not much over 80 m.p.h. and a governed engine. Charles Jarrot's account of his experiences in this race in his memoirs, *Ten Years of Motors and Motor Racing* (he was third on a De Dietrich) is one of the finest pieces of motoring writing I know. One lives the excitement of the race with him, and feels the terrible anxiety and suspense hanging over the first arrivals at Bordeaux, where the race was stopped, as first the rumours of nameless horror and then the confirmatory telegrams begin to come in.

I am glad that he gives an account of Madame du Gast's chivalry. She was going very well in her 24-h.p. De Dietrich with every chance of winning, or at least finishing well up in her class. Lorraine Barrow, driving one of the big racing De Dietrichs, got a dog in his steering and had a terrible crash. Madame du Gast stopped, gave him first aid, and stayed with him till he was safely in an ambulance. She had deliberately thrown away her chances, and finished in sixty-third place.

It was a fascinating race, the last of the capital-to-capital races. Fresh study of contemporary accounts invariably brings forth new and fascinating details. For instance, Jenatzy's new 90-h.p. Mercedes which could, on form, have won, would not run quite right. It did not seem like carburation trouble, but finally, in desperation, he and his mechanic dismantled the carburettor, and found an enormous fly lodged in it. By that time he had lost over an hour – and the race. Fifty motor-cycles entered, only fifteen finished the course, and a woman, Mademoiselle Jollivet, was third, barely half an hour behind the winner!

Undoubtedly the finest effort was by Louis Renault, who won the light-car class, accomplishing the Paris–Bordeaux journey at an average speed of 62·3 m.p.h. But the triumph was nothing for him, as his brother, to whom he was devoted, was killed. Marcel Renault was only thirty-one, tall and slight, with a sandy beard, and very modest. Everybody liked him.

When S. F. Edge, the previous year, had won the Gordon Bennett trophy from the French, he set a problem for the Automobile Club of Great Britain. Under the terms laid down, the next race had to be held in the country of the winner of the last. Of course, with the tremendous anti-motoring bias of Parliament, it was hopeless to ask for permission to hold the race on English roads. So a course, centred on Athy, in Ireland, was arranged through the liberal-minded Viceroy of the day, and legalised by a Bill in the House of Lords. As Napiers had won in 1902, they were allowed two places in the team and the third was to be decided by eliminating trials held at the Duke of Portland's estate, Welbeck. J. W. Stocks on a Napier, beat Charles Rolls and Mayhew on Napiers and Lisle on a Star, to win the coveted place in the British team. The other two members were Edge, the last year's winner, and Charles Jarrott. America sent two Wintons and a Peerless, driven by Owen, Winton and Mooers.

The French sent two 80-h.p. Panhards and a 70-h.p. Mors. The dispute over the German team could not have been more amusing. The German Daimler Company wanted to enter their five new 90-h.p. cars with works drivers, who were mechanics promoted from the fitting bench. The Deutsch Automobile Club were horrified. These man were not "hochwohlgeboren"! The German entry must be driven by *gentlemen*. A first-class wrangle ensued, but eventually a compromise was made with Jenatzy and Hieronymus, who apparently, although engaged in trade, just qualified. The remaining place might have gone to Charles Rolls or Foxhall Keene. As the former was the son of a lord, and the latter a Master of Foxhounds, they would have been more than acceptable to the German committee. But the whole question was resolved by a disastrous fire which destroyed most of the Mercedes works and all the 90-h.p. racing cars, except one that had been sent to W. K. Vanderbilt in America, and could not be returned in time.

As the works team had gone up in flames, amateurs took over. Foxhall Keene and Baron de Caters drove their own

60-h.p. cars, and Gray Dinsmore lent his "sixty" to Jenatzy.

The race itself resolved itself into a struggle between Jenatzy and the Chevalier de Knyff's Panhard. My mother watched this race and knew several of the participants, so I have a clear picture of what happened. Jenatzy was a magnificent but reckless driver, and hitherto he had mostly driven "forlorn hopes" that nobody else would touch. The result was that, although he usually went very fast for a time, he almost invariably finished the less usual way up in a ditch, or broke down.

The Chevalier de Knyff was a very experienced driver indeed, who had driven since the very beginning of motor racing. In fact his detractors said that he was already too old. His Panhard was fast but had given trouble in the "Paris–Madrid" and he reckoned that, by not pressing it too hard, he could beat everybody except Jenatzy, who would undoubtedly eliminate himself. What he had not reckoned with was that, for once, Jenatzy had, in his borrowed 60-h.p. Mercedes, a car which was not only worthy of him, but which was absolutely reliable. In fact half a century later an identical car was driven from Sussex to Stuttgart without any serious mechanical trouble.

It was not till the race was well over half-run that the Chevalier realised that Jenatzy was well in the lead. De Knyff then drove as hard as he knew how, but he was unable to make up the lead Jenatzy had gained, and he came in nearly twelve minutes after the winner, in second place.

The Belgians ran the Circuit des Ardennes again, once more dividing the cars by weight. The Voiturettes and Light Cars regulations were the same as before, but the Heavy Cars were now allowed to weigh 1000 kilogrammes plus a further 7 kilogrammes for a magneto if fitted. It was very well run; there were no bad accidents, and it had a profound influence on public feeling which would, after the "Paris-Madrid", have called for the banning of even circuit racing on the public roads. It is interesting to compare the average speeds of the winners of the various classes.

Heavy Cars	Baron Pierre de Crawhez	70-h.p. Panhard	54.3 m.p.h.
Light Cars	Baras	40-h.p. Darracq	48.9 m.p.h.
Voiturettes (Shorter course)	Wagner	20-h.p. Darracq	43.1 m.p.h.

I think that the year's racing in 1903 must have shown manufacturers that a hotted-up touring car was no longer in the running, and that if they wished to win races, then special racing cars would have to be built.

In the English law courts there was an interesting aftermath to the "Paris–Madrid". The beneficiaries of the life insurance of Lorraine Barrow, who died of his injuries, had to sue the insurance company for their money. The insurance company held that Barrow had not disclosed that he was a racing motorist. For occupation he had simply put down "Gentleman". The judge ruled that motor racing was a normal occupation for a gentleman and that the money must be paid.

One of the three ladies competing in the "Paris–Madrid" was Madame Lockert, driving an Ader car. Later in the year she drove her Tony Huber car from Paris to St. Petersburg. Considering the state of the roads this was no mean achievement, and she had many adventures. Needless to say, she was held up for a day or so at the frontier by Russian officials, who in Czarist times were as passionately devoted to "red tape" as they are today. They maintained that her passport covered entry into the Russian Empire by rail or water, but not by road!

In America, car designers were still thinking originally, for production was small, and designers were not yet slaves to the toolroom and conveyor belt. Mr. Winton made a fast coast-to-coast run from San Francisco to New York in one of his cars.

In England several long-distance reliability trials were held and those cars which did well, especially new makes which did not have a long waiting list, found that success had a most beneficial effect on their order book. At the Crystal Palace, special dust trials were held.

There were several motor shows in 1903. At the beginning

of the year Cordingley's Automobile Exhibition was held at the Agricultural Hall. There were also exhibitions in Berlin and Vienna. It is a solemn thought, looking at the plan of the Cordingley Exhibition, that a large number of the exhibiting manufacturers no longer exist, although there were quite a number who kept going until the lean times of the 1930s which put so many of the older, smaller makers out of business. Notable features of this show were external contracting brakes, either on wheels or transmission, reinforced or all-metal chassis, and a considerable increase of shaft-drive and mechanically operated inlet valves. Most of the newly established small makers used proprietary engines, largely de Dion. Electric cars were quite popular, in spite of their short range; particularly electric broughams, which were very smart and built on strictly conventional carriage lines. Gobron-Brillié showed their opposed-piston-engined car for the first time in England. The press were unstinting in their praise, some even going as far as to suggest that it might be the engine of the future. The Americans showed, among others, a very solid, workmanlike three-speed, shaft-driven 18-h.p. two-cylinder Peerless. The French as usual sent over a number of makes, and from Trompenburg in Holland came two-and four-cylinder Spyker cars. The excellence of their workmanship was freely commented on, and an English motor firm, The Bradford Motor Company, contracted to take the entire output of the Spyker Company for the subsequent three years.

The Paris Show was held, in 1903, during the fortnight before Christmas. The following statistics are interesting, as they show the trend in design. Fifty-five per cent of the cars had four cylinders and the remainder had one or three cylinders. There were no sixes, and Charron, Girardot and Voigt had just built what must have been one of the very first eights, but they did not show it.

The pressed steel frame had gained popularity during the past year and now accounted for forty-six per cent of the chassis. Thirty-two per cent still clung to the old "armoured wood" type, while fourteen per cent were of tubular design. Chain drive had declined sharply to sixty-two per cent, but mechanical inlet valves had increased from forty-five per cent the previous year, to sixty per cent. The old system of governing, by impeding the valves from shutting, was now completely abandoned in favour of a governor acting on the throttle.

Tyres had made considerable progress, and Michelin brought out a "non-slipping tread". This, they claimed very honestly, did not pretend to abolish the dreaded sideslip, but minimised the risk.

As far as coachwork went, the show was stolen by a British-built M.M.C., almost the last product of the Lawson empire. The closed body, with curved glass windows, was lushly upholstered in the most luxurious materials. There were folding tables, a barometer, a speaking tube and a clock. There was also a ship's telegraph, to indicate the passenger's wishes to the driver.

Among the oddities there was a Spyker whose offset engine drove all four wheels. The Janvier had six wheels, in rather

The belt-driven Fouillaron, 1903

unlikely places, and steered with most of them. From the data available I do not really understand how it was supposed to work, but the most extravagant claims were made for the vehicle. However, in spite of these – Monsieur Fouillaron's car with a sort of Zenith Gradua belt-drive and a few other unorthodox designs – there was no doubt at all that, in the year 1903, motor cars had started to conform to a standard pattern.

1904

Soon after the turn of the century, it became abundantly clear that motoring had not only come to stay, but that it was already within the financial grasp of the professional classes. It was also clear that, even if it did not spread any lower in the hierarchy of Edwardian wealth, an almost limitless market was opening up. A year or two earlier the buyer's choice had been restricted to a few of the earliest manufacturers, and a few cars equipped with proprietary engines, but by the spring of 1904 almost a hundred new firms were actually in production. It is true that some only produced a very few cars in a year, but the large Continental firms, like De Dion et Bouton or Benz, were producing in a very big way indeed, and in England several makers were turning out five or six cars every week. So great was the pressure by would-be purchasers that certain popular makes, notably Panhard and Renault, commanded a substantial premium for immediate delivery. There was a delay of twelve months on any new Mercedes.

Indeed, the choice that lay before the prospective purchaser was bewildering in its profusion. Even in the under £200 class, he had some forty different models to choose from.

Although a number of steam cars were exhibited during 1904, it was quite apparent that the popularity of this motive power was already on the wane. A sort of "Gallup poll" taken in 1903 and 1904 showed that its adherents had fallen by fifty per cent in a year. As regards transmission, the majority of automobilists mistrusted the comparatively recently introduced shaft-drive and preferred chain-drive, but a few, about two per cent of the total, still preferred belt-drive.

Now that people of moderate income were taking to the road in large numbers, the question was heard on all sides, "What does it cost?" Experienced automobilists came forward with carefully kept accounts. These varied enormously, but here is a fairly typical one for a 10-h.p. car, over 7065 miles:

	£	s.	d.
Lights, oil, grease	3	5	6½
Petrol	22	12	8
Repairs and replacements	12	9	11
Tyres	27	15	3
Sundries, licence, stable and washing	14	10	1½
	£80	14	4

This works out at 2·72 pence per mile, which compares quite favourably with the cost of a horse and trap, which, by general consensus of opinion, cost about 6d. per mile. A chauffeur cost 30s. a week and his food; a groom, trained to drive and do simple maintenance, rather less. But a really first-class engineer who could do all the necessary fitting work on a car, commanded at least £2 a week and his food. A 7-h.p. car running on solid tyres cost about £20 less per annum, but for anything over 12 h.p. the costs rose alarmingly, owing to the price of tyres. In fact, for a sporting 40-h.p. car, weighing a good ton and a half, the annual 'tyre bill might run into several hundreds of pounds.

It is rather curious that the many budgets which remain from 1904 do not include fines, as they must surely have been appreciable. Police prosecutions for exceeding the 20-m.p.h. limit were increasing, for the local authorities were beginning to find them a very useful source of revenue, and savages fines of up to £15 were imposed – a big sum in Edwardian times. None of the anti-motoring feeling, so strong in England, was apparent in Germany or France. In the former, the Emperor declared public holidays for major motor races and, in the latter, the Post Office were planning to replace their horse-drawn vehicles with those mechanically propelled.

Women had been driving cars since Frau Benz and her young sons made the first long run ever achieved by any self-propelled vehicle. So far they had not been numerous but by 1904 the automobile had become so reliable that the number of women drivers increased by leaps and bounds, and The Ladies' Automobile Club was formed. My mother tells me that at this time it was considered dashing to the point of being "fast" for a lady to be seen driving alone, unaccompanied by a chauffeur, or at least some form of liveried servant.

The internal combustion engine was also now considered sufficiently reliable to adapt to farm tractors. This was by no means the first attempt, but in 1904 they began to be manufactured in appreciable quantities. In this year, too, cars were first used to take electors to the poll.

A vast improvement in the engines of 1904 was the fact that they could now tackle long ascents without either boiling themselves dry or ruining their bearings. The crude horizontal engines of 1899 would run indefinitely, but the early vertical engines ran into all kinds of trouble, particularly with their lubrication. That this problem was now being overcome was proved undeniably by Max de Martini who, with the Englishman, Captain Deasy, drove a car of his own make over most of the passes in the Alps.

Ordinary cars that could go quite fast, 40 m.p.h. and more, were beginning to be sold to the public. Anyone who has driven a fast car of this date knows what a highly skilled business it is. The temptation to "put one's foot down" seems to have been irresistible to many drivers with only a few month's experience. As a grim warning, papers of the time were full of the most terrifying pictures of cars reduced to a sort of metallic omelette. Although there had been Schools of Motoring for three or four years there was no driving test or other means of checking the competence of a driver.

A car had been used in the Boer War, and the armies were beginning to take an interest. Germany had, quite early on, a Motor Volunteers Corps, as did the British. But in the manœuvres of 1904, cars really participated seriously in appreciable numbers, under the command of Major B. F. S. Baden-Powell, the brother of the founder of the Boy Scout movement, who was a very keen automobilist and airman. The High Command were extremely pleased when they found that the powerful acetylene headlamps could be used for long-distance signalling.

The second-hand advertisements columns in the motoring papers for this year make fascinating reading, from the good, reliable little Benz and De Dions at £30 to the following:

"For Sale 60 h.p. F.I.A.T. Four speeds and reverse, magneto ignition. Fitted two seated racing body, or five seated tonneau, painted white, red upholstery, complete with two Bleriot Elliptique lamps, spare tools, tyres, etc, price £1500; a most powerful car and exceptionally easy to drive."

It is typical of the strict social segregations of this epoch that privately owned cars and those offered by dealers were in separate sections of the papers.

Danny Weigel, who later built an elaborate and not very successful car on his own, made a sporting effort this year. He drove a 20-h.p. Talbot car with no windscreen or hood for 2000 miles non-stop. To drive a modern car this distance, nearly the full distance of the modern Monte Carlo Rally, would be quite an achievement. He did 2,017 miles in 124½ hours, and was rewarded with a silver cigarette case containing a £100 note, presented by Lord Shrewbury and Talbot.

Club events for sporting motorists were rapidly growing in popularity. Probably the most important of these were the Sunrising Hill Climbs run by the Midland Automobile Club, founded in 1901, and the Blackpool and Bexhill Sprint Trials. The latter were run off in heats of two cars at a time. From the very beginning, private and trade entries were run in different classes.

The great transcontinental races across Europe had been stopped, following the "Paris–Madrid" disasters. Automobile clubs had not yet learned the difficult business of spectator control, that is to say, preventing the spectators getting mixed up with the motor racing and vice versa. I do not think that even today the layman has an idea of the amount of man-hours of really hard work that goes into it, even when the racing is limited to a circuit of a few miles. No government, least of all the French, was going to permit any more of the great races between the capital cities.

The next best thing was the Gordon Bennett race. Jenatzy's win in Ireland had brought the Gordon Bennett trophy to Germany. Jenatzy was a Belgian, but the award went to the manufacturer, not the driver. He was freely tipped as a likely winner for a second time. A number of nations were competing but only two, England and France, had so many potential entrants that eliminating trials were held. Both these countries had governments who were far from enthusiastic about motor sport. In England the organisers did not even attempt to argue with the embattled reactionaries of Westminster but approached the House of Keys, the separate parliament governing the Isle of Man, who proved much more co-operative. For this elimination trial, three Wolseleys, three Napiers, and the three "British-built" Darracqs were entered. The three Huttons were not completed in time to start. It seems that the Darracqs were sent over from France in pieces and assembled at Messrs. Weir's factory at Glasgow, and that this satisfied the Gordon Bennett regulations. Opel did much the same with a Darracq in Germany. Mercedes had two strings to their bow. They could enter three cars for Germany and another three for Austria because they had factories in both places.

The English trials in the Isle of Man were not run as a straight race, but marked on a rather complicated system of points. There was one bad crash caused by the brakes jamming on Clifford Earp's Napier. His brother, who was riding as mechanic, was seriously hurt. The judges worked out from the points that England should be represented by S. F. Edge on a Napier, with Girling and Jarrott in the horizontal engined Wolseley "Beetles". John Hargreaves, M.F.H., and J. W. Stocks were in reserve with their Napiers.

At first the French government refused to permit a road race, and the Belgians offered a circuit to the promoting club. But the proud Marquis de Dion would have none of this, and he persuaded the House of Deputies to pass a Bill legalising a race in the sparsely populated Argonne district. I have always heard that the Marquis said privately that if anyone seriously opposed the Bill he would take it as a personal insult. The ready passage of the Bill may not have been entirely unconnected with the fact that the Marquis was one of the most deadly duellists of his day.

Of the twenty-nine French starters, only ten completed the

course. It is interesting to observe that Le Blon, driving a steamer, who finished fifth, averaged 61·4 m.p.h. as against the winner Théry's 74·5, for the flying kilometre. Steam-power was dying out in 1904, but it was by no means dead.

Panhard tried out a V-radiator which was a failure, and they were eliminated. France was represented by Richard-Brasier, Mors and Turcat-Méry.

The Germans, on the Kaiser's orders, did the race in style; every amenity was provided, and for the first time in history much of the course was fenced off against spectators. The competitors were started off at seven-minute intervals, and although Jenatzy drove his very best, Théry, on a Richard-Brasier, gradually increased his lead on him until in the end he beat Jenatzy's Mercedes by nearly eleven minutes. Baron de Caters on a Mercedes had, as a result of a protest, to yield third place to Rougier in a Turcat-Méry. It must have been a terrible disappointment for Jenatzy, as his American backer, Gray Dinsmore, had promised him £4000 if he won. But the moral was obvious, I think. The Richard-Brasier had shock absorbers and the springs of the Mercedes were undamped. However well Jenatzy had driven, he could not have won. The British team all had mechanical trouble and did poorly. In fact Jarrott had so much go wrong with his Wolseley that it was an heroic feat that he finished at all.

This is an interesting period for, although racing cars were driven for long periods at an average speed of 60 m.p.h. and more, they still had governed engines and low-tension ignition and, as we have just seen, shock absorbers were a novelty.

The Gordon Bennett Cup, by Théry's win, was returned to France, which put the French in a very awkward position indeed. Now they were bound to stage a race which they had publicly and violently condemned.

There were three other major races this year, the Circuit des Ardennes in Belgium, the Florio Cup in Italy, and the Vanderbilt Cup in America. The Ardennes race must have been an exciting one to watch, for the large field was evenly matched and the lead constantly changing. 90-h.p. Panhards, with the new pressed-steel chassis, were first and second.

64

Darracqs were first, second and third in the Light Car Cup. The fact that they were not a long way behind the winning vehicles does not seem to have impressed racing-car designers. During the next couple of years, and even later, they were competing one against the other, seeing who could fit the biggest engine into a chassis, regardless of all else.

The second Florio Cup was won by young Lancia driving a 75-h.p., four-cylinder, chain-driven F.I.A.T., which seems to have been "inspired" by the 60-h.p. Mercedes, even to a steel spring spiral clutch. (The next year, with their 16·2-litre racing car, F.I.A.T. did a lot more thinking for themselves.) Teste, who averaged the astonishing speed of 74 m.p.h., should have won the race with his 90-h.p. Panhard, but was penalised three minutes for filling up with petrol in a control. Florio, driving a 60-h.p. Mercedes into third place, missed winning his own cup by just over five minutes.

W. K. Vanderbilt Jnr., who had raced both Mors and Mercedes, gave a magnificent cup to be contested by national teams, rather after the manner of the Gordon Bennett Trophy. In this race France was very strongly represented by a team of professionally driven 90-h.p. Panhards. Most of the other cars, including the F.I.A.T.s, the Mercedes and three American entries, Pope-Toledo, and Royal and Simplex, were driven by American amateurs. The race was run over a triangular course on Long Island. Heath won it on a Panhard, young Clément was second in one of his father's Clément-Bayards, and Herb Lytle did extraordinarily well to get third place with his Toledo.

And so ended a most interesting year. Not only had the motor-car established the fact that it had really come to stay, but a basic design had been evolved which was to remain constant for the rest of the Edwardian period: honeycomb radiators, forward-mounted vertical multi-cylinder engines with mechanically operated valves, shaft-drive for all but the most powerful cars, and, of course, wheel steering and pressed-steel chassis. The detachable rim was already foreshadowed by the Stepney rim which fitted alongside the punctured tyre, and, in Stuttgart, Gottlieb Honold was already putting the high-tension magneto into production for Robert Bosch. Automobile production and sales were booming, to meet a demand that was to last for another three years.

18/22-h.p. four-cylinder Mercedes tourer

5

The Years of Consolidation, 1905-1909

1905

THE experimental years were over and motor-car designs had settled down to the basic principles that were to govern their construction for the next two decades. Electrics and front-wheel brakes were yet to come, and chain drive would gradually give way to shaft drive, but basically there would be little change. The year started with young Mr. Siddeley, now Lord Kenilworth, setting off in a snowstorm to prove the reliability of a 12-h.p. two-cylinder chain-driven car of his own construction, by driving it for 5,000 miles. In London, motor-buses were beginning to run with reasonable regularity. These were horse-bus bodies mounted on commercial chassis. The wealthy now made the trip to the Riviera with little trouble, except for the inevitable punctures, blowouts and accompanying tyre changing.

In India, the Delhi–Bombay trials excited the greatest interest, and there was a royal rumpus about the marking, with protests by the competitors on all sides. In America crowds were flocking to see young Barney Oldfield race his famous "Green Dragon". Another popular attraction was Webb Jay's racing steam car "Whistling Billy". In 1905 the Americans built over 24,000 cars, and started to sell them on hire purchase.

At home in England a fascinating contest was held at the Crystal Palace in February. A large area was well greased with soft soap and Thames mud, and a non-skid trial was held. It sounds the greatest fun.

As a result of many complaints that fresh recruits to motoring were being swindled, *The Autocar* briefed inspecting engineers, who would give a detailed report on any car for 2 guineas for small cars, or 4 guineas for large ones.

In 1905 there was no easy way. Tyres had to be changed

on the beaded edge rim of non-detachable wheels, and another curious competition was held in London. The winner, an employee of the Wolseley Motor Company, changed one tyre, including removing and replacing safety bolts, in five minutes, forty seconds. Truly an heroic effort.

The world's speed record, although it was not yet called that, was creeping up. Macdonald, driving a Napier at Ormonde beach in America, took it by a fractional margin, from Baras (Darracq) who had in his turn captured it at Ostend the previous year from Rigolly on his evergreen opposed-piston Gobron-Brillié. It now stood at 108·4 m.p.h.

Early in the year a Frenchman, Claudel, brought over a most ingenious carburettor with dual float chamber that would vaporise alternately petrol or paraffin. Soon he went into partnership with H. M. Hobson, later agent for Delahaye cars, and the great firm of Claudel-Hobson was launched.

That versatile engineer, F. R. Simms patented and sold "bumpers" exactly like those in use today, except that they were made of heavy rubber. He was also making the Simms-Welbeck car.

As cars got faster and more numerous, so the police began to reap an increasingly rich reward. Not that convictions were by any means universal. The country policeman, earning anything from a guinea to thirty-five shillings a week, was hardly a match for some of the best and nimblest brains in the country who, in court, pulled to bits his rough-and-ready "handkerchief and stopwatch" methods. Some of the benches were, however, so anti-motoring that no matter what garbled evidence the police gave, or however inaccurate their timing, a conviction was a matter of course. Electrical timing was tried, but the apparatus was so crude that an expert witness could show, in court, that it was very far from infallible.

The anti-motoring crusade was more or less at its zenith. Motoring was not only unpopular with some of the old die-hard squirearchy. The annual turnover of industry directly connected with the horse was, in 1905, £4,000,000,000. The fact that the London registration "A" was already full, and had gone into double letters, showed the remarkable growth of motor traffic. There were many rich and influential people who drew their incomes from this £4,000,000,000 turnover and it was in their interests to recall the man with the red flag.

The fight was on, in grim earnest. Already a few private individuals, led by Charles Jarrott, had organised volunteer cycle patrols for just such an emergency. Subscription was 1 guinea per year and motorists flocked to join. How the Motor Union and A.A. grew into the mighty Automobile Association of today is a fascinating story, particularly in the Edwardian days. It has all been ably set down in *This Motoring*, written by Stenson Cooke, who was its Secretary for so many years.

Exhibition runs were quite usual, and received a good deal of publicity. A Napier was driven the 91 miles from London to Coventry without using the clutch and so was a Coatalen-designed Humber using no gear except top. In America a White steamer was driven from Los Angeles to San Diego by a route reputedly impassable to wheel traffic since the days of the Conquistadors. Judging by contemporary photographs this may, for some of the way at least, have been quite true. In Australia the largest and longest reliability trial ever run there was won by Mr. Tarrant driving his 10-h.p. Argyll. Tarrant became, subsequently, the first Australian car manufacturer.

Young Siddeley had, in the meantime, joined up with the Wolseley Tool and Motor Company, and built a 100-h.p. racing car for Mr. Leopold de Rothschild, which Girling was to drive in the forthcoming Gordon Bennett race. It got no further than the eliminating trials in the Isle of Man. The three which did qualify for the race were Clifford Earp's Napier and two Wolseleys driven by Charles Rolls and Bianchi, who had been Jarrott's mechanic, respectively. These Wolseleys had 90-h.p. horizontal four-cylinder engines, and were otherwise similar to the "Beetles" of the previous year.

But these eliminating trials in the Isle of Man were by no means the only excitement. The Scottish Reliability Trials were run over what was a very long and tough course for 1905 cars, and great store was set by the results. The winners of their respective classes were a 6-h.p. Wolseley, a 16-h.p. Albion and a 20-h.p. Ariel. At South Harting Hill Climb the fastest time of the day was made by a Daimler, and the very exciting Bexhill Speed Trials were won by Algernon Lee Guinness's 100-h.p. Darracq with Cecil Edge's 80-h.p. Napier second and Sir Ralph Gore's 100-h.p. Mercedes third.

But, as always, the great classic races took place on the Continent. The French tried to transform the Gordon Bennett race into a French Grand Prix, but this was firmly quashed by the other competing nations. The expense of staging an international motor race had now become so huge that the promoting club had to hold it in whichever district the local authorities would put up most money towards the expenses. Highest bid came from Clermont Ferrand, where the Michelin Brothers made tyres. So the course was laid out in the Auvergne, regardless of the fact that hotel accommodation was quite inadequate for the thousands of people who flocked to see the spectacle.

A grandchild of these famous brothers told me that at about this time one of them looked over the shoulder of a clerk and saw that, instead of making entries in his ledger, he was drawing a fat, jolly man composed entirely of motor tyres. Michelin promptly took the artist off his clerical duties and set him to elaborate the world famous antics of the new-born "Monsieur Bibendum".

The French Eliminating Trials showed that the Panhards who had, this year, crammed a 120-h.p. engine into the 1000-kg. limit were no match for the Richard-Brasiers of smaller cubic capacity and more advanced design. This relatively small (11·3-litres, 160 mm. × 140 mm.) engine developed over 100 h.p. at peak (1350) revolutions. It weighed 994 kg. The French team consisting of the first three were Théry and Callois on Richard-Brasiers and Duray on a De Dietrich. The latter had, for the first time, a pressed steel chassis, instead of the old "armoured wood" chassis to which De Dietrich had clung long after others had abandoned it.

And so the last Gordon Bennett race was run over the twisting, hilly Auvergne course. The Auvergnard peasants being what they are – ask any Frenchman – stole the telephone wire between the controls, which caused much confusion among the officials. Jenatzy started as fàvourite but he was dogged with troubles on his new 120-h.p. Mercedes. The Americans had sent over two Pope-Toledos of a modest 60 h.p., driven by Lytle and Dingley, and Joe Tracy on a 90-h.p. Locomobile.

The 16·2-litre F.I.A.T.s made their début. These very advanced cars had push-rod-operated overhead valves set at 90° to each other. Drivers were two youths, Lancia and Nazzaro, with Cagno not a lot older.

Théry ("The Chronometer"), won from Nazzaro and Cagno. The British team did not do well, Charles Rolls, the best of them, finishing eighth.

Now the French were in worse trouble than ever. As winners they were bound to hold the Gordon Bennett the following year, but they had already declared that they would take no part in it. However, after a great deal of discussion, a formula acceptable to all the other national clubs was found for a French Grand Prix for 1906.

The next race of international importance was the Circuit des Ardennes, which did not attract as large or as important an entry as it had done a few years earlier. The most interesting point was the entry of a shaft-driven 112-h.p. newcomer from Italy. The Itala Company, founded in Turin by one of the Ceirano family, had made its début with a light car in the Coppa Florio the previous year, but did not put a big racing car in the field till the Circuit des Ardennes of 1905. The race was won by Héméry on a "light" Darracq of a mere 80 h.p.

Raggio, an amateur and a newcomer, driving one of the new Italas, then proceeded to win the third Coppa Florio, still being run on the Brescia circuit. There was another new Italian make in this race. The 120-h.p. Isotta-Fraschinis were entered, but either failed to start or did not survive the first lap. These cars are reputed to have been designed by Ettore Bugatti for the newly formed company. This is supported by the fact that De Dietrich, who had retained Bugatti as a consultant designer for a number of years, were associated with Isotta-Fraschini.

1906

This year is distinguished by two far-reaching events. Detachable rims appeared, and as we shall see later in this chapter, small-car racing was reborn. The year started with the news that the stout and genial American, Charles Glidden, was driving a Napier car round the world a second time; a feat attempted unsuccessfully some four years earlier by Dr. Lehwess in the huge and cumbrous Panhard "Passe Partout". Australia had started early to build her own cars. Mr. H. Tarrant, winner of many reliability trials, was now in production with his 8-h.p. two-cylinder. In England there was considerable trepidation as it was feared that Louis Renault's "Master" patent in shaft-driven transmission might cause all British manufacturers to be forced to pay him royalties. However, it was proved that the idea had been anticipated by many years in this country. It was also found that the gate change, patented by Mercedes, had been anticipated.

Two very significant happenings were taking place, which really showed that by this year, 1906, motoring was fast becoming part of our way of life. One was the almost universal use of motor-cars in the general election, the other that cars with chauffeurs could now be hired to tour to any part of the British Isles. One paid £5 a day, all-in except chauffeurs' meals.

And, just to show that there is nothing new under the sun, a Frenchman called Constantin built a pair of roller skates, each one with a tiny petrol motor. 30 m.p.h. was claimed. The petrol tank and ignition were strapped on the inventor's back!

A Motor Show was held in March at the Agricultural Hall. There was little that was very novel, and the keynote of the show was a battle between low- and high-tension ignition, and the number of makers coming out, probably in view of the immense success of the Napier, with six-cylinder engines. Shaft-drive was on the increase, often described by the rather fancy name of "chainless drive", but virtually all the really powerful cars still used chain-drive. It would not be till the following year, when Rolls and Royce led the way with the 40/50-h.p.

"Silver Ghost" that shaft-drive for big cars began to gain ground. Many cars were still "governed", but the governor now operated on the carburettor, and not by partially lifting the exhaust valves as of yore.

As far as coachwork went, the landaulette body was rapidly gaining ground, and a few "doctors' coupés" were beginning to appear. Lieutenant Windham had patented a "transformable" body which was to be very popular during the next few years. The front seats remained permanently anchored to the chassis, while various alternative types of landaulette, brougham or touring coachwork, which were stored hanging from the garage roof, could be lowered down and bolted into place.

A question in Parliament throws an interesting light on international commerce of the day. During an average month, we exported two British-built cars to France, but imported four hundred, or even more, French-built cars from France! It is interesting, *en passant*, to note that British motorists touring in France not only had to comply with very strict customs formalities, but had to wear French number plates. Channel-crossing for a car did not cost a great deal less than it does today. Something of the order of £4 each way, plus a fee for use of crane for landing.

Acetylene lighting was still very much the order of the day. A great deal of ingenuity and fine workmanship went into this equipment. The better-class types, such as "Rushmore", had optically ground mirrors for reflectors. I remember them well. The whole secret was to keep the burners and generating plant, in which water dripped slowly on to carbide, scrupulously clean. They gave a very pleasant soft light, and it was quite safe to drive behind them at anything up to 40 m.p.h. on a good road.

Steam cars, although on the decline, were by no means defunct. A White steamer made fastest time of day, 80·6 seconds, at Shelsley Walsh (cf. Charles Jarrott, 60-h.p. De Dietrich, 105 seconds).

Among the amateur fraternity, Algernon Lee Guinness bought the 200-h.p. Darracq that had been the first car in the world to do two miles in the minute, and H. R. Pope with his Itala had captured the London to Monte-Carlo record from

73

Jarrott and Rolls. Miss Dorothy Levitt was driving her 90-h.p. Napier with great success in competitions. Police trapping was as virulent as ever, but by now counter measures were well under way. Not only were maps published and details given in the motoring press, but the Motor Union, whose membership was growing, was getting a worthwhile number of Scouts out on to the road. There was a famous test case, in which the A. A. Scout was held not guilty of obstructing the police in their duty by warning motorists of a trap.

At the end of 1906, a Motor Exhibition was held at Olympia. As at the Spring show, there was nothing startlingly new, virtually all touring cars were now side-entrance, and there was a vogue for three-quarter elliptic springing. That is really almost all that can be said about the Show this year.

Now let us go back a little and have a look at the racing year. Small-car racing, which had languished for some years, began to have a separate entity of its own. From these early voiturettes it is easy to trace an unbroken line of development to the Aston Martins, Lancias and Porsches of today. L'Auto, the French paper, did sponsor a Coupe des Voiturettes the previous year, but it was more in the nature of a series of one-day trials, based on Alexandre Darracq's works at Suresnes, than a race.

In 1906, however, it was definitely a race; run round a triangle at Rambouillet near Paris. The main regulation was that the bore should not exceed 106 mm. for a single-cylinder engine, or 90 mm. for a twin. This was not nearly as crazy as it sounds for, to develop maximum power, the competitor had to have either longer stroke or higher engine speed. It was the latter that the organisers sought to encourage. In point of fact it worked the other way at first, producing strange monstrosities like the 1910 Lion Peugeots. But later, with the assistance of Ettore Bugatti, Louis Delage, Marc Birkgit and the 1208-c.c. Isotta-Fraschini and other cars, the foundation of the post-Kaiser war sports cars was laid. In fact Lionel Martin ran one of these little Isottas in 1913/14, and from this the early Bamford and Martin, later to become the Aston Martin, was partially developed.

74

The start of light-car racing was the beginning of the end for the great bolides of the heroic age. By 1912 a 3-litre Sunbeam was lapping the Grand Prix circuit almost as fast as a 15-litre F.I.A.T. After this the engine designs of the young Swiss Ernest Henry, who coaxed 90 b.h.p. out of 3-litres at just under 3000 r.p.m., and his followers, rendered the big-engined cars as out of date as a full-bottomed wig.

Altogether 1906 is full of interest. In January, at Ormonde, Daytona, Marriot drove his Stanley steamer over the flying mile in 28½ seconds. That is to say 127 m.p.h. Then Cavaliere Florio, a wealthy Sicilian vineyard owner, who had sponsored the Coppa Florio races at Brescia but never managed to win his own cup, decided to stage a race round his native island.

The story goes that competitors complained during practice that they were being almost continually sniped at round the 93 miles of wild mountain course. There was quite enough hazard in motor racing, they said, without rifle bullets going past their heads. So Cavaliere Florio sent for the three principal brigands of the island and made them STEWARDS OF THE MEETING, and sent them back to the hills with strict instructions to see that none of the lesser brigands indulged in rifle practice on the tempting, swiftly moving targets. The instructions have been carried out to the letter to this day.

The entry regulations are of considerable interest, and could well be copied by many racing organisers today. The cars had, within clearly defined limits, to be stock models that could be bought by anybody at a fairly modest ceiling price. The toughness of the course can be gathered from the fact that the winning Itala, piloted by Cagno, a consistently successful driver of F.I.A.T. cars, averaged less than 30 m.p.h.! This was the 40-h.p. production sports model, not to be confused with the bigger Grand Prix car but even then it was no sluggard.

The first Targa Florio only drew a small field, but the names are interesting. Rigal, one of the greatest drivers of the late Edwardian period, was making his début in one of the new Italas. Baron de Caters, a great sportsman of the early days of racing, was making almost his farewell bow on the same model, which had the most exciting lattice-work chassis. Bablot, later crack Delage driver, was driving one of his first big races in a Berliet. Lancia, now at the top of his form but, as ever, dogged by bad luck, was still driving a F.I.A.T. A superb driver, he must have been frustrated, by circumstances beyond his control, from winning more races than any other racing motorist before or since. This time it was a split petrol tank.

The great excitement of the year was, of course, the French Grand Prix, which had now superseded the "Gordon Bennett". For the record, although we today usually think of this as the first Grand Prix, the Automobile Club de France held that it was, taking into account the following, the ninth. Paris–Bordeaux 1895, Paris–Marseilles 1896, Paris–Amsterdam 1898, Tour de France 1899, Paris–Toulouse 1900, Paris–Berlin 1901, Paris–Vienna 1902, Paris–Madrid 1903.

Officially, because it was one of the birthplaces of the French automobile industry, but probably for quite a number of other reasons as well, the circuit was laid out near Le Mans in the Sarthe district. The local authorities, realising that the great crowds drawn by a motor race would bring money into a not very wealthy agricultural district, spent a small fortune on the course, including, for the first time, a tunnel for the spectators to pass under the course.

The previous year Louis Renault, who had stopped building racing cars after his brother's death in the "Paris–Madrid", had started again. Marcel Renault's mechanic, Szisz, of Hungarian extraction, who started life as an engine-driver, was the firm's official driver. The car was a very sound conventional 90-h.p. four-cylinder, and the engine was not so heavy that the safety factor of chassis parts had to be skimped to come within the 1000-kg. limit, as in the case of the monstrous 18-litre Panhards and De Dietrichs arrayed against it.

There was a sharp divergence from the rules of the "Gordon Bennett", in so much that all repairs and tyre changing should be done by the driver and mechanic. The latter was, as anyone who has changed beaded-edge tyres on the road-wheel knows well, something very like hard labour, and I remember Charles Jarrott saying to me, "The two real hardships of the early days you youngsters have never experienced – the dust and the troubles."

Possibly as a result of this new ruling, Brasier, F.I.A.T, Itala and Renault all appeared with the first detachable-rim wheels ever seen.

It is only natural that the first two places in this race went to cars with detachable rims and significant that no 18-litre cars could do better than sixth place. The advantage of the detachable rims was emphasised by the tropical heat of the June day which played havoc with the tyres. Three-speed gearboxes were not really an innovation, but a number of builders of racing cars, notably Renault, Brasier, Darracq and Itala, had adopted them to save weight. The race was won by Szisz, with young Nazzaro on a F.I.A.T. second. Third place went to Albert Clément, driving one of his father's Bayard cars which was a fine effort, as he did not have detachable rims.

And so ended a very happy Grand Prix for the French. The race had been run according to rules of, more or less, their own drafting; it had been won by a Frenchman, and the German-entered Mercedes had finished last. What more could a Frenchman want?

The two remaining big races on the calendar were the Belgian Circuit des Ardennes, and the Vanderbilt Cup at Long Island. The Coppa Florio at Brescia had to be abandoned as the Italian Government feared bigger crowds of spectators than ever before, and declined to detail troops to keep them off the course. I am delighted to report that the populace of Northern Italy, even then enthusiastic on motor racing, staged some quite sizable riots to protest against the Government refusing them their fun.

The Circuit des Ardennes, which had not been run since 1902, produced nothing new whatsoever, but it must have been a most exciting race to watch; for although chassis design was improving immensely, the engines were still about 16- or 18-litres, achieving peak power at about 1200 r.p.m.

The designers of the American cars were uninhibited in 1905, and in 1906 they were even more so. Fifteen cars were entered for the eliminating trials for the Vanderbilt Cup, and with the exception of Tracy's Locomobile and the Thomas cars, which were more or less copies of current French practice, each one was more odd than the last. Even Lytle's 120-h.p. Pope-Toledo, normally a reasonably conventional car, had a most peculiar chassis, and shared one valve spring between each pair of valves. The twelve-cylinder Maxwell had a horizontal engine and no flywheel, the Christie was bigger and more unorthodox than ever, and the Fryer Miller was a stripped chassis carrying an immense air-cooled engine with its centrifugal fan, two bucket seats and little else.

The remarkable thing about these freaks is that some of them ran, and ran very well. But the race itself was, of course, a walk-over for the tried and tested Continental cars and drivers who had come over for the race. The only two American cars left running at the finish were a Thomas, driven by Le Blon, who had been brought over from France, and the Locomobile driven by Tracy. The race was won by Wagner's Darracq, followed by a string of European cars down to eighth place, which was occupied by Le Blon's Thomas, the first American car.

And that was the end of the year's racing. the Commission Sportif, in an attempt to curb the installation of bigger and bigger engines in inadequate, unscientifically designed chassis, based the formula for 1907 on petrol consumption. Unfortunately, this excellent idea has never been repeated.

Nearly 200,000 people attended the Olympia Motor Show held in November. General tendencies were the increase in popularity of six-cylinder engines, and increased use of pump lubrication, pressed steel frames, quadrant changes and ball bearings. As far as coachwork went, a side entrance as opposed to a rear entrance or swinging seat was now essential. For open cars, much ingenuity had been expended on the Cape Cart Hood, which was still difficult to erect, and a few very crude side curtains were seen. In fact, on all sides real efforts were beginning to be made for the comfort of both driver and passenger during the long journeys that were beginning to become the order of the day.

The Locke-Kings were a wealthy couple. Among other possess-
ions they owned Mena House Hotel in Egypt which, in those
days, paid formidable dividends, and they decided that England
needed a high-speed test track. The motor manufacturers, when
approached, were very luke-warm about the project, and gave
little or no financial support. Both Jarrott and Edge, however,
were keenly enthusiastic and were largely responsible for the
form in which the Brooklands Track was laid out at
Weybridge in Surrey, at the cost of a quarter of a million
pounds. Designed by Colonel H. C. L. Holden, R.E., one of
the most remarkable things about the track was the speed with
which it was built. The contractors, Price and Reeves, brought
2000 men on to the site and special trains brought building
materials and 200,000 tons of cement. Work was started late
in 1906, and in the incredibly short time of about nine months,
the track and the clubhouse were open. There is a first-rate
history of Brooklands, written by William Boddy, the editor
of *Motor Sport*.

As far as I know, the first practical self-starter was made by
Monsieur Mors in 1905. There may well have been earlier
isolated attempts of which I am unaware. The French sponsored
a competition for self-starters, and many weird and wonderful
devices were shown. Curiously enough, among the least successful varieties were those operated by electricity. There were a
number of perfectly practical compressed air starters. Typical
of these is a "Letombe", imported from France by Charles
Jarrott and Letts, where compressed air was stored in a metal
bottle. The compressor, a beautiful little bit of work, was
permanently coupled to the engine. It was therefore possible
by means of a simple rotary valve, built integrally with the
compressor, to admit compressed air from the bottle to each
cylinder, in the correct order, as the piston came past top dead
centre.

I do not think many of us realise that, under the 1896 Act
and the Local Government Regulations referred to in it, a car
had to carry a white light on the off side showing forwards and

a red light showing to the rear. It was about this time, too, that His Majesty King Edward VII, always a keen motorist, had granted the Automobile Club the prefix "Royal". Early in this year, too, was the Crystal Palace Motor Exhibition. This old-established show was so badly supported by manufacturers that the organisers were forced to include an exhibition of second-hand vehicles.

With the increase in the number of cars on the road to over 60,000 from 45,000 the previous year, attention was focused on two, to us, long-forgotten nuisances – road dust and smoky exhausts. The Royal Automobile Club ran a "vapour emission" competition, which was won by a 32-h.p. Pilgrim with a 20-h.p. Lanchester, Albion, Belsize and Chenard-Walcker as runners up. Many trials, experiments and conferences were held on the subject of road surfaces. Coachbuilders experimented and published their findings, with several variations of the "tulip-back" body to see which raised the least dust. But both these controversial problems died a natural death, the former because of the increased use of force-feed lubrication pumps to replace the old "splash and dip" or "drip" systems. The latter was gradually solved, over a period of years, by the surfacing of main roads with tarmac.

One of the most fascinating events of the year was the Pekin to Paris race, sponsored by a French daily paper. The competitors faced almost unbelievable difficulties ranging from obstruction by dignified Chinese officials, to thousands of miles of almost impassable roads across Czarist Russia. Added to these were, of course, the usual ailments from which 1907 cars suffered. The winner, Prince Borghese, who drove an Itala, wrote the most enthralling book about his adventures.

The Tourist Trophy was run again under slightly different regulations. There was also a "Heavy-touring" class run concurrently for cars fitted with larger and more commodious bodywork. The latter was won by a Beeston Humber. It is interesting to observe that this was the lightest car in its class, as was the 20-h.p. Rover which won the Tourist Trophy itself.

Speed trials and hill-climbs (Shelsley Walsh was held for the first time in 1905), were on the increase in England, but

80

undoubtedly the event of the year was the opening in June of Brooklands, the first banked motor racing track in the world. There was, of course, no established method of running a meeting on this kind of circuit, and horse-racing procedure was adopted almost in its entirety.

Soon after the first meeting S. F. Edge did his famous twenty-four hours' run round the track at an average speed of over 60 m.p.h. He himself drove the whole time, and at night was guided by storm lanterns placed at intervals round the circuit.

In Europe there was a very full racing calendar which began with the Targa Florio. The formula stipulated that four-cylinder cars should have a bore of between 120 mm. and 130 mm. The minimum weight allowed was 1000 kilograms, plus 20 kilograms for every millimetre of bore over 120 mm. This seemed to favour the Italians, for out of forty-six starters, F.I.A.T. were first and second, with Itala third and fifth and Isotta-Fraschini seventh. The only foreigners in the first twelve were the French aces Duray and Gabriel on De Dietrichs.

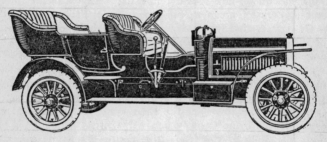

Tourist Trophy winner, 1907: the 16/20 h.p.,
four-cylinder Rover

We have noted the resurgence of "voiturette" racing in 1906. This year Vincenzo Florio, always in the forefront of anything new, organised a race for small cars of limited bore, round the same circuit as the Targa Florio. Naudin, driving one of the new and unorthodox Sizaire Naudins, which had been bought by Florio, won it, with Florio himself second, on his racing single-cylinder De Dion; soundly trouncing the Lion

81

Peugeots, so called because they were built at Belfort, a town whose crest is a lion.

Next, Kaiser Wilhelm II of Germany offered a large prize to the winner of a race for what we should call "sports cars". Engine capacity was limited to 8 litres, and the supplementary regulations ensured that real racing cars should not compete. This "Kaiserpreis" attracted an enormous entry, many manufacturers building cars specially for it, including the English Daimler Company. So vast was the number of entries that two eliminating races were run, each between about forty cars. The circuit was 73 miles round, and took in some of the old "Gordon Bennett" course. One of the cars to be eliminated was the Mercedes-Mixte, an extremely clever adaptation by a young Austrian, Ferdinand Porsche, of a Mercedes with his own electric transmission. F.I.A.T., who had built cars specially for this event, did very well indeed. Lancia won one eliminating race, Nazzaro the other and the final. A long-forgotten Belgian car which had been racing since 1901, the Pipe, was second. This was an 80-h.p. four-cylinder car with overhead valves and high-tension magneto, built specially for the "Kaiserpreis".

Of course, the French Grand Prix still held the blue riband of the motor-racing world, and attracted a large entry. The only British entries were two 15-litre, straight-eight Weigels. Weigel had left the Talbot Company and had started to build motor-cars on his own. It seems, by all accounts, that they were not very good cars. He did not last long as a manufacturer on his own, and a year or so later he became associated with the Crowdy car. Mr. Christy brought his remarkable 20-litre, V-4 front-drive racing car from America, but did not start. The French put in every car they could, including Rigolly's ancient opposed-piston Gobron-Brillié, which had been built in 1903, and which was still going very well indeed. The Italians entered three F.I.A.T.s and an Aquila Italiana at the last moment, paying double fees to do so. Young Albert Clément was killed in practice, but in spite of this terrible tragedy, his tough old father, Adolphe Clément, insisted that the rest of the Clément-Bayard team should run in the race.

Although the winner was Nazzaro driving a 16-litre F.I.A.T., the keynote of the race was that cars of more moderate capacity went as fast, and faster, than some of the really big-capacity cars.

Three weeks later came the Circuit des Ardennes, divided this year into two races: one for Grand Prix formula cars, the other for "Kaiserpreis" formula cars. The former was won by Baron de Caters, the first major event he had won in ten years of racing. Happily, he was driving his first and great love, a Mercedes. Kenelm Lee Guinness on a 120-h.p. Darracq was second. The "Kaiserpreis" race was a notable victory for England and Minerva. Moore-Brabazon (now Lord Brabazon of Tara) won, Lee Guinness also driving a Minerva was third, Warwick Wright, sixth. The only non-English driver placed was Koolhoven, also on a Minerva. These Belgian Minervas, specially built for racing, cannot be identified by their radiators, because instead of having flat ones luxuriantly curved on top, they had very sharp V-radiators, not dissimilar to a Métallurgique, but at a considerably more acute angle.

It will be recalled that the previous year the Coppa Florio could not be run at Brescia because of the refusal of the Government to draft in additional police or soldiers to keep spectators off the course. Cavaliere Florio recruited his own corps of marshals, and two races, to "Kaiserpreis" and Grand Prix formulae, were run off round a slightly shorter circuit of 38 miles. The Americans experienced the same trouble, but presumably owing to the fact that the cost would have been so much higher in the U.S.A., they were unable to solve it as easily as the Sicilian Cavaliere, with the result that there was no American Grand Prix in 1907.

The "Kaiserpreis" formula for the Coppa Florio was a notable victory for a young man who will be remembered as a driver of great ability in the 1920s – Minoia. This was his first year in *grandes épreuves,* and he was driving an overbore short-stroke (145 mm. × 120 mm.) Isotta-Fraschini, by no means the largest engine capacity in the race.

Cagno, driving a large 120-h.p. Itala, put up a magnificent show in the Grand Prix formula race. Although delayed eight minutes early on, with magneto trouble, he worked his way right through the field and won. This was really wonderful driving because the duration of the race was little over half an hour. On one lap he averaged 71·8 m.p.h. on a circuit that was so curly that there were quite a number of accidents. Baron di Martino was killed in his Züst, and Duray and Shepard, the American amateur, who had forsaken Hotchkiss for Clément-Bayard, both ran off the road.

And so ended an outstanding year's racing, if only because of the variety of formulae. The Kaiserpreis limited the cubic capacity to 8 litres, the Targa Florio and Coupe des Voiturettes limited the bore and the Grand Prix formula was based on petrol consumption.

In those days of cheap skilled labour, it was quite in order for a firm like F.I.A.T. to build three separate teams of racing cars, one for each formula. This, in fact, they did, winning Targa Florio, Kaiserpreis and Grand Prix.

At the end of the year, the Coupe des Voiturettes was run again at Rambouillet. Up to quite modern times there have been a vast quantity of small cycle-car builders, employing two or three men, in little sheds all over France. The Frenchman is an extremely original thinker. If two find that they think alike, they form a political party. It was much the same over cycle-cars. Sometimes, as was the case of Monsieur Naudin and the Sizaire brothers, they built very good ones. But most of the thirty different makes from which the sixty-one starters were drawn on that damp late autumn morning in 1907 were obscure then, and have been forgotten for forty years.

Looking down the list, Sizaire Naudin, Delage, Peugeot, Doriot-Flandrin (Parant had not yet been taken into partnership) and Corre la Licorne are the only names that strike a chord, most of the others, even to a serious student of early racing cars, convey very little.

The regulations held that the bore must be 20 mm. less than in 1906, but still put no restriction on stroke. The strokes of most cars had not yet been increased to the fantastic dimensions of three or four years later, but even then, at an engine-

84

speed in excess of 2000 r.p.m., piston speeds must have been exciting.

The exception to this was that those voiturettes fitted with proprietary De Dion Bouton single-cylinder engines retained a conservative bore/stroke ratio.

The circumstances under which the "trial" was run could not have been more French. In order to get permission from the Ministry of the Interior to run on public roads, the organisers had to pretend that it was a reliability trial for fully equipped low horse-power touring cars. Of course, the Ministry knew perfectly well that the cars were miniature racers stripped down to two bucket seats and highly tuned. The fact that the exhaust pipes in most of the cars were open-ended stubs was purely coincidental. By various polite subterfuges the fiction was maintained, and Parliamentary face was saved. Monsieur Naudin won, in spite of being held up. A lot of other competitors thought that they should have won and protested that Naudin had "doped" his petrol with picric acid; a charge he was easily able to refute.

And so ended 1907, a year more remarkable for good sport than for spectacular technical progress.

1908

The idea of producing a large number of interchangeable parts for assembly, instead of making every individual component separately for each car, appears to have come into being in the American Civil War for the manufacture of rifles for the Northern Forces. Mass production was applied to other forms of machinery and there seems very little doubt that, as far as quantity production of automobiles goes, the Americans were leading European makers by five or six years. The first manifestation of this in England was when several Cadillacs were assembled, under very strict R.A.C. supervision, from "scrambled" parts and then driven round the track. For this they received the Dewar Trophy.

Some interesting research was done by S. F. Edge on the relation of the frontal area of a car to its performance at high speed. These experiments were many years ahead of their time and cannot be said to have borne much fruit in the Edwardian period.

Certainly the greatest technical development of the year was the sleeve-valve engine. English-born Charles Knight worked in America but, as he could find no sale for his revolutionary engine over there, he brought it to his home country. Percy Martin of Daimlers saw it and was much impressed by the idea but not by the way in which Knight had executed it. In a matter of months, an incredibly short space of time for this sort of work, he had drastically modified the engine and got it into production. Towards the end of 1908 Daimlers were appearing with the famous "Silent Knight" engine. This was, of course, the double-sleeve engine. Shortly afterwards, patents were taken out, both in America and Europe, for single-sleeve engines.

Although some may well have been made earlier, the first electric horn actually in production appeared in 1908. It was a diaphragm-type operated by electric magnets, not dissimilar to those made today. As for lighting, acetylene had now reached its highest pitch of development and all sorts of ingenious and beautifully-made contraptions such as shutters and mechanical dimmers were available to mitigate the glare when meeting another car. Electric lighting was making a very shy and barely noticed appearance. The first and, at that time, principal manufacturer was C. A. Vandervell, who preceded Lucas on electrics by some years. The earliest sets simply derived the current from a 60-ampere-hour battery, which had to be removed from the car for charging as there were as yet no car dynamos in production, although one or two engineers wrote to the technical press saying that they had adapted small dynamos and cut-outs for their cars. One of the earliest firms to make one specially for the job was E.I.C.

As for the engine and chassis, chains were fast giving way to the live axle and low-tension ignition was now almost obsolete. Gate change was rapidly gaining popularity, and would soon be almost universal, although some of the French makers retained the quadrant change for many years. There was also a tendency towards the idea pioneered by Daimler many years earlier, of building engine and gearbox in one unit.

In America production went up and up and hit an all-time peak of 63,500 cars in a year.

A lot happened there of great interest commercially and very little of technical interest. William Crapo Durant founded General Motors. Fred and Charles Fisher founded what was to become the mammoth Fisher body combine. The first Model T Ford chuffed out of the Detroit works, the first of fifteen million to be built in 19 years. Coupled with the birth of the Model T was one of the technically interesting achievements; the development of vanadium steel for this car. The other American achievement in the technical field this year was the development and production of helical gearing.

The Americans, inspired by the Pekin–Paris race of the previous year, held a New York–Paris race. It was not very well supported in the way of entries, and only one car, a Thomas Flyer, got through.

In Europe, the cost of motor racing was rising rather sharply, and most of the manufacturers seem to have tacitly agreed to economise by not supporting the Targa Florio, which was won by Trucco on an Isotta Fraschini, with Lancia on his F.I.A.T. as inevitably second as Girardot in years gone by.

Héméry put up a most fantastic performance in the St. Petersburg–Moscow race. He drove an enormous Benz to victory over 438 miles of road with a surface like the mountains of the moon at an average speed of 51·4 m.p.h. Anyone who has averaged over 50 m.p.h. over any distance on the road knows that one has to be doing about 80 m.p.h. a great deal of the time. Couple this with 1908 springing and Russian roads and this really does sound an achievement to bracket with Monsieur Levassor's feat in the "Paris–Marseilles".

The French Grand Prix was well supported with no less than forty-six entries and was run once more on the Dieppe circuit. For the first time, pits were built for the mechanics. They really were pits, below ground level, and the name persists to this day. The regulations this year stipulated a minimum weight of 1100 kilogrammes and a maximum bore of 155 mm. for four-cylinder engines and 127 mm. for six. The Germans put a very strong team in the field. Not unnaturally, with the soaring costs of building and racing special cars, both Mercedes and Benz (completely separate entities till the amalgamation of the two firms in 1926) made periodic attempts to abstain from racing. But every time either of them did this, their sales started to drop in the most alarming manner, so they had to start again. This year both firms sent teams, driving 1908 models, as did the firm of Adam Opel, a huge cycle-making concern, who had now been making cars for some years. Fritz, one of the partners, had started this off by building Darracqs under licence.

France was represented by Lorraine de Dietrich and Panhard who showed little evidence of fresh ideas, and by Clément Bayard and Renault who did. Mors and Brasier made a not very successful come-back to the Grand Prix racing. Italy put in F.I.A.T.s and several Italas, and England was represented by Austins. The Belgians also put in a team. Napier had tried to enter a team of most interesting and advanced cars, but the A.C.F. would not accept them on the childish pretext that their Rudge-Whitworth patent detachable wheels were unsafe.

Mercedes made a brilliant come-back, so did Benz. In fact if Héméry had not had his goggles smashed by a flying stone and got a splinter of glass in his eye, he might well have won the Grand Prix for the latter firm. It was a most exciting race, and George Monkhouse of Kodak has a copy of a film of it which is, discounting the jerky action, tremendously thrilling. But the race was really decided on tyres. This was one of the periods when the speed of racing cars had outstripped the inventiveness of the tyre manufacturers. By the time young Lautenschlager was on his final winning laps not one single spare cover was left in his Mercedes pit.

There was not a French car in the first three home, and most of them finished well down the list. As a result of this cataclysmic defeat the French manufacturers got together to sabotage their own Grand Prix as thoroughly as they had done the Gordon Bennett race. They signed a pact to abstain from Grand Prix racing and induced most of the leading German and Belgian makers to sign as well. When the A.C.F. tried to organise a Grand Prix for 1909 all the entries they received were from Monsieur Mors who, good for him, had firmly refused to sign the "black pact", and from a few of the lesser-known makers. So it was abandoned and there was no French Grand Prix, discounting the rather inadequate affair at Le Mans in 1911, until 1912.

The Italians staged some racing at Bologna in September for the Coppa Florio and the Targa Bologna. It was a very fast and exciting race, with the best lap by Lancia at an average speed of over 82 m.p.h. Most of the cars were retired French-built Grand Prix cars, driven by up and coming Italians, a combination that certainly makes for thrills and spills. It was won by Nazzaro on a F.I.A.T.

In England, about the same time, the "four-inch" race was run in the Isle of Man, so-called of course, because of the limitation of the bore. Napier did not have a suitable car, but they were represented in a way because, although for some unknown reason it was always kept extremely dark, the Huttons were built in the Napier works. The race was, most of the way, a tussle for the lead between Watson's Hutton and two Darracqs. On the last lap it looked as if George, one of the Darracq drivers, had won the race, but a mile or two from the finish his carburettor caught fire which held him up long enough to let Watson on his Hutton into first place. At least one of these "four-inch" Huttons is still in existence.

In America, a couple of years earlier, A. L. Riker of the old-established firm of Locomobile, built a four-cylinder (7¼ in. × 6¼ in.) overhead-valve racing car of advanced design. Any hope it may have had of victory against strong European opposition in the 1906 Vanderbilt Cup was killed by tyre trouble. The car was entered again in the 1908 Vanderbilt Cup and George Robertson, after a terrific 100-m.p.h. duel with Herb Lytle's Isotta, brought it home the winner. This historic car, preserved like new, is now the pride and joy of Peter Helck, the famous American artist.

A little later the American Grand Prix was run at Savannah. All the European crack drivers brought their cars over and swamped the natives. There was not a single American car amongst the first fourteen; Ralph Mulford's Lozier came in fifteenth. Wagner won on a F.I.A.T.

At the end of 1908 we can reach a number of conclusions. Although chassis had not changed a lot, racing-car engines were getting much more efficient and the benefit of this would be passed on to the production cars of the following year.

But perhaps the most significant thing was that France had now definitely and irrevocably lost the lead in motor-car design which she once held over the rest of the world.

And finally, during the next few years, firms whose reputation had been built on racing learned, as they should have from their earliest attempts to do so, that it does not pay to stop racing. Mercedes lost so many sales that they had to discharge men. Many great names of the first ten years of motoring declined into small and obscure firms, a number of whom went out of business.

1909

For the previous two or three years motor-car designers had been behaving rather like Charles Lamb's fabled Chinese who, whenever they wanted roast pork, put a pig in a house and then burned the house down. They were, in fact, achieving simple effects by very complex methods. One typical example of this is that in 1909 L-head engines, with all the valves on one side, were beginning to replace the almost universal T-head engine, so that only one camshaft was necessary instead of two. A great deal of external tidying-up was done to engines and drilled ducts were replacing the complex network of copper pipes (which used to harden with vibration and break) for the conveyance of oil to where it was needed.

Apart from the two processes above, there was little basic change in the engines of 1909, although detail improvements evolved during the previous year's racing paid dividends. There were two general tendencies. Now that it was a normal thing for crankshafts to revolve at a speed in excess of 1000 r.p.m., increasing numbers of manufacturers were beginning to fit central bearings. The other tendency was a striving after mechanical silence, particularly with relation to valve gear.

Napier, Rolls-Royce and the other makers of high quality cars had achieved this some time ago, but now it was being eagerly sought by all.

The trickle of weird and wonderful alternatives to the conventional four-stroke engine, that was to become a flood during the next year or two, had already started. Very few got further than one experimental model, and many never beyond the drawing-board and patent rights. There were, however, a very few exceptions, notably the Valveless car – a somewhat unorthodox two-stroke which had appeared in 1908 and sold in quite considerable quantities up to the outbreak of war in 1914. Another exception was the piston-valve Bentall, built at Heybridge, Essex, up to 1912, which was well spoken of in the technical press. Even Riley, usually producing rather a conventional car, brought out a sleeve-valve engine of their own design.

Although high-tension magnetos were almost universal, people were still a bit mistrustful of them. So Maudslay and some other makers mounted them on the driver's side of the dashboard. This fashion only lasted a very short time till Ettore Bugatti revived it in the early 1920s.

Early in this year the French suddenly realised the unpalatable fact that they were no longer the leading nation of automobilists in Europe. Their press published with great dismay that although nearly ninety thousand cars were registered in Great Britain there were not thirty-eight thousand in all France. In France, chain-drive retained its popularity. In England only about one-eighth of the cars were still chain-driven, in comparison to a quarter of the cars in France.

An interesting sign of the times was the beginning of a movement to standardise screw threads to some extent. Admittedly some manufacturers, Talbot for instance, would supply the owner, at an extra cost, with a set of stocks and dies of their own particular threads, but it does not need much imagination to envisage the appalling confusion. It also goes a long way to explain why, in the old days, practically every car repairer, however humble, was equipped with a small screw-cutting lathe. Yet another innovation this year, which grew

91

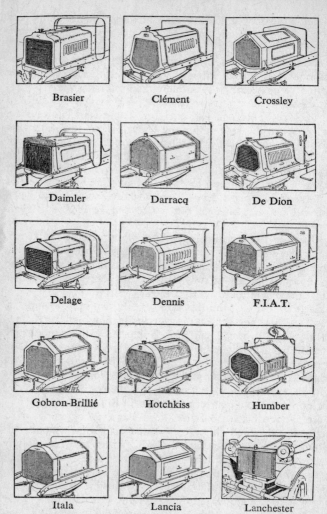

Brasier   Clément   Crossley

Daimler   Darracq   De Dion

Delage   Dennis   F.I.A.T.

Gobron-Brillié   Hotchkiss   Humber

Itala   Lancia   Lanchester

SOME RADIATOR DESIGNS OF 1909 [*Not to the same scale*]

into great things, was the erection "as an experiment to determine whether or not they were of any value" of three roadside telephone call-boxes for the use of motorists. These appear to have been sponsored by private firms and not by the Automobile Club.

An enterprising German, Lieutenant Graetz, motored across Africa. It took him over nine months. The main reason for his not very good time was the fact that whenever he came to a river — and these were both wide and frequent — he had to round up natives to build him a raft.

The British company handling Mercedes attempted to enforce certain basic patents such as the gate-change, but the days of Lawson, Pennington and Selden were gone for ever, and they failed to do so.

In March the Nice Automobile Week was run off in pouring rain. It no longer had the international flavour of earlier days, for most of the entrants and all the winners, with a couple of exceptions, were French cars. Relatively new makers, however, still sent works teams, in the hope of catching the eye of wealthy patrons. But almost all the old names, except various manifestations of Clément, were absent.

The abstention of the major manufacturers from racing made for rather a dull entry for the Targa Florio. It was won by Baron Ciuppa driving an S.P.A. (Societa Piedmontese Automobili) with Cavaliere Florio, for once getting very near winning his own race, on a F.I.A.T. There was also a voiturette race over the course in which long-stroke Lion Peugeots driven by Goux and Guippone came first and second. Goux also won the Catalan Cup presented by King Alfonso of Spain. He must have judged the speed of his Lion Peugeot nicely, as the roads were terrible and broke up the cars that tried to go any faster than he did. In the French Coupe des Voiturettes, the only major race in France now that most of the manufacturers were abstaining from racing, Lion Peugeots were first and second. This time the winner was Guippone, with Goux second. The British Calthorpes finished well down the list. Gaillon hill-climb was one of the last wins for a Brasier car driven by that up-and-coming young driver, Bablot.

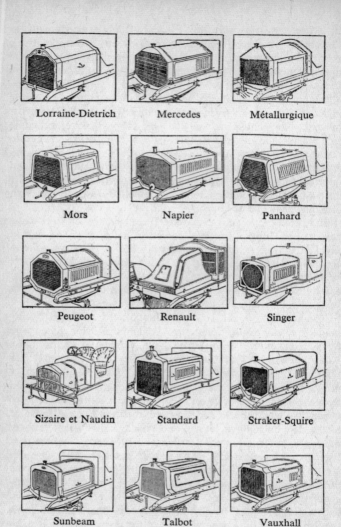

Lorraine-Dietrich Mercedes Métallurgique

Mors Napier Panhard

Peugeot Renault Singer

Sizaire et Naudin Standard Straker-Squire

Sunbeam Talbot Vauxhall

SOME RADIATOR DESIGNS OF 1909 [*Not to the same scale*]

Continental racing was sparse and dull in this year, but in England Brooklands showed splendid sport, and the club meetings were very well supported. A wager match, in the Regency manner, between two amateurs for a couple of hundred guineas, was quite a normal spectacle which never failed to delight the crowd. The Scottish Reliability trial, run over a very stiff course, aroused great interest.

The "war" between police and motorists still went on in England quite undiminished, and there were many fascinating battles. The most amusing of these were when clever lawyers absolutely tied the police in knots over identification of drivers. The bench, relenting somewhat, agreed, rather surprisingly, to accept the position of the maximum speed hand on the instrument as legal evidence. However, in spite of this, everybody wanted to motor, and a normal charge for a course of twelve driving lessons was 3 guineas. Prices were coming down in the most satisfactory way. Here are the running costs of an 18/24 h.p. Austin over 10,164 miles:

	£	s.	d.
480 gals. petrol (21·17 m.p.g.)	22	10	0
Tyres: repair and renewal	37	9	3
Insurance and tax	20	17	5
Repairs, etc.	4	18	0
31 gals. lub. oil and grease	5	0	5
Charging batteries, carbide, etc.	1	7	0
	£92	2	1

which works out at 2·175d. per mile.

Early in 1909, His Majesty the King bought a 65-h.p. four-cylinder Mercedes landaulette which, judging from the contemporary press, he seems to have used in preference to his fleet of Coventry Daimlers.

The Motor Show held at Olympia in November had a bigger attendance than ever before. Dealers started, for the first time, to take old cars in part exchange. There was a very large number of outstandingly handsome closed cars of the chauffeur-driven variety and the two-seater and coupés are, in a curious way, attractive. The majority of the touring coachwork was, however, remarkably ugly. The general trend of design of 1909 made sure of that. What pretty touring bodies there were, such as Lord Vernon's La Buire, really belong to a year later; though some of the attractive Rolls bodies belong to a style of a year or two earlier. For touring coachwork and quite a number of other things, including racing, 1909 could certainly not be described as a vintage year.

16   An alternative to the landaulette body on a 1907 16/20-h.p. Sunbeam

17   A 10-h.p. F.N. (Fabrique Nationale). See pages 114 and 115

18, 19 Record-breakers: *above* Camille Jenatzy at the tiller of his Jean-taud electric car *La Jamais Contente* after raising the world's flying kilometre record to 65.79 m.p.h. in 1899. *Below* Arthur MacDonald in the 90-h.p. six-cylinder Napier with which he took the world's speed record in America in 1905. The car was subsequently driven by Earp in the 1905 Gordon Bennett Race

20   A 1903 12-h.p. four-cylinder F.I.A.T. with Giovanni Agnetti at the wheel.

21   "A spin in the motor": six-cylinder Darracq at Brighton, 1907

22 Scottish Trials, 1906: the competitors at Inverary

23 Anglo - American Vintage Rally, 1954: Model K Ford at Goodwood

24, 25 Lord above (and below): Lord Lonsdale arrives at Brooklands in his Mercedes and Lord Montagu of Beaulieu, a motoring pioneer, drives Dr. Poltrier's Brasier; 1907

26, 27   Targa Florio, 1907: *above* single-cylinder De Dion-Bouton in the
voiturette race. Note the condition of the roads.
Below the Isotta-Fraschini "pits"

28 Claude Grahame-White, the pioneer aviator, at the wheel of a Kissel Kar during a visit to America in 1910

29 President Theodore Roosevelt riding in a 30-h.p. White steam car in 1908

6

The Years of Refinement, 1910-1914

APART from the appearance of front-wheel brakes on Arrol Johnston and Isotta-Fraschini cars, there was little new in 1910. These brakes, by the way, were fitted more with the idea of steadying the car, and most of the braking was still on the back wheels.

Admittedly, a Mr. Morgan designed an internal combustion turbine which was described and illustrated very fully in *The Autocar*, but no more was heard of it. A wireless telegraphy installation was fitted to a car, but as this took up most of the back seats and there were, in any case, very few transmitting stations to listen to, it was somewhat premature.

More notable were the developments in coachwork. Scuttles started to be almost universally extended backwards to protect the legs of the occupants of the front seats. Some were hinged, as the Lanchester brothers had done years earlier, to give easier entry. In this year, too, the ingenious and practical Lanchesters pioneered the storing of tools in flap-down panels on the doors. Flat-sided touring bodies were becoming very popular and were in a rather ugly transitional stage between the graceful *Roi des Belges* bodies of a few years earlier and the better-looking touring bodies of 1913/14. One of the most important coachwork developments of this year was the introduction of pressed-metal domed wings to replace the carriage type, some of which, even as late as this, were made of wood or leather.

One eccentric nobleman amazed the motoring press, and probably scandalised his more conservative peers, by having his Delaunay-Belleville landaulette built with glass side-screens in front to protect the chauffeur and footman. Such a thing had never been heard of before.

There were interesting developments in tyres. A few of the larger and more luxurious cars fitted as an optional extra very much larger section tyres than ever before, mostly Palmer cord 915 × 175, high pressure of course. Although tyre prices had dropped tremendously during the last five years, these were still very expensive. Some cars carrying large and heavy coachwork came out with twin rear wheels.

While on the subject of coachwork, it is interesting to observe that the French introduced in this year, or at any rate not much earlier, long-distance trips by motor coach. And the bodywork of these vehicles was wonderfully luxuriously finished. Unlike the early charabancs of a decade later, the seating was completely enclosed. Large windows gave excellent visibility and the heavy real leather upholstery and appointments generally were reminiscent of a Pullman-car of the same era.

Although there was little basic change in engine or chassis design in 1910, and engines still turned at speeds around 1200 to 1700 r.p.m., gadgets and accessories were greater in number and ingenuity than ever before. Vulcanisers for tyres were appearing everywhere, and a multiplicity of exhaust whistles, organs and bugles augmented the more usual bulb horn. Brown Brothers, the factors, introduced a service whereby one rang them up on the telephone, and they would blow these various exhaust-operated instruments in front of the mouthpiece, so that one could make one's choice then and there. Klaxon-type horns, operated by winding a handle, could also be bought, but these, I am told, were not considered at all good form, except for a near-racing car. At Bilston, in Staffordshire, John Sankey and his works manager evolved a steel wheel, pressed in two halves and welded together in a jig. This was the father of the pressed-steel wheel that was, for the next two decades and more, to replace the more costly hand-made wooden ones.

As far as lighting and starting went, electrics were gaining ground, but many people still preferred acetylene lamps, and the wealthy bought compressed-air starters. Throughout the years there have been sporadic and unsuccessful attempts to introduce headlights swivelling with the front wheels. The first recorded instance I can find of these being offered is in this year.

There is not space to chronicle the very large number of

accessories that were now becoming available. One of the most attractive was a set of piston-type pneumatic shock absorbers, of bulky design, but many years ahead of their time. At the tail end of the year, however, Newton and Bennett brought out the first hydraulic (oil) shock absorbers. Quite the silliest accessory was the Jangley carburettor which was mounted beside the driver's seat, so that he could twiddle the knobs by hand, and fed the engine through an induction pipe some four feet long exposed to the open air!

Motoring produced some fierce Parliamentary clashes at this time. A bill to tax petrol was defeated. As a general election was imminent, *The Autocar* published a list of members who had voted for the bill. As there were by this time over 800,000 motor vehicles on the road it cannot have done much good to the Government votes. The new Government then set up a Road Fund from taxation based on the bore of the cylinders and R.A.C. h.p., and promised that it would be used for the improvement and maintenance of the roads.

The war between motorists and the police was still raging fiercely, and every week the motoring papers published names of places where the police not only ran speed traps, but were encouraged by higher authority to report insignificant petty offences. In France, driving tests were inaugurated, to be passed before a licence was granted.

I do not think it is generally known that in 1910 a number of people became interested in the preservation of early and historic motor-cars. A Panhard Levassor of 1894, probably the first to come here, was discovered and bought for £100 by public subscription, and presented to the National Science Museum in South Kensington. A committee of pioneer motorists, headed by Edmund Dangerfield with Sir David Salomons, Colonel Holden and Claude Johnson, collected a number of very early motor-cars and placed them on exhibition in the old Crystal Palace. When this building was required for storage during the 1914–18 war, these priceless specimens were thrown out, dispersed, and many of them destroyed.

The motoring world was genuinely grieved by the death of that lovable monarch, Edward VII. He had done so much by his Royal Patronage to overcome the prejudice against motor-cars in their early days. Soon afterwards, Charles Rolls was killed in an aeroplane crash. Actually, his aircraft only fell about 20 feet and Rolls was quite uninjured, apart from the fact that his head got one bump, on a fatal spot, when it hit the upper plane.

The sporting year opened with an Australian, G. White, beating the Melbourne to Sydney (577 miles) record with a time of twenty-one hours, nineteen minutes, which was very good going over bad roads. The car was a sturdy 25-h.p. Talbot. The Catalan Cup in Spain was won by a small four-cylinder Hispano-Suiza. Brooklands was going strong, and a youngster called Malcolm Campbell, driving what looked like a hotted-up touring Daimler, was racing against the pioneer Jarrott in a Benz. Jarrott had long since retired from Grand Prix racing, but he was not averse to an occasional day out at the track.

The first big Continental event was the Prince Henry of Prussia tour, which was won by young Ferdinand Porsche, driving an Austro-Daimler of his own design. But the highlight of the trial was not the Benz, the Métallurgique or the Mercedes (who were going through one of their bad periods), but the immortal "Prince Henry" Vauxhalls designed by Laurence Pomeroy, senior. At the Gaillon hill-climb, the veteran Fritz Erle rocketed up in a great Benz to beat the record established by Lee Guinness in 1906. He also beat Jenatzy, on a 135-h.p. Mercedes, who is shown by a photograph to have shed his famous red beard.

In America, stock-car racing was gaining great popularity. The rules were so worded that there was virtually no such thing as an amateur driver, for if he accepted a prize after winning it he lost his amateur status. The Vanderbilt Cup race was won again this year, as it had been the previous year, by Harry F. Grant driving an Alco (American Locomotive Co.), Dawson on a Marmon was second. The winner averaged 65 m.p.h. over a 278-mile course. Spectator control, both during the race and approaching the course, seems to have been at an all-time low, and the terrible casualty list reads like the "Paris–Madrid". Motor racing in America seems quite coincidental to the 1910 boom in the American automobile industry, which was producing 99 per cent touring cars.

Although no French Grand Prix was run in 1910, the Americans had one again at Savannah. Bruce Brown won it in a big Benz, beating Héméry in a similar car by only two seconds in a five-and-a-half-hour race – a very close finish. At one time Nazzaro, who had brought over a F.I.A.T., looked like winning, but he went out of the race with a broken chain.

In the Autumn, the Motor Show was held at Olympia. As has been said earlier, it was a year of general improvement rather than startling innovation. With regard to engines, the only new thing, apart from a number of curious and ephemeral valve-gears exhibited, was that instead of having pipes outside the cylinder blocks, the exhaust and inlet passages were now being cast integral and connecting straight into manifolds. Carburation was greatly improved and much experimental work was being done on shock absorbers. Steering was improved by the almost universal adoption of ball races to take the thrust in the steering box. A few cars, now including Argyll, had front-wheel brakes. The Germain had a chain-driven overhead camshaft which was progressive, and Jackson anticipated modern practice by pressing the chassis so that it formed the lower half of the body. A young "blood" with a large bank account would have been very hard put to it to choose between the "Prince Henry" type Austro-Daimler exhibited, and the "Prince Henry" Vauxhall, although neither of these delectable cars was in anything like the highest price range. Apparently the demand for Rolls-Royce cars must have rather exceeded the supply, for dealers vied with each other to advertise "early delivery".

1910 closed with the Paris Salon, held a few weeks before Christmas. Like our own show, many weird and wonderful forms of valve gear were exhibited, although it is unlikely that they ever went into production. One was shown by a maker who subsequently did very well indeed with more conventional engines, Monsieur Ballot. As for the coachwork, there were few pretty bodies, and more than a few outstandingly ugly ones. Every year has its own particular style. Sometimes it lends itself to beautiful coachwork, at other times it does not. That of 1910, like the "bulboid" style of the late 1940s, very definitely did not.

1911

This was not a very dramatic year; rather one of steady progress. And not really much progress in performance, for though engines were becoming more efficient this was counteracted by the fact that bodywork was getting heavier. However, to get the greater efficiency, more r.p.m. were necessary, and this led to makers paying considerably more attention to the dynamic balancing of crankshafts. Also faster-turning engines seemed to suffer more from inhaled road dust and grit than their predecessors. Another bugbear, due to the large increase in the use of electric lighting and the immensely improved acetylene headlamps (Bleriot was advertising 10,000 candle power), was dazzle. Many and ingenious were the suggestions for dealing with these two problems.

A lot of cars this year had electric side-lamps and acetylene headlamps; others, including the Royal Daimlers, were all electric. The Royal Daimlers of 1911 seem to have set the style of coachwork for the King's state cars, for this remained more or less unchanged right up to the death of Queen Mary in 1953.

The real progress made in 1911 was not so much in the flat-sided bodies, on which the advertisements of that year laid so much stress, but in dashboards! The dashboard of earlier years had housed an impressive polished brass and glass lubricator tell-tale, with later additions of a speedometer and, perhaps, a clock. The lubricator drip box had now disappeared, leaving space for a most comprehensively equipped dash. Some cars had glass-topped scuttles for better lighting of the instruments.

One remarkable fitting was a reservoir of battery acid on the dash, connected with the accumulators, containing an hydrometer. From this, the driver knew when to cut off his dynamo to avoid overcharging his batteries. It was a year or so before this was done automatically. There was one very remarkable dashboard, designed by Mr. Ferguson of Belfast, later to become the tractor tycoon. The instruments, instead of being mounted vertically somewhere round the driver's feet, were grouped on an oval facia placed much in the same position as they are today!

But Ferguson was not the only one to anticipate present-day practice in 1911. A Mr. Vincent designed an infinitely variable hydraulic transmission similar in principle to those in use today. A Mr. Wright designed hydraulically operated front-wheel brakes. On paper this system looks perfectly practical, but I can find no record of any manufacturer adopting it. Further, there was a system of hydraulic tappets which could, it was claimed, be fitted to most types of side-valve cars.

Two innovations that have remained with us through the years instead of disappearing for a decade or so were the electrically operated klaxon horn and the A.T. magnetically operated speedometer. Electric sirens, like those used by the American police, could be bought.

There was also, as there had been ever since Knight had cashed in on the sleeve-valve, a prodigious number of alternatives to the poppet valve being patented. There were reciprocatory-valves and many other varieties. Few got beyond the prototype stage, but Itala made most practical and efficient rotary-valve engines. This device might be described as a plug containing ports, rotating in an extension of the cylinder bore, and kept gas-tight by conventional piston rings.

It was a great year for radiator mascots. Nobody could say that 1911 was a year of great taste when it came to the building and decorating of houses, and, though a few of the mascots were charming, most of them were about on a level with contemporary architecture.

A number of them were finding their way on to Rolls-Royce cars, which did not please the directors at all, so they commissioned a well-known sculptor of the day to design a special Rolls-Royce mascot. Frederick Sykes produced the world-famous silver lady. She is, to my mind, so incomparably more beautiful in her original 1911 form than she is in her later adaptations, that I have kept the original from my first "Silver Ghost", and used it on my later Rolls-Royces.

Rolls-Royce cars must have been in considerable demand in this year, for an agent advertised on 4th February that he had a chassis for delivery on 12th April, so anyone who wanted it must apply immediately.

Another emblem of a different kind which had made its appearance in 1906 was the A.A. badge, much as we know it today, but in heavy polished brass.

The two first Motor Shows of the year were at Brussels and New York. There was also one at Manchester and another in Edinburgh. The feature of the former were "inside-drive limousines", or, as we should call them, close-coupled coupés. At the latter show every manufacturer tried to get maximum publicity out of driving his show model from London to Edinburgh non-stop.

The Brussels Show was full of novel and exciting ideas, whereas the New York Show was very barren of them. It looked as if the Americans waited for a year or two till a new idea had got over its teething troubles in Europe and then adopted it. A case in point was worm-drive. This was the *dernier cri* in Europe and a great talking point on any of the many cars that had come out with it. On the other hand, it was still giving a bit of trouble. Not a single American car at the New York Show had it. Anyway, I suspect that the American manufacturers were so jubilant that the Selden Patent case had been overthrown on appeal that they did not really mind much about anything else. But six-cylinder engines, now they had proved themselves in Europe, were fast gaining in popularity in U.S.A. The car of the show seems to have been the Pierce-Arrow, and European observers wrote that the workmanship and really superb finish were as good as anything they had seen at home.

1911 was a great year for America, marking the opening of the Indianapolis track and the first 500-mile race. It was won by a locally built car, a six-cylinder Marmon, of about $4\frac{3}{4}$ litres, in six hours forty-two minutes. Lozier and F.I.A.T. were second and third, and curiously the two last cars were a Stutz and a Mercer! The enthusiasm was enormous; people had come from hundreds of miles round about to see the race, and the gates had to be forced shut an hour before the start, as all the enclosures were full to overflowing.

At home, Brooklands was all the rage – the flying as big a draw as the motor racing. George Boillot brought over one of the immensely long-stroke Lion Peugeots and took a lot of class records. A very pretty girl, Miss Esmé Stewart, also made an unsuccessful attempt on class records driving "Mephistopheles I", an ex-Nazarro F.I.A.T. (not to be confused with Mephistopheles II which is with us today), which had been bought by Noel Macklin. Herb Lytle, the American racing driver, came over to have a look at Brooklands and was, it seems, much impressed.

Racing-car builders were making considerable, if rather primitive, efforts to streamline their cars. Gregoire, however was experimenting with models in a smoke tunnel and produced a saloon not dissimilar to the Burney Crossley of the 1930s. The Germans announced with great glee that they had built the first anti-aircraft gun mounted on a lorry, and that it now completely neutralised the aeroplane as a weapon of war. Many years later I heard from an old man in Germany, who had been concerned with it, that it was absolutely useless.

In Europe there was plenty of competition motoring, in which English cars were beginning to participate, in France at least. However, they did not get as far as the Targa Florio, which was won by one of the Ceirano clan driving a car of his own make, a S.C.A.T. This car grew up into the Ceirano of the 'twenties.

The Prince Henry tour was unique in so far that the course lay both in Germany and England. In the latter country it included visits to such stately homes as Welbeck and Badminton (in those days in the full flower of Edwardian hospitality), and finished at Brooklands.

We also had another distinguished visitor, Bordino, who brought over an immense streamlined F.I.A.T. and electrified the crowds by doing 120 m.p.h.! All over England there were hill-climbs, now almost one every week-end during the season.

It had been proposed to run a race round the Isle of Man circuit for "touring cars" with bores limited to three inches, but the Island authorities vetoed this. Instead, a race for production cars was run at Brooklands, which was a great success.

But the highlight of sport for the year, as far as England was concerned, was the French Coupe des Voiturettes, or Voitures Légères. It seems to have been called both, but in any case it means the same thing, and it was, as usual, sponsored by the paper *L'Auto*. The successful French light cars – Sizaire, Lion Peugeot, Delage, Gregoire, Alcyon, Côte (two-stroke) – were there in force. The Belgians sent some Excelsiors and a long-defunct car called F.I.F., which, from its appearance, looked very good indeed. Britain sent teams of Calthorpe, Vauxhall and Arrol-Johnston. There was also one Sunbeam. Birkigt, whose Hispano-Suiza had won the previous year, rested on his laurels and Zucarelli, his driver, had been snapped up by Peugeot. It is interesting to observe that former drivers of the great bolides, Duray, Wagner, Gabriel, Hémery, Hanriot and others were now all driving *voitures légères*. The old-stroke singles and twins were no longer allowed; only four- and six-cylinder cars. Germany was represented by a solitary Mathis from Strasbourg.

The race, which has progressed from a Cinderella, pushed to the end of the race calendar, to one of major importance, was now held in June on the Boulogne circuit, running 32 miles through the forests. There was a most exciting finish between Boillot's Peugeot and Bablot's Delage, with only twenty-seven seconds between them. Bablot won at an average speed of 55·2 m.p.h., a slightly slower speed than the previous year. The British cars were never in the picture, although all three Arrol-Johnstons finished. The best placing was made by Burgess who brought the sole surviving Calthorpe into sixth place.

Several history books imply that there was no French Grand Prix in 1911. There was, but it was a tame affair. The cars were mostly at least three or four years old and the drivers had no works backing. The race was won by Hémery on a hotted-up touring F.I.A.T. Far the most interesting car in the race was Ettore Bugatti's 1½-litre type 13, driven by his mechanic Friderich, which went nearly as fast as some of the bolides.

The Motor Show at Olympia produced nothing startlingly new, but there was a tendency towards much smaller bore engines with a long stroke, turning a little faster than before. These engines called for, and usually received, four-speed gearboxes. Silent chain-drive for camshaft, magneto and pumps was on the increase. A rather remarkable mechanical engine-starter was shown, which wound up a large powerful clock spring to rotate the engine when released, but, as electric starting was to come the following year, it had little chance to prove its usefulness. Automatic advance and retard for magnetos began to appear. Multiplate clutches had been made for a number of years, but the buying public was still mistrust-ful of them, and the old leather-faced cone clutches were still holding their own. Parry Thomas, later a famous Brooklands driver, had patented an immensely ingenious, but very com-plicated electro-mechanical transmission. Wooden wheels were, however, fast losing ground to the pressed steel type produced by Sankey.

Probably the most advanced engine at the Show, although not a particularly successful one, was the 26-h.p. V-eight de Dion, which looks as modern as can be.

The American Stanley steamer was shown, and it was being built here under licence at Gateshead-on-Tyne.

Taken by and large, it was not an exciting Show, but for one thing: the radical change in coachwork design. The previous year the flat scuttle, so long in vogue, had its top turned over and extended backwards. Now attempts were made to merge it into one with the bonnet. Some like Daimler were conser-vative and did not really try; others tried much too hard and produced outstandingly hideous results. It was not easy, for the tops of radiators were still a long way below the bottoms of windscreens. The logical conclusion was, of course, to raise the radiator, but that was not to come for a few years. The "Lon-don–Edinburgh" Rolls-Royce brought the scuttle almost down to the level of the radiator cap, and it was one of the most attractive-looking cars ever built. Isotta-Fraschini, which looked like a baby Benz, and Austro-Daimler, produced harmonious lines. A particularly good job was done by Maythorn, the Biggleswade coachbuilder, on a 24-h.p. Lancia chassis. But generally speaking, most attempts at the "New Look" were hideous, from any angle.

In spite of police persecution, which had increased with the number of motorists on the road, the quantity of cars in use was increasing by leaps and bounds. Membership of the recently opened Royal Automobile Club was full.

The reason for this increase is quite simple. In 1911 a modest trap or carriage with one horse cost about 10d. a mile to run. A 6-h.p. car cost 5d., a 10- to 16-h.p. 5½d., and anything bigger, except the very largest and most complicated cars, 5¾d. This does not include a small rebate on petrol tax to the large number of doctors who were becoming motorists.

1912

The cycle-cars of five and six years ago had become *voiturettes,* and from that had grown into relatively expensive motor-cars. Now in 1912 a fresh crop sprang up to take their place. It seems one of the laws of nature that a cycle-car cannot for ever remain in the tadpole stage, it must either grow up into a motor-car or else perish. The long-established A.C. was now a light car. Many new makes of very lightly built cycle-cars had just appeared. Morgan, now grown up, is still with us; so is G.N. – now Frazer Nash – but there were a host of others who perished. To name a few: Bedelia, Wall, Crouch, Enfield, Sabella, Crecent, Rollo, Eric and New Hudson. All these were born about 1912. Another, of interest because of its extreme lightness, was the Beacon. It had a tubular frame and a wickerwork body. The whole vehicle, including a twin-cylinder J.A.P. (J. A. Prestwich) engine, weighed just over 6 cwt.

The American scene at this time is rather curious. Technically, with a very few exceptions, the cars were two or three years behind European practice. For example, in 1912 the American automobile builders were only just beginning to replace T-heads with L-heads. But when it comes to appliances to make life easier for the driver, they were way out ahead.

The reason for this was, of course, that with the higher

wages paid in America, fewer people than in Europe could afford to employ a paid driver. The 1912 New York Show is an excellent example of this. Not a single car costing *under* $2500 did not have some means of starting the car from the driver's seat. Cars costing over that were bought by an income group who had paid drivers. There was, at this time, 45 per cent import duty on foreign cars into the U.S.A. Many of these high-priced cars did not have self-starters, or they were listed as optional extras. Fred Bennett claimed, and I think he was right, that the Cadillacs he imported in 1912 were the first production cars to be marketed in Great Britain with electric starter as standard equipment.

For the same reason – owner-driver convenience – anti-freeze to mix with the coolant was readily available in America long before it was here.

Rudge detachable wheels, held on by a simple locking cap, as are in use today, were first produced about this time, and were not only widely used in Europe but imported into America for use on the racing Mercers. Production in America was getting enormous; nearly a quarter of a million private cars, not counting trucks or buses, were built in 1912.

At the Brussels Show, where many new cycle-cars were shown, coachwork displayed a new trend. Radiators were raised in height to straighten the line to the base of the windscreen. This was accompanied by a most unfortunate and, mercifully, short-lived trick of also raising the back of the body, giving a hideous, truncated-wedge effect. An example of this was the 90-h.p. Mercedes which could have been an outstandingly attractive car. As it was, it could not have been uglier. Isotta, on the other hand, kept their lines straight, parallel with the ground and down to radiator level. The result is a remarkably handsome motor-car. As is usual in any period of coachwork transition, when change is more important than truth and simplicity of line, those builders who kept as closely as possible to the old carriage lines came off best.

At the Manchester Show in England, undoubtedly the most handsome car was the 38-h.p. Lanchester touring car, and the most-sought-after sports car was the "Prince Henry" Vauxhall, now on sale to the public at the extremely modest chassis price of £495. This meant that it could cost, with quite respectable light sporting coachwork, under £600.

I wonder how many people know that the Targa Florio was once won by an Englishman from Manchester? Newton and Bennett were concessionaires for the S.C.A.T. cars, also a handsome 20/30-h.p. Nazzaro car of simple but advanced design that young Felice had just started to build on his own. Cyril Snipe was sent out by Newton and Bennett to Turin as resident tester, to make sure that the chassis exported to England were one hundred per cent perfect. He was given the wheel of one of the S.C.A.T.s entered in the Targa Florio and won the race handsomely, finishing an hour and a half ahead of the next man, Garetto on a Lancia! This year the race was run over the long, intensely gruelling 700-mile circuit.

The French made a great song-and-dance about their 1000-mile Tour de France. But really the conditions were so ridiculously easy for 1912 cars that it proved absolutely nothing.

The Austrian trials were a different matter and very tough going indeed. There was a large entry ranging from the 8-litre Benz, Graf und Stift and Rolls-Royce cars down to Julius Weiner's 1·31-litre Bugatti. As for drivers, a fair proportion of the Almanach de Gotha were taking part, including Prince George William of Cumberland, a cousin of our King. He was unfortunately killed in a car crash in Denmark just before the trials. It was an extremely gruelling trial and a rather difficult one to decide who "won" as a number of competitors finished with no penalty marks. The City of Vienna prize went to Willy von Guttman in a large sporting Mercedes. Why, I do not know, as contemporary reports do not indicate whether or not some final eliminating test was run.

In England, speed hill-climbing was as popular as ever, and a record crowd attended Shelsley Walsh to see Higginson (for whom the father of all 30/98 Vauxhalls was built the following year) go rocketing up in his 80-h.p. La Buire in one minute eight seconds. A little Mathis (65 mm. × 100 mm.) went up much faster than any small car had done before, and indeed much faster than a lot of big ones. Unless some historian does

110

a good deal of research, we shall never know just how much of it came from the drawing-board of Ettore Bugatti. By some accounts, quite a lot.

The Automobile Club de France could not help seeing that the Coupe de L'Auto for light cars of the previous year had been an unqualified success, and that the Grand Prix de France most certainly had not. So the A.C.F. persuaded *L'Auto* that the two races should be run together in June on the 47-mile triangular Dieppe circuit. The winners of the previous year, Delage, entered but then withdrew. Peugeot, on the other hand, brought two types of car to the line, 3-litres for the light-car race and 7·6-litre cars for the Grand Prix. These latter were designed by a young Swiss engineer called Henry, who the following year was to set a fashion in engine design which lasted through two decades.

Great Britain sent over a very strong team for the 3-litre class (both races were run concurrently this year): Sunbeam, Calthorpe, Arrol-Johnston, Vauxhall and Singer.

It was Sunbeam's finest hour. They finished one, two, three, in line ahead in the Coupe de L'Auto, and were only beaten by the first two of the Grand Prix cars – Boillot's winning Peugeot and Wagner driving a monster F.I.A.T. of rather retrograde design. They would also have been beaten by David Bruce Brown, the American ace, driving a similar F.I.A.T., if he had not been disqualified. As Charles Faroux said at the time, "Sans Peugeot, quelle terrible defaite pour nous." What he really meant was, "What a pity that only Peugeot, among the firms that once led the world, are prepared to spend money on winning our own Grand Prix."

The American Vanderbilt Cup was run that year at Milwaukee. Tragedy clouded the meeting, for that cheerful driver, much loved both sides of the Atlantic and twice winner of the American Grand Prix, David Bruce Brown, was killed in practice for the race, which was won by C. S. Bragg in a F.I.A.T. Ralph de Palma ditched his Mercedes and broke both his legs.

At the Gaillon climb in France, Fritz Erle, the veteran German driver, made his farewell appearance, tearing up in a

"Blitzen" Benz to break the record for the hill. At Gaillon, too, there was writing on the wall, for a tiny 1·4-litre Bugatti won its touring-car class.

At home, Brooklands produced some excellent racing; and Gordon Watney, at his house nearby, had built up a fine business, buying up second-hand Mercedes cars with heavy unwieldy coachwork, hotting them up, and fitting them with ultra-light sporting shells, which were made for him by the Ewart Geyser Company. A Gordon Watney Mercedes was very much the thing for a young blood in 1912. Watney raced consistently and quite successfully at Brooklands, where the man of the year was probably Hornsted, driving the Benz cars of Arkwright, his wealthy patron. There were also a number of class records taken by Star, Vauxhall and other makers. In this year, also, that pioneer of pioneers, S. F. Edge, severed his partnership with Napier and retired from the motor world to farm his pigs in Sussex.

In England, a great deal of research was going on over the question of silencers. Cut-outs had been forbidden by a law passed early in the year, and a silencer with a minimum of back pressure was eagerly sought. Considerable research and experiment was taking place in shock-absorber design and other means of damping the springs. Petrol prices had risen slightly and several makes of carburettors were on offer, including some with two float chambers that could be switched from petrol to paraffin. A pleasant innovation this year was a small electric lamp that lit up the running-board when the door was opened. A curious device of 1912 was spring-mounting for headlamps. Lamps had been getting steadily bigger and heavier and their weight vibrating caused the brackets even of the best "Lancashire" iron to fracture, so spring mountings were tried, but never achieved much popularity. Another novelty this year was an unburstable inner tube, which apparently worked perfectly well.

In France, a competition was held for devices preventing motor-cars splashing pedestrians. There were a large number of entries, most of which make Heath Robinson look rather orthodox, but it does appear that some worked quite effectively.

Now, let us take a look at the general tendencies of the exhibits at the Olympia Show, held that year in November. Two things were immediately apparent. Firstly, that most of the seekers after the philosopher's stone of valve-gear alternatives to poppet design had disappeared. They must all have run out of money, or given it up as a bad job. Only well-established makers such as Daimler, Itala, Minerva, Darracq and others continued. Most of them had been making alternative valve-gear for four years or more, and it had now proved itself. This had made a tremendous impact on the makers of poppet-valve engines. They had been scared into doing tremendous research into both camshaft design and the metallurgy of the valves themselves. Valves were bigger, longer-lasting and now mostly all enclosed. The effect was most salutary.

Secondly, the single-cylinder engine was now virtually dead, but the multi-cylinder engines this year tended to have a slightly larger swept volume, strokes particularly being longer. Designers generally seemed to have sought to avoid "crankshaft whip" by making them heavier and stronger. Monobloc casting for cylinders was now, except for some of the American cars, virtually universal. As detachable heads had not yet arrived, decarbonising these was quite a major operation, which some people tackled with special tools, and others with an oxygen process or a chemical preparation that was reputed to do the job. Piston design was receiving a great deal of consideration, and some go-ahead makers were beginning to make them out of steel.

A great variety of carburettors with float feed were offered. Only Lanchester remained faithful to their primitive but amazingly efficient wick carburettor.

Worm drive was waning in popularity, largely because makers had, in the past year, learned the secret of building a bevel drive that ran as quietly as a worm one.

The Adams car, always full of original ideas, featured not only electric lighting and starting, but electrically operated jacks as well.

As far as coachwork went, what has been said earlier in this

113

chapter about the Belgian Show applies equally for Olympia. There were two innovations; V screens were seen for the first time, and a hideous practice appeared of projecting the roof about 18in. forward of the top of the windscreen. There were such a number of cars with extremely good lines that it is difficult to choose any one, but far the most beautiful closed car was a D-fronted limousine, built to very conservative design by Barker, on a "Silver Ghost" chassis. A polished mahogany torpedo tourer was seen for the first time, but it had none of the elegance of line with which we associate later examples of coachwork in this medium.

The year ended with a spate of letters in the daily press emanating from embittered diehards, who complained furiously that, although it was perfectly easy to get hold of a motor-cab, the horse-drawn variety, which they preferred, was becoming so rare as to be virtually unobtainable.

1913

Motoring costs were coming down with a run. A typical owner-driver's budget over three years on an 8/10-h.p. F.N. (Fabrique Nationale) is shown on page 115.

Admittedly this is a light car, with the owner-driver doing his own maintenance and vulcanising his own punctures, but the average figure is one we may well envy today, $1\frac{1}{2}d$. per mile! The car would have cost new about £250 complete, so even depreciation does not make the running a great burden. Trade was good, and by early 1913 some British manufacturers had their order books full for the year. With the number of cars on the road increasing daily, craftsmen were needed for their maintenance and several responsible bodies were sponsoring schemes for the proper training of youths before they entered the industry. There may well have been more to it than that. Although prosperity was at its height and Europe was gay and apparently carefree, there were war clouds on the horizon and full-scale manœuvres took place in Russia, Germany, France, Austria, Hungary and England. In all these manœuvres the motor-car played an increasingly important part. It is probable that far-sighted people at government

114

1910 (5,144 miles)	£	s.	d.		£	s.	d.
Sundries	1	13	11				
Repairs			8				
Renewals		nil					
Petrol (296 gals.)	17	10	11				
Lubricating oil	3	11	9				
Gear oil		10	0				
Grease		8	10				
					23	16	1
1911 (7,040¼ miles)							
Sundries	1	0	10				
Repairs			10				
Renewals			8				
Petrol (362 gals.)	21	12	2				
Lubricating oil		19	0	(now bought in bulk)			
Gear oil		18	9				
Grease		8	6				
					25	0	9
1912 (5,867¾ miles)							
Sundries		17	5				
Repairs		3	3				
Renewals	1	15	3				
Petrol (305 gals.)	22	15	5				
Lubricating oil	1	0	3	(now bought in bulk)			
Gear oil		9	10				
Grease		6	6				
					27	7	11
Tyres for 18,052 miles					43	18	9
					£120	3	6

level saw that a necessity might arise not only for cars but for men to service them.

Neither the Brussels, Scottish nor Manchester Shows brought forth much that was new and the coachwork was, in the main, supremely uninspired. The three "cars of the year" as far as looks went, were not exhibited. The 100-h.p. Isotta-Fraschini was by far the best-looking sports car built pre-1914. An open four-seater body was built on a "London–Edinburgh" Rolls-Royce chassis, of such peerless and classical beauty that it is really ageless. Among the closed cars, most of them were not at all attractive, though J. W. Stocks, the pioneer motorist, built himself a limousine on an eight-cylinder De Dion chassis which would have still been considered handsome two decades later. Three of the ugliest cars of the year were Rolls-Royces built for the Maharajah of Alwar.

One fitting did appear which made for better-looking closed coachwork and that was a mechanism for winding up windows by turning a handle instead of pulling them up on a strap. A form of streamlined torpedo called "the dogfish style" was pioneered by the French. Although it was to be greatly modified into a far-better-looking form in time, it was really remarkably ugly before 1914.

Two neat gadgets appeared; one a simple thief-proof device which locked the gear lever in neutral, and the other an engine stand, on to which one bolted the engine to be worked on. The engine could then be swivelled and locked in any desired position.

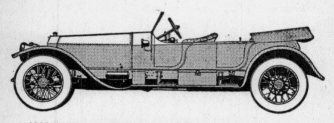

1913/14 "London-Edinburgh" Rolls-Royce "Silver Ghost"

Our friend of 1911, Vincent's infinitely variable hydraulic transmission, reappeared, no longer on paper, but installed in a six-cylinder Napier chassis. It seems to have behaved perfectly well on test, but there is no record of any manufacturer taking it up.

The R.A.C. held extensive trials of various forms of petrol. It was found that a mixture containing Benzole was immensely beneficial, and within a matter of months was on sale all over the country. The mysterious pills with a secret ingredient that, when dissolved in the petrol, increase the performance of your car, are nothing new. They were investigated at the R.A.C. petrol trials, and the general opinion seems to have been that if they did not do much good, they did no harm either.

Warming the car by means of exhaust gases was still popular, although it was no longer as necessary as it had been when it was introduced a few years earlier. Then the exhaust pipe had been passed up near the steering-wheel to warm the driver's hands, and it had been even suggested, probably as a joke, that exhaust-heated suits might be made!

As well as petrol trials the R.A.C. held tyre trials, and it certainly seems that competitions and the publication of the results went a long way to improving tyres. It will be noted that the light F.N. car mentioned earlier did 18,000 miles on a set, a figure that would be good today.

A young man called Morris was offering his "Oxford" light car with a proprietary White and Poppe engine. In two-seater form, including all equipment, it sold at £175 and was well received.

Direction indicators appeared for the first time in 1913. Two kinds were offered, one was a bold arrow revolving in a drum, the other a white celluloid hand. Both were operated by Bowden cable.

In the sporting world records were falling like ninepins. Brooklands was by far the finest track in Europe, and European drivers were constantly coming over. Percy Lambert did 103 miles in the hour on a Talbot car specially designed for the job by a Scotsman, George W. A. Brown. This was the first time 100 miles in the hour had ever been accomplished. A month or two later Goux and Boillot brought over one of the 7·6-litre Peugeots built for the 1911 Grand Prix, and winners of that race in 1912, and beat Lambert's record. For this attempt they were equipped with single-seater bodies.

The Perrot-designed Argyll, in the hands of Hornsted, also took some world's records. The two most remarkable things about Brooklands in 1913 were the large number of newcomers to the sport, and the tremendous progress made in streamlining the cars. In fact, looking at some of the streamlined cars it would be hard to tell if they had been built in 1913 or 1925.

117

The continental year started, as usual, with the Targa Florio. It looked at one stage as if a relatively unknown driver, Marsaglia, was going to win with his Aquila-Italiana (a long-since defunct Italian make which used to be quite well-known in racing), but he fell back to let Nazzaro, whom he had been leading by half an hour, come on to win with one of his own cars. Quite the most extraordinary thing about this race is that fourth place was taken by an anonymous amateur, racing under the name of "Berra", who prepared and drove what had been initially a standard eight-cylinder touring De Dion!

Christaens, the Excelsior driver, took one of the previous year's racing cars from Brussels to St. Petersburg at an average running time of over 50 m.p.h., presumably as an advertising stunt. Considering the state of the roads, this must have needed quite a lot of doing.

In America, Indianapolis was a bigger crush than ever. Although the seating had been enlarged to take 90,000 spectators at a minimum charge of $2, it was packed to capacity. Guyot brought over a Sunbeam. It was not an official works entry. Everyone remarked how smoothly and regularly it ran, and I can testify to this as I owned the car about fifteen years later. But it was not fast enough to do better than fourth place. Goux won with a Henry Peugeot, with Spencer Wishart's Mercer and Mertz's Stutz in second and third places. Curiously enough, the Peugeot did not go as fast as the American car which had won the previous year.

There is no doubt whatever that when Mercedes make one of their periodical returns to racing, there are no half measures. No money or pains were spared on their 1913 racing cars. Various engines were installed in chain-driven chassis with a view to trying them out under actual racing conditions. These cars had front-wheel brakes which were dropped the following year. But unfortunately the A.C.F. barred their entry in the French Grand Prix on a technicality.

This was a great pity, as what was a good race – Delage versus Peugeot, with Sunbeam a strong challenger – would have been even better with the experimental Mercedes taking part. The regulations were somewhat different this year. There was no limit on engine capacity – the day of the monsters was over – but petrol was rationed to about 14 miles to the gallon and weight was restricted to 1100 kilogrammes maximum and 800 kilogrammes minimum. The circuit was a short one, a mere 20 miles round, near Amiens.

The maximum weight limit did not suit the Itala team at all. Their rotary-valve engines were running like clockwork, but the Itala had always been rather a heavily built car and, to get it down to this year's weight limit, the chassis and transmission had been weakened enough to put them out of the race well before the end.

First two places went to Peugeots, driven by the great Boillot and Goux. If the third of that great triumvirate, Zuccarelli, had been driving, they would probably have finished one, two, three. But he had been killed in a road accident some months before, and his place taken by a very able but rash driver, Delpierre, who crashed.

1913 Adler, with "Special Design Side-Entrance" coachwork by Morgan

Let us examine these successful Henry-designed Peugeots that were to influence racing- and sports-car design on both sides of the Atlantic so profoundly. Although 1913 might well be called Henry's year, Boillot, Goux and Zuccarelli all deserve credit for the car, for they worked with Henry on design, research and development. In fact, it seems that these three men, all engineers working at Peugeot as well as race drivers, originally prevailed on Robert Peugeot to engage the brilliant young Swiss Henry.

By means of skilful head and port design, this double over-head camshaft engine achieved greater volumetric efficiency than anything previously built. 3 litres was relatively very small indeed for 1913, and Henry made them yield 90 h.p. at just under 3,000 r.p.m. This power was very ably taken up by a crankshaft supported in three places by ball bearings. This extremely advanced engine was also a pioneer of forced dry-sump lubrication. As the whole car only weighed 16 cwt. un-laden, 100 m.p.h. plus brilliant performance was well within its capabilities.

There is no point in giving a full detailed description of this epoch-making car as this has already been done by Laurence Pomeroy in *The Grand Prix Car, 1906–1939*. Undoubtedly the man of the year was Henry, for this car was the *beau ideal* of all designers for years to come. One immediate result was that Louis Coatalen bought one of the Grand Prix Peugeot team cars and imported it to England, where it served as a basis for both racing and sporting Sunbeams till the late 1920s.

There is no doubt that the Motor Show at Olympia pro-duced a most attractive collection of motor-cars. Engines were of an advanced monobloc type with improved lubrication and valve gear, and with better balanced and supported crank-shafts. In fact they were similar to, and as good as, most engines made for some years after the Kaiser war. Steel pistons were no longer a novelty, four-speed gearboxes were now in the majority and carburation was greatly improved. About this time the S.U. "piston regulated" carburettor came on the market and in basic principle it was the same as it is today. Other innovations coming into more general use were torque and radius rods, and worm-and-nut steering was featured by Rolls-Royce and Sizaire Berwick. Triplex safety glass was still a novelty, but a very popular one.

For coachwork also it was a vintage year. The closed bodies that did not attempt to be ahead of their time were really lovely, and open bodies, after the hideous examples of the previous year, had blossomed into great beauty. In fact, at the risk of repetition it may be said that to 1913, more than any other year in the period covered by this book, the much over-worked word "vintage" may be truthfully applied.

1914

Historians as yet unborn will have to judge in what period the most aesthetically satisfying motor-cars were built. Certainly the "pressed ware" of the 'thirties and the bulbous American vehicles, whose designers' one desire seems to be to emulate a "space-ship" as closely as possible, will be near the bottom of their list. It is my personal opinion that the palm should be awarded either to the last few years of the 1920s or to the immediate pre-Kaiser-war period. Certainly in this latter epoch we have a wonderful and harmonious marriage between the carriage-builder's art, refined to perfection, and reasonably practical mechanism, still finished – for costs were low – in the nineteenth-century engineering tradition.

The Manchester Show held in January 1914 did not produce as attractive a selection of coachwork as the London Show of three months later. There was, however, one interesting innovation, a boat-shaped body with mahogany decking, of the type so popular in the middle and late 'twenties. Unfortunately, the scuttle and bonnet did not carry through the excellent lines of the body. It was mounted on a 15/20 Straker Squire. Very much the same remarks apply to several car shows at Brussels. The Scottish Show was rather dull, and produced nothing new at all.

Self-starters were now the rule rather than the exception, but a number of cars had them placed, incredibly stupidly, in the position usually occupied by the starting handle. This naïve belief in their infallibility led to a spate of protest when they failed and the cars had to be started by towing, or jacking-up and turning the back wheels. Another evil effect of the advent of electric starting was that some makers took advantage of this to make starting handles, mostly still fixed, both too small and horribly inaccessible.

Some curious cars were built in 1914, including a three-ton gyro-car which was built at Wolseley for an eccentric Russian nobleman who never collected it.

Two rather surprising things happened in 1914. The Russian

Government announced that foreign motorists might tour in Russia without even customs formalities provided that "they notified a police station of their proposed itinerary". The other was the erection in Kent of experimental flashing lights at a dangerous crossroads. This must have anticipated the next attempt by a long, long time. Now that screw threads were beginning to be standardised, an attempt was made to standardise rims.

Early in 1914 the A.A. and R.A.C., in spite of their rivalry, agreed to combine to fight anti-motoring bills brought by private members in the House of Commons.

In Australia, incredibly tough inter-state trials were held. These were won by a Benz. In America, the Vanderbilt Cup was run at Santa Monica, California, and was won by Ralph de Palma on a 9½-litre Mercedes, probably one of the old 1908 Grand Prix cars. Barney Oldfield on a Mercer ran him a very close second, followed by a Mason, a Stutz and a Touraine. Marquis on a Sunbeam might well have won, for he was leading by a long way, but he rolled his car over and was terribly injured.

In June, the Russians ran a Grand Prix round a 20-mile circuit near St. Petersburg. It was won by a "Blitzen" Benz of vast capacity at over 70 m.p.h., with a "Prince Henry"-type Vauxhall a fairly close second, over a course of about 150 miles. A very strong contingent of European drivers went over for the Indianapolis 500-mile race, which was won by René Thomas on a Delage. The Americans did not really have a look in, the only one to finish in the first eight was Barney Oldfield on a Stutz, who was fifth. In Europe, Nazzaro won the Coppa Florio at great speed on a most interesting car bearing his name.

The last pre-war Tourist Trophy race over the Isle of Man course was a most exciting race involving the most fascinating cars, some of which still survive. It was won by Kenelm Lee Guinness on a "Henry"-type Sunbeam. The Humbers were every bit as much inspired by Henry, but did not do so well. One of them was driven by Burgess, the designer. Harry Lawson, full of years and money, presented the winner with a cheque for £1000. The Minervas, the only sleeve-valve cars in the race, did very well indeed, but used ten gallons of lubricating oil *each* during the race. The other Belgian cars, the Savas, were not so successful, nor were Star, Crossley or Vauxhall, but a Straker Squire managed to get fourth place. W. O. Bentley, driving a D.F.P. (Doriot, Flandrin et Parant), a French firm with whom he was associated as English representative, finished well down the list.

It is interesting to look back and observe that winning the Tourist Trophy never brought much success to the victorious model. The two-cylinder horizontal-engined Arrol-Johnston that won the first Tourist Trophy did not sell in any quantity. The four-cylinder Rolls-Royce that won the second was suppressed to make way for the "Silver Ghost". The 18-h.p. Rover, the next winner, enjoyed limited but not great popularity, and the Hutton, almost immediately after its victory, went out of production.

The Austrian Alpine Trial, if only there were space, would need a chapter to itself, for the competitors contended with everything – floods, mud and even fire. It was a saga of apparently insurmountable obstacles overcome amid breathtakingly beautiful Alpine scenery. There were quite a few English entries, though the redoubtable James Radley, with his glorious Labourdette-bodied Rolls-Royce "Continental", was the only one to gain an award, the prize of the City of Vienna.

Much has been written about the dramatic 1914 French Grand Prix and how the great Boillot, driving brilliantly in his last race, broke down just before the end, and allowed the white Mercedes to come in, one, two, three, as easily as three white ducks waddling down to the home pond. I am afraid that the lovely story that the British Secret Service stole the winning car is quite untrue. It was bought by Gordon Watney, who had entered it for the August Brooklands meeting (which, of course never took place).

Whether or not it was actually the winning car which was delivered to the Mercedes showrooms in Long Acre is obscure. Several people who ought to know say that it was not. At any rate, it was on exhibition there when war was declared, and it was promptly handed over to the experimental department at Rolls-Royce, where it yielded valuable data for aero engines.

In August the Army Motor Reserve (as the Motor Volunteer Corps had become the previous year) were mobilized. Motor owners all over the country gave their cars for ambulances, and the Duke of Westminster hurriedly armoured his Rolls-Royces to harry the Uhlans. Europe was at war. It was the end of an era. Gracious living in the grand manner as our fathers had known it was gone, never to return. One of the casualties of European tumult was the superlative craftsmanship that made the Edwardian car what it was. This lingered on for a decade, diminishing yearly, after the cessation of hostilities, but it was never quite the same. Just as the furniture of Chippendale and his contemporaries links us with the elegance of the eighteenth century, so the careful and loving restoration of Edwardian cars today is surely born of the nostalgia for those days when a man took real pride in his work, and was not primarily concerned with the length of time it took.

1914 12-h.p., 4-cylinder Rover two-seater

7

British Cars

A.C.

IN 1900, John Weller and John Portwine set up a small workshop to build motor-cars. Weller was the engineer, and Portwine, a butcher who owned a chain of shops, was the capitalist. A 20-h.p. Weller car, chain-driven, with engine, gearbox, silencer, radiator, etc., all mounted on a sub-frame, appeared in 1903. There were four separate cylinders. This car is fully described in three successive issues of *The Autocar* commencing 6th June 1903. But in spite of the glowing eulogies given to it in the motoring press, it did not sell well, and by 1907 the company had turned their attention to the little "Autocarrier" of which, at one time, there were many hundreds on the streets of London. This became available with a single seat in place of the carrier box. The A. C. Sociable, where the driver and passenger sat side by side, arrived in 1909. There was also, in 1913 and 1914, a four-wheeled "Sociable" with its single-cylinder now in front.

In 1914, the first of those wonderful little four-cylinder (59 mm. × 100 mm.) A.C.s appeared. It weighed only 10 cwt. and the few of them that were built before the outbreak of war had French-built "Fivet" engines. Anzani engines were not fitted till after the 1914–18 war.

CROSSLEY

The old-established oil-engine firm of Crossley Brothers, Openshaw, Manchester, decided, in the early years of the century, to enter the motor industry. In 1903, J. S. Critchley designed a very sound, conventional, 22-h.p. chain-drive, four-cylinder car. They did not propose to market it themselves, but entrusted this to the newly formed firm of Charles Jarrott and Letts. Jarrott we know already as the pioneer racing motorist. Letts was also a pioneer driver, although not in races, who in 1898 worked for a year or two in America, and returned with the agency for Locomobile. In 1903 he gave this up and joined forces with Jarrott to handle Oldsmobile, De Dietrich and the new Crossley car. Some years later, Jarrott withdrew from the business. In 1904 the 22-h.p. model was supplemented by a chain-driven 28-h.p. car. The following year a 20-h.p. model was built, primarily for the Tourist Trophy race, but the cars were not ready in time. Jarrott drove one from London to Edinburgh in twenty and a half hours, which was very good going indeed. The coachwork on these early Crossleys was particularly pleasing. At the end of 1905 they started to build, as well as the models mentioned above, a 40-h.p. chassis for 1906. This car looked very much like a F.I.A.T.; it had a conventional T-head, four-cylinder engine (121 mm. × 150 mm.), with two separately cast blocks. The makers claimed that they had paid particular attention to the suspension. Charles Jarrott broke the London to Monte Carlo record with one.

In 1910, the automobile division was separated from the Crossley Oil Engine Works, and William Letts was appointed Managing Director. The selling firm of Charles Jarrott and Letts was bought up as a subsidiary by Crossley Motors. It is interesting to note that although there was a tremendous vogue for six-cylinder cars, Crossleys, right up to 1914, never built anything but fours.

Up to 1910 they concentrated on the 20-h.p. and 40-h.p. cars only, but after that they introduced 12-h.p. and 15-h.p. models, and the 40-h.p. was dropped. By far the most popular of their products was the 20/25 which, although not a very inspiring performer perhaps, was of good, solid workmanship throughout.

The 15-h.p. car did very well indeed at Shelsley Walsh hill climb, and just prior to the outbreak of war in 1914 a range of sporting but very comfortable "15-h.p. Shelsley Models", with the famous bull-nose radiators, were offered for sale. From 1913 onwards, Rotax electric lighting was available as an optional extra at a cost of about £30.

In August, 1914, Crossley Motors were fortunate in getting

War Office contracts for staff cars, lorries and tenders.

DAIMLER

A young English engineer called F. R. Simms was selling
aerial cableways in Germany in about 1890. He demonstrated
one at an exhibition at Bremen where Gottlieb Daimler was
showing his petrol-driven tramcar, and the two struck up
a firm friendship which was to last till Daimler's death in
1900. In 1893, Simms formed, in London, the "Daimler
Motor Syndicate", an agency for selling Daimler's patents in
England. No manufacturing was envisaged. Now the financier,

The first "Coventry" Daimler

H. J. Lawson, comes on the scene. Ruthless, spectacular and
a great showman, he saw the potentialities of the horseless
carriage and attempted no less a coup than to corner the
master patents covering them. He did not succeed in this, but
he founded the Daimler Company as we know it in England
today. He formed "The British Motor Syndicate" who took
over the Daimler patents at a very substantial profit to Simms.
The following year the "Daimler Motor Company Limited"
was formed. For some time, until they got their works going,
this firm imported quite a large number of German-built
Daimler cars, being rather careful to conceal the fact that they
had not made them in the new Coventry works. King Edward

VII tried one in 1898 and bought one of the first British-made models in June 1900. From that moment they never looked back.

To say the internal affairs of the Directorate were stormy would be an understatement. The Company was re-formed in 1904 and in 1910 the "Daimler Company Ltd." was launched to take over the company of 1904 and also the Birmingham Small Arms Company, which stems from a seventeenth-century trade guild. Apart from accepting an honorary directorship, Gottlieb Daimler never had anything to do with the administration of the British Company.

By 1901 the Coventry factory was in full production, making 6-h.p., 8-h.p. and 12-h.p. cars and taking active part in competitions and races. Also, and this was very progressive, they opened up a London service station. The next year a 22-h.p. car was built and a succession of increasingly powerful poppet-valve chain-driven cars were built till 1909. In 1908 Percy Martin, the works manager, saw an experimental sleeve-valve car built by a young Englishman called Knight, who had emigrated to the U.S.A. Martin was not impressed by the way the car was built but liked the idea. With the approval of his directors he did a year's development work and so the famous "Daimler Silent Knight", on which the Company's fortunes were founded, was born. In that year F. W. Lanchester was appointed Consulting Engineer to the Company, and by November 1909 not only were the big sleeve-valve cars in production but so was the little 15-h.p. Daimler, the smallest sleeve-valve car ever made at that time. The big poppet-valve cars continued to be made for another year and then faded out. In the years up to 1914 a very large variety of models was available, all sleeve-valve, from the little 12-h.p. to the 57.2 h.p. six, and the first of the vast luxurious 45-h.p., so long used by Royalty, with a wheelbase in excess of 12ft. To drive one of these is like steering a big steam yacht, and there is great charm in their majestic progress and complete indifference to all but the steepest hills. With an effortless cruising speed of 38/40 m.p.h., the back-wheel brakes are quite adequate except for very dense, present-day traffic. Corners should, however, be treated with the greatest respect as there is a tendency, with heavy coachwork towering to a height of 9 ft., to "lie down on the door handles".

DENNIS

John Dennis, in 1895, greatly daring, threw up his secure job in an ironmongers and started his own little cycle business in Guildford. The "assembly line" was an old pear tree behind his shop, where he hung the frame of a bicycle as he built the various components on to it. Cycle business was good, and soon his brother Raymond came to help him, and then, instead of assembling bought-in parts, they started to make all the components themselves. The old pear tree had to go, to make room for a workshop.

In 1898 the brothers decided to fit a De Dion engine into a tricycle, and in 1899 John Dennis was fined for riding it "furiously". By 1902, they were building a very practical little quadricycle with a seat over the front wheels, the engine over the back axle, and the driver sitting on a bicycle saddle on top of that. On these 3-h.p. tricycles and quadricycles, Raymond Dennis won many minor racing awards.

Then they made a sturdy, primitive little car, which not only went well, but sold quickly: 200 in less than a year. It still had a proprietary engine. This model was followed by 12/14 touring cars, 16/20 four-seaters, broughams and hansom cabs, as well as by a 40-h.p. racing car with a Simms engine. At the 1904 Crystal Palace Show they did incredibly well, taking nearly £30,000-worth of orders. During this year they were one of the earliest firms to introduce a worm-drive axle. In 1905 John Dennis and his manager, Reggie Downing, entered two cars for the Tourist Trophy race in the Isle of Man. These were not, like most of the other cars, specially built racers, but tuned up 14-h.p. touring cars, weighing 17 cwt. They finished 16th and 18th, and recorded the remarkable petrol consumption of 26·73 miles per gallon.

The 20-h.p. Dennis did so well in the 4000-mile Reliability Trial of 1906 that the firm was awarded the Dewar Trophy. In 1907, one could, by paying £25 extra, have a silent chain-type gearbox instead of the normal sliding cogs. This, coupled with the worm-drive axle, made for a very silent transmission indeed. Also, many years ahead of its time, a free-wheel was available.

The Dennis limousines and landaulettes won a number of prizes for luxury and flexibility. In 1910 they were building a 24-h.p. four-cylinder (100 × 120 mm.) with a White and Poppe engine, specially made for them. The popular 18-h.p. model continued, now with a four-speed box, direct-drive on third. Two large and luxurious chassis were also built; a 40-h.p. four-cylinder (127 mm. × 130 mm.) and a six-cylinder 60-h.p. of the same bore and stroke.

In 1904, Dennis built a delivery van for Harrods, and during the next nine years the commercial vehicle side of the business developed so rapidly that it outstripped the passenger vehicle side. So, in 1913, the directors of Dennis decided to stop building motor-cars altogether, and concentrate entirely on lorries, fire-engines and other commercial vehicles.

HORBICK

How many people have ever heard of the Horbick? Yet, in its day, 1900 to 1909, it was quite well known and successful in competitions, so I have included it because of its curiosity value. The firm of Horsfall and Bickham of Pendleton made, and I believe still do, specialised machinery connected with textiles. In 1900 they made a car more or less for fun. Friends of the directors wanted one like it, so part of the works, under William Snow, was turned over to building them. In 1902 they exhibited a car at St. James Hall, Manchester. They ran a car in the 1000-mile trial in 1903, and in 1904 produced a range of one- and two-cylinder shaft-driven cars. At first, proprietary engines – Forman and also Johnson, Harley and Martin – were used. In 1905 they used a White and Poppe three-cylinder engine. This car, the "Minor" 10/12-h.p. had a radiator rather like an early Royce car and sold at £300. The four-cylinder 15/20-h.p. "Major", with a radiator like a Léon Bollée, sold for £500, and the 22/28-h.p. for £600. In 1906, the "Minor" still had a White and Poppe engine, but a completely different radiator, and the "Major", now fitted with their own engine, looked externally much the same. In 1907, 18/24 six-cylinder and 45/60 six-cylinder models were added to the range. Both had Horbick-built engines. Cylinders were cast in pairs and maximum r.p.m. was 1000. In 1908 the cars were similar but better equipped.

In the meantime, Horbicks had been gaining considerable successes in hill-climbs and trials, driven by the sales manager, the late "Doc" Cranham. More orders than they could possibly handle came in, including one for 2000 taxicabs. The directors of Horsfall and Bickham decided that they had to expand enormously or to cease production and stick to their real métier: textile machinery. There were a number of serious difficulties in the way of expansion, so they chose the latter course. Production ceased in 1909. Had they chosen otherwise, we might still have Horbick cars on the market today.

HUMBER

The cycle-manufacturing firm founded by Thomas Humber, which was connected with H. J. Lawson's British Motor Syndicate, first became interested in motor vehicles in 1896. This year saw the second motor exhibition to be held in London, at the Imperial Institute, where Humbers showed two tandem bicycles fitted with Kane-Pennington engines mounted behind the rear-wheel. However, it was not until 1899 that the first four-wheeled vehicles officially made by Humber appeared at the Stanley Show. The exhibits included an M.D. voiturette, which was a quadricycle with a 2½-h.p. De Dion engine, front-wheel-drive and rear-wheel steering; a lighter quadricycle of 1¾-h.p., and two Phaetons with 5- and 8-h.p. horizontal engines.

The Company was re-formed in 1900 and had no further connection with Lawson's Syndicate. They continued to manufacture the same models as before with a few minor modifications, but with the interesting addition of a 5-h.p. water-cooled car with four speeds and reverse – the first of the "Humberettes". In 1901 an improved version of the car was shown. It had a De Dion engine, and the radiator was mounted on watertight hinges so that it could be swung aside when

131

working on the engine. It had shaft-drive with universal joints, a three-speed and reverse gearbox and three brakes. Two of these were handbrakes on the rear wheels and the foot-operated third brake worked on the driving-shaft. This braking system was continued on Humber models almost to the 1914–18 war.

Louis Coatalen had joined the firm in 1901 and designed a new 12-h.p. chassis which was shown in 1902 carrying a limousine body with curved windows of plate glass! It had four cylinders, cast in pairs, electric and tube ignition and a four-speed gearbox. At its selling price of about £300, the 12-h.p. was excellent value and the model was very successful. An 8-h.p. two-cylinder car was also exhibited.

By 1903, a new factory at Beeston was in production and the practice of building the larger and more expensive models at Beeston, and the cheaper or lighter models at Coventry, was introduced. Another new design appeared in this year: a 20-h.p. four-cylinder machine with mechanically operated inlet and exhaust valves on opposite sides of a T-shaped combustion chamber.

Production of the 5-h.p. single-cylinder "Humberettes" continued both at Beeston and Coventry, and by 1905 alternative engines of 5-h.p., 6½-h.p. and 7½-h.p. were being offered. The range continued with 10–12-, 12–14- and 20–25-h.p. models, most of them being made at Coventry. Beeston was producing "8–18" and "16–20" cars.

During the next couple of years all motor manufacturers found a multiplicity of models uneconomic, so this wide range was reduced to two models for 1906. The Beeston works continued the "16–20" and Coventry with the "12–14". Both cars had four-cylinder engines, with a pressed-steel frame and four-speed box on the Beeston car, and a three-speed box and tubular frame for the Coventry version. Humber cars scored a success in the 1906 Tourist Trophy when they were the only cars to complete the course. The two-model policy was revised next year when a new 15-h.p. Coventry-built machine was added. My mother told me that the Beeston-built cars were always considered vastly superior to the Coventry-built ones.

A large new factory was opened at Coventry in 1908, and the Beeston and old Coventry works were gradually amalgamated in the new premises. The range now included a two-cylinder 8-h.p., a 30-h.p. "six" and five four-cylinder models of 12, 15, 20, 22, and 28 h.p.

Financial difficulties, brought about by a combination of poor sales and heavy expenditure on the new factory, caused the Company to be re-formed again in 1909 with an entirely different Board with the exception of one member. The new company altered the range of models once more by eliminating the 22-h.p. and 28-h.p. cars altogether and by replacing the "15" with a new 16-h.p. with detachable wheels. These were also fitted to the "8". The terms "Beeston Humber" and "Coventry Humber" were dropped as all the cars were now made at Coventry.

In 1910 the 8-h.p. model was replaced by the two-seater "10–14" and a new 28-h.p. made its appearance. Wire wheels were standardised on all models except the "12" which was given a new frame and torque tube, fitted with rear-wheel shock absorbers, and called the "12–20". Two years later, in 1912, came the 11-h.p., four-cylinder Humber which claimed to be the first monobloc "four" ever produced. A special streamlined version, known as the "Golden Bug", broke three international class-records at Brooklands in the hands of W. G. Tuck.

Variations in the engine sizes of the models offered continued during 1913 and the "Humberette" reappeared, this time as an 8-h.p., air-cooled V-twin. It weighed under 7 cwt. and was therefore classed as a cycle-car by the R.A.C., but it was essentially a miniature motor car. It had rack-and-pinion steering, a three-speed gearbox, propeller shaft with bevel-gear transmission, half-elliptic springs for'ard and quarter-elliptics at the rear. In two-seater form, complete with hood, screen, horn and lights, it cost £125. The car enjoyed considerable popularity and it was said that over 2000 "Humberettes" were in daily use by mid-1914, by which time it was being offered with an alternative water-cooled V-twin engine.

For the 1914 Tourist Trophy race, F.T. Burgess designed the first, and only, team of Humber racing cars to be specially built. The Tourist Trophy Humbers had four-cylinder engines (82 mm. × 156 mm.), and twin overhead-camshafts operated two inlet and two exhaust valves per cylinder. 100 b.h.p. at 3200 r.p.m. was claimed. The gearbox was separate from the engine, carried on a sub-frame in the usual Humber manner, and behind it was a propeller-shaft brake, heavily ribbed to assist cooling. There were no front-wheel brakes but a hand-wheel for rapid brake adjustment was fitted close to the mechanic's seat.

The cars were driven by Tuck, Wright and Burgess and all three retired from the race, two with valve trouble and one with a seized piston. Those driven by Wright and Burgess gave a good account of themselves, however, and it is unfortunate that the outbreak of war prevented development of these interesting cars.

For the greater part of the period Humbers were producing motor-cycles as well as cars, and they began to manufacture aircraft in 1910. It is also of interest that their war-time activities included the development and first production of the B.R. 4 rotary aero engine designed by W. O. Bentley.

LAGONDA

The firm of Lagonda was founded at Staines by an American, Wilbur Gunn. Although he had served an engineering apprenticeship at the Singer Sheepshearing Co., Inc., the family firm in Ohio, his real ambition when he came to this country just before the turn of the century was to become an opera singer. Be that as it may, his house, which stood in the middle of the area which was later to become the Lagonda factory, took on the aspect of a workshop. After a steam launch, allegedly built for a bet on a speed contest with a fellow American, a number of motor-cycles were produced which he called Lagondas, after the name Lagonda Creek, his childhood playground by the Great Lakes.

Another engineer, A. H. Cranmer, joined the firm and at the end of 1904 they began production of a twin-cylinder tri-car. Apart from the Longuemare carburettor no proprietary parts were used, and even the nuts and bolts – for Gunn was a stickler for detail – were made by the firm. About 30 tri-cars a year were built and they achieved no small success in contemporary trials. In the 1905 Reliability Trial of the Auto-Cycle Club, Gunn, driving himself, not only won the only Gold Medal to be awarded, but carried off the Appearance Contest as well.

The last of the tri-cars were finished early in 1907 but already the first Lagonda cars were in production. Two models were made, a four-cylinder of 20 h.p. and a larger model, with an extra dual-cylinder block added to an enlarged crank-case, rated at 30 h.p. All the early production cars were sent direct to Russia and apart from one or two that were sold to friends of the directors they were not available in this country until 1912. Perhaps their most interesting feature was the rear suspension. The axle, made up of sleeves of cast mild steel, was supported by four rods. These rods, the two outward ones being above the axle and the two inboard ones below it, were constructed in a parallelogram formation similar in principle to the modern trailing-link suspension, so that movement was limited to the vertical. Great tyre economy was claimed and certainly the Gold-Medal-winning 20-h.p. model was the only car in the 1910 Russian Reliability Trial to complete the 3000-verst course on its original set of tyres.

In late 1913 an entirely new Lagonda was offered to the British public. This was an 1100-c.c. light car, priced at £135 for a two-seater cabriolet. The engine was a four-cylinder 67 × 78 m.m. monobloc with overhead-inlet and side-exhaust valves driven from a single nearside camshaft. The earliest cars had the inlet valves operated by short rockers working fore-and-aft down the line of the engine but, after these had been found to cause undue wear in the valve guides, they were soon replaced by long-rockers (No. 1's pushrod was behind No. 2 cylinder and No. 2's in front of No. 1) that gave the appearance of a succession of exposed-beam engines.

The body and the chassis of the Lagonda light car were constructed as a single unit. The body panels extended downwards to be attached to rather than to brace the two thin angle members that constituted the chassis frame. The whole design was born of economy rather than an insight into the monocoque technique and, indeed, the frame members owed their rigidity, not to the thin panelling between them, but to the extremely light weight of the car (9 cwt.) and a substantial cast transverse member that supported also the rear of the engine and the front of the transmission assembly.

Direct steering, that required but a third of a turn to move the front wheels from one end to another of an ample lock, was not this model's most endearing feature, but 50 m.p.g. was claimed and contemporary descriptions indicate that this last figure at any rate was no exaggeration. All this for £135 gave Gunn a real chance to capture the cheap-car market but no sooner had production got into its stride than the 1914–18 war came and the factory turned to other things. At the end of the war, Gunn was seriously ill and the battle for supremacy was never seriously rejoined and in 1920 the founder of the firm died. A very large, very generous, good-humoured man and always immaculately dressed, he took as much interest in local affairs as he did in his own factory.

NAPIER

D. Napier and Sons of Vine Street, Lambeth, were specialist weighing-machine makers, and the fact that they made coin-weighing machines for the Bank of England gives an indication of the high level of accuracy of their work.

"Old Number 8", the Panhard on which Merkel came second in the Paris–Marseilles race of 1896, was bought by H. O. Duncan for 30,000 francs and brought to England for Lawson, on whose behalf he was acting. It later became the property of S. F. Edge. Young Montague Napier converted her from tiller- to wheel-steering and also built an engine for her. He did both these jobs so well that he was asked for more engines and, by 1900, he was building complete cars. Edge and Charles Rolls drove a 16-h.p. Napier together in the Paris–Toulouse race of 1900, but withdrew owing to ignition troubles.

Montague Napier built, in 1901, a 50-h.p. racing car for Edge in the "Paris–Bordeaux", also for Rolls, Edge and Eliot Zborowski for the first Gordon Bennett race, which Edge won the following year.

Apart from the racing cars, Napier was building medium-powered four-cylinder touring cars. Not only were they very good cars but Edge, now associated with the firm, was a salesman in a million. The resultant demand for cars encouraged Napier to buy a large tract of land at Acton Vale, on the outskirts of London, and to erect a big new works. In 1903 Edge gave a dinner at the Trocadero Restaurant to announce a new model for the next year – one of the very first six-cylinder cars ever put into production. About this time, also, Napier started to build large petrol engines for racing motor-boats, which were very successful indeed.

By January, 1904, the Acton works were in full production. It is interesting to note that the engines were run-in by being driven on the bench for many hours with "rotten stone" mixed with the lubricating oil. Napier and Edge tried, like Bollée, to build an engine that was really silent, and to a large extent they succeeded. The big model, although expensive, was the most popular both with Royalty and with wealthy people.

In 1903 it was fitted with a remarkable device whereby the amount of air admitted to the carburettor was governed by the flow of cooling water, i.e. the greater the revolutions, the weaker the mixture. Napiers are reputed to have been built under licence in U.S.A., but whether this was so, or if they were only assembled there, does not seem clear.

In 1906, four models were offered, the 18-h.p. (89 mm. × 102 mm.) four-cylinder, the 45-h.p. (102 mm. × 107 mm.), and two six-cylinder cars: the 40-h.p. (102 mm. × 102 mm.) and the 60-h.p. (127 mm. × 102 mm.). These were priced at £650, £1000, £1050 and £1500 for the bare chassis. In 1910, they marketed rather belatedly, what is described as a Grand Prix Napier. It seems to have been more of a sports car than an actual racer, but it certainly did not lack power, for the low bonnet hardly had room to contain the immense six-cylinder engine rated at 90-h.p. (126 mm. × 154 mm.). The wheelbase was only 9 ft. 8 in. Pricing was interesting. Chassis cost £1500, the body £25, and the hood £40. They sold a few, but this model was not on offer the following year.

by 1911 prices had come down with a run. One could buy a 45-h.p. "Noiseless Six" Napier touring car, complete with accessories, for under £850. They were also making many smaller cars ranging from the 16·9-h.p. four-cylinder taxicab chassis to the 30-h.p., 45-h.p. and 65-h.p. cars, all of which now had live axles. They also made colonial versions of these of which many hundreds were exported. In 1912, S. F. Edge sold his shares in S. F. Edge Limited to Napier. The story goes, I cannot vouch for its veracity, that they had made, very early on, an agreement that Edge, who had a very fine selling organisation, took the entire annual output of the Napier works. In 1912 the output had become so large that even Edge would not handle it, so he sold out all his interests.

By 1914, Napier had cut their models to five – three four-cylinder cars, 15-h.p., 16/22-h.p., and 20-h.p. and two sixes, the 30/35- and the 45-h.p. Obviously, by reducing the number of models and in other ways, they had cut their costs considerably, for at the outbreak of the 1914 war the most expensive Napier made cost only £850 for the chassis, exactly half what the most expensive chassis had cost in 1912.

ROLLS-ROYCE

Henry Royce was an engineer making electrical cranes in Cook Street, Manchester. He bought, at the turn of the century, a car of French manufacture and was really horrified by its mechanical crudity, so he set to work and built himself a two-cylinder car of modest power, but of great refinement, which soon went into production.

Charles Rolls, Lord Llangatock's son, was also, in his dashing way, a perfectionist. In the very earliest days of motor racing he was a consistent competitor on Panhard and Mors cars. He also had a motor business for the sale of Panhard, Minerva and other continental cars. Rolls was delighted with the Swiss-watch-like precision of the little Royce car and the world-famous partnership ensued. The power of the two-cylinder model was raised to 10-h.p. and this was speedily joined by a 15-h.p. three-cylinder and a 20-h.p. four-cylinder. These are all Rolls-Royce cars as opposed to the original two-cylinder

138

Royce. The three Rolls-Royce cars, of early 1904, had a radiator like a Panhard, but the three-cylinder brougham presented to Dr. Warre, headmaster of Eton, at Christmas of that year, had a radiator approaching the traditional Rolls shape.

In 1905 Charles Rolls was second in the Tourist Trophy race with a 20-h.p. four-cylinder car and in 1906 he won it. In 1905 the range was augmented by a fascinating car, not one single specimen of which is known to exist – the 30-h.p. six-cylinder. The engine was virtually the 20-h.p. with two more 5-h.p. cylinders added, on a crankcase already suggestive of the "Silver Ghost". The whole range of cars had overhead-inlet and side-exhaust valves. Each crank revolved in its own chamber formed by baffle plates so that it was impossible for the front "splash-feed" bearings to starve on a hill. Water was positively circulated by pump. Rather a nice contemporary touch is that inspection doors, like those on a marine engine, were bolted to the sides of the crankcase so that any bearing could be viewed separately. The clutch, very like that of a "Silver Ghost", drove through a three-speed box (direct-drive top) to a live axle of the usual complexity and beautiful workmanship which one expects in a Rolls.

On 3rd November 1905, the firm of Rolls-Royce gave a dinner-party at the Trocadero to announce a new model. This was at once the most remarkable and the least-known which they ever produced. This car was built for the express purpose of doing everything required of a town carriage as well as, or better than, an electric brougham. The engine, a 90° V-eight, 83-mm. bore and 83-mm. stroke, was mounted inboard like a Lanchester. The valves were side by side and, being operated on a vertical plane, were at an angle of 45° to the line of the cylinders.

The object of this design was to obtain maximum torque throughout the whole engine range, so that the lower ratios of the three-speed box should only be necessary for the steepest hills, and, indeed, it could normally start away in top gear. Most motor-cars of this date were lubricated through adjustable drip feeds on the dash, and any spectator of the London-Brighton run will recall the smoke barrage often caused by this arrangement. Royce was determined to obviate this and had a fully automatic pump lubrication system even to the extent of a drilled crankshaft!

People who saw this remarkable car in action say that it was absolutely successful in all it set out to do, that it had a steering lock like nothing ever seen before and that its silence was really uncanny.

Not many of these fascinating cars were built and it seems fairly definite that none remain in existence. There does appear, however, a very long sporting chance that one of the 30-h.p. cars described above, of which many more were made, might conceivably turn up.

In 1906 Claude Johnson, a supremely able man who had joined the firm, laid down a one-model policy. In 1907 the immortal "Silver Ghost" appeared and remained, with surprisingly minor modifications, in production for nineteen years. It was so perfect and acquitted itself so well in every event from its first appearance in the 1000-mile trial that, in spite of the high price (£950 for chassis only), the car was an instantaneous success. The very first ones had "square" engines, 114 mm. × 114 mm., giving 48 h.p. at 12000 r.p.m., a four-speed box with direct drive in third, and then a rather noisy overdrive. The lubrication was years ahead of anything except the 30-h.p. six and V-eight Rolls, and the dual ignition, designed by Royce, years ahead of anything at all.

In 1909 the stroke was lengthened to 121 mm., overdrive was no longer fitted (three speeds only) and rear suspension was altered from semi-elliptic to cantilever in 1912. Then one of the most fascinating cars in the world was built. This was the four-speed high-compression model which became known in 1913, because of its success in the Alpine Trials, as the "Alpine Eagle". It was not as fast as, say, the 100-h.p. Isotta of the same year, but it had more charm than any other Edwardian, coupled with a most deceptively useful performance. Anyone who is, as I have been, lucky enough to drive one counts it as a really great and unforgettable experience, like tasting a noble Burgundy or seeing St. Peter's lit up with a myriad of candles for Easter.

Charles Rolls was killed in a flying accident and Henry Royce, like Gottlieb Daimler a decade earlier, was killing himself with overwork. But aided by a few men of the calibre of Claude Johnson they built a tradition for perfection which has lasted, even after Royce's death in 1934.

ROVER

Coventry has always been a city devoted to light industry. During the first half of the nineteenth century two of the leading products were silk and watches, but during the next twenty years or so both these articles were imported so cheaply from abroad that the Coventry factories were forced to close down. The availability of cheap skilled labour attracted a number of new industries to Coventry, among them the manufacture of bicycles. Among the earliest cycle-makers were J. K. Starley and William Sutton who built "Penny farthing"

Rover single-cylinder, 8 h.p. coupé, 1907

bicycles, with one enormous wheel in front and a tiny wheel trailing behind, as early as 1877. They also made the "Meteor" tricycle. Starley dissolved partnership with Sutton and in 1884 was among the pioneers of the modern "safety bicycle" with its rear-wheel driven by a chain from the centrally mounted pedals. Their bicycles were both good and popular

141

and were exported all over the world. An expedition to Tibet in 1904 found that a Rover bicycle had preceded it!

Around 1888, Starley built a motorised tricycle, with a horizontal engine under the seat, but the firm did not go into production of any power-driven vehicles till 1903, when they started to build a 2¼-h.p. motor bicycle. It was followed in 1904 by an 8-h.p. single-cylinder car. This was the genesis of the 8-h.p. Rover that was to prove one of the most reliable, economical and popular light cars for many years to come. This car, curiously enough, was thought "too powerful" and was shortly supplemented by a similar 6-h.p. car. The 8-h.p. engine had a bore and stroke of 114 mm. × 130 mm., and the 6-h.p. 95 mm. × 110 mm. The designer was E. W. Lewis from Daimler.

The 8-h.p. car had three speeds forward and reverse, giving 8, 16, and 24 m.p.h., with a maximum speed, under favourable circumstances, of 30 m.p.h. The consumption modestly claimed was 35 m.p.g., but a large number of owners wrote in to say that this was nonsense, that they had checked and counter-checked and were getting 40 m.p.g. The carburettor on both 8-h.p. and 6-h.p. cars was "Rover patent automatic", of a remarkably simple and modern design. It was controlled by the accelerator pedal and not, as with so many contemporary cars, by a governor. Ignition on both cars was by high-tension trembler coil and wipe contact, operated off the clutch because the twin flywheels revolved inside the crank case. On both cars, also, the gear-change quadrant was in the modern position under the steering wheel. The chassis was of seasoned ash supported, where necessary, by steel flitch plates, and front springing was transverse on the 8-h.p., not on the 6-h.p. An adequate radiator, coupled with pump circulation, accounted for efficient cooling under any circumstances – a very rare thing in those days. The steering on the early models was of the wire and bobbin variety; with rack and pinion, which soon superseded it, as an optional extra.

The 8-h.p. car sold as a two-seater for £210. The more robust export version with higher ground clearance known as the "Indian and Colonial Model", was available at £225.

The 6-h.p. car, its three speeds giving 8, 15 and 22 m.p.h., sold at £130, but a cheaper version, with wire wheels, small tyres and less elaborate coachwork could be bought for 100 guineas. This really does seem outstandingly good value. All this, and, as the Rover Company put it so charmingly, "Deferred Purchase by arrangement".

Both these grand little cars won many awards in trials and continued in production till 1912.

In 1906 the single-cylinder cars were joined by a range of four-cylinder models. There was the 10–12-h.p., a very bad car, and the 16–20-h.p. Two of the latter were entered for the 1906 Tourist Trophy races, but were excluded on the technical grounds that they arrived too late for scrutineering. The next year one of these two cars, driven by Mr. E. Courtis, won this race in the most abominable weather. This was really an achievement, as the car was basically a standard four-seater selling at £400, and it beat many other cars costing three and four times that money.

These 16/20 Rovers had each cylinder (95 mm. × 110 mm.) separately cast. They had many features reminiscent of the 8-h.p. and 6-h.p., including transverse springing forward, and the Rover "Patent engine brake" which manipulated the camshaft so that the inlet valve could be permanently closed when the engine was used for braking. The ignition was by coil, but a high-tension magneto was optional at increased cost. Three speeds were standard, but a four-speed box with overdrive top could be had for an extra £250. They also built a 30-h.p. model which never went into production. In 1906 the 16/20 had a radiator rather like the early Standard cars, but in 1907 the famous Rover "shield" shape was adopted.

In 1908, one could buy a "Tourist Trophy Replica" Rover, which now had dual ignition, for £450, and the 8-h.p. single cylinder could be had with a glorious little hansom-cab town coupé for £250. The Rover Company bought the old-established coachworks, Hawkins and Peake.

In 1910 the range was much the same, except that the cars had detachable wheels, many extras were now standard, and the prices were slightly higher. Also the four-cylinder had now grown up into a 15-h.p., and was available with a range of owner- and chauffeur-driven coachwork. This car won a Gold Medal in the non-stop trials of 1909. Rovers, by the way, built not only the chassis, but all coachwork as well.

In 1912 the two single-cylinder cars were replaced by a 12-h.p. four-cylinder car (75 mm. × 130 mm.), of sound and progressive design. The engine was monobloc and magneto and camshaft were driven by silent chains. A metal-to-metal clutch ran in oil driving the worm-gear back axle. It was a wonderful car, though not a startling performer, selling at £350 with dynamo lighting. I can testify personally to its excellence. The old doctor who brought me into the world bought one of these cars new, with a Rover-built drophead coupé body, and ran it to the day of his death in the 1930s. He claimed, perfectly truthfully, that in a quarter of a century he had never had an involuntary stop, apart from an occasional puncture. Owen Clegg, who came from Wolseley, designed this car.

After 1912, the Rover Company produced few new models before the outbreak of the Kaiser war. There was an 18-h.p. model and also single- and twin-cylinder "Silent Knights", but none of these was successful and only a few were built. However, almost every car they built in the decade 1904–14 justified the Company's motto – *Aut Optimum Aut Nihil*.

SINGER

In 1868, the Coventry Sewing Machine Company received an order to make 300 velocipedes – quaint two-wheeled machines which were proving a "craze" on the Continent. The company's name was changed to the Coventry Machinists Co., and velocipede manufacture began. The Directors soon found that a knowledge of sewing-machine manufacture did not guarantee the production of faultless bicycles. To overcome this, a number of mechanics were imported. From Penn's of Greenwich came a young man called George Singer, who had an original turn of mind, and who soon became convinced he could design a better machine than the bicycles already on the market.

In 1876 he set up his own concern to build the world's first

144

safety bicycle. Thus it was, seventy-nine years ago, that the infant Singer Company entered, on wheels, the industrial scene.

As far as the Singer Company was concerned, the internal combustion engine and the twentieth century arrived at the same time, and at the Motor Vehicle Exhibition of May, 1901, Singer's were showing a "Gent's" Motor Bicycle, a Lady's Motor Bicycle and a "Gent's" Motor Tricycle. One gathers that Ladies had no need of a third wheel. The catalogue proclaimed:

"In the Singer motor-cycles there is no smell, owing to the admirable system by which perfect combustion is secured."

These machines were well ahead of their time – about fifty years ahead. The engine was mounted inside the wheel and looked very similar to those fitted to push-bikes today. Furthermore, the engine ran on roller bearings – a development neglected, I believe, until Ettore Bugatti began building motor-cars, although a few years later Mercedes built a ball-bearing engine.

These motor bicycles were designed by two men named Perks and Birch, and Singers took them over.

Simultaneously, body-builders began designing passenger accommodation and the tri-voiturette appeared. This was a tricycle with enclosed seat for passengers. By this time, however, motor-cars were no longer a novelty and in 1904 the Singer Company began building its first car. Although built in 1904, the vehicle was not marketed until early in 1905. After all, Singers were selling plenty of bicycles and motor-cycles, and car production was then of secondary importance. Unfortunately, this first Singer no longer exists.

By 1909 there were four models, ranging from the 7·9-h.p. twin-cylinder to the 24·8-h.p. four-cylinder. The same year, the name of the firm was changed to Singer & Co. Ltd. with a capital of £50,000. At the Olympia Show of 1909, six models were shown, the most popular being the 16/20-h.p. The winner of class "D" in the 2000-miles Reliability Trial was shown as a two-seater.

Singer's had entered competitions with their earliest cycles and continued with motor-cycles. The cars, also, were soon taking part in races and speed trials. In 1910 and 1911 there were a number of successes. Some of the more outstanding were the 15-h.p. record at Brooklands at an average speed of 77·108 m.p.h. The half-mile from a flying start was covered at 81·25 m.p.h. Three firsts in succession at Brooklands, winning the 76-m.p.h. and the 100-m.p.h. handicaps, first place at the Aston Hill Climb and first place at Shelsley Walsh (closed class).

During the Brooklands 76-m.p.h. handicap, Mr. Herbert's Singer raced against a Hanriot monoplane. Both entered the finishing straight together. The Singer was topping 78 m.p.h., the aircraft, flat out, reached 40 m.p.h.

1912 was a vintage year for the firm. The most important development was the introduction of the Singer Ten. The four-cylinder engine was of 1096 c.c., bore 63 mm., stroke 88 mm. The three-speed gearbox was incorporated in the differential casing of the back axle. It cost £195 – or with electric lighting, 195 guineas.

Whit-Monday, 1912, found a Singer Ten lapping Brooklands at 64 m.p.h. Brooklands was also the scene of a number of triumphs for Singer 15-h.p. models, a team of three being raced throughout the season. Three new models emerged in 1913, the 10-h.p. runabout, the 14- and the 25-h.p. cars. Meanwhile, the 15- and 20-h.p. cars continued with little alteration. Most interesting of the new cars was the Fourteen. The four cylinders were cast *en bloc*, the camshaft was chain-driven, and the inclined valves were actuated by adjustable fibre-headed tappets.

The Fourteen was also one of the first cars in which the engine was supported by a comparatively rigid chassis, instead of being mounted in a rigid sub-chassis, allowing the main chassis to flex under road shocks. Chassis price of the Fourteen was £315. With the standard two-seater body it cost £350.

In those pre-war days there was no such thing as one standard body for any particular chassis. The 1913 customer,

146

when ordering his chassis, had a wide choice of body styles. Most of these names have vanished from today's motoring vocabulary, but they make a fascinating roll of the coach-builder's craft. There was the Single Landaulet Coupé, the Three-Quarter Landaulet Coupé, the Limousine Coupé, Single Landaulet, Limousine-Landaulet, the Three-Quarter D-Front-ed Limousine with Dome Roof and a Cabriolet.

The 1914 models showed little change from the previous year, although there were a few detail improvements. A water-heated carburettor, for example, an attachment for driving a dynamo, and a petrol gauge.

At this time one Singer owner, a Miss Blore of Llandudno, planned to astonish the motoring world by ascending and descending Cable Hill, Great Orme, which had, in parts, a gradient of 1 in 3. The car, a Singer Ten, passed this test with flying colours, but the event passed unnoticed by the motoring world. The lady, unfortunately, had timed her achievement badly. She chose early August, 1914.

STANDARD

R. W. Maudslay was educated at Marlborough and trained as an engineer. He was then apprenticed to Sir John Woolf Barry and played an important part in the construction of Barry Dock near Cardiff. In 1903, inspired by the Americans, he decided to start a motor-manufacturing firm, building a very limited number of models with, as far as possible, standardised and interchangeable parts, catering for the low-price market. Hence the name of "Standard". He took over a small works in Much Park, Coventry. He is not to be confused with his cousin of the same name who built very fine powerful cars for the luxury market and was a pioneer of overhead-camshaft multi-cylin-der engines.

The first Standard car was a 6-h.p. single-cylinder, with shaft-drive and a three-speed gearbox. It had an extremely short stroke, 3 in. in relation to its bore of 6 in.

This very short stroke policy was carried on in the 12/15-h.p. two-cylinder car which appeared early in 1904, and had a 5 in. bore and 3 in. stroke. This produced a remarkably flexible

147

engine which, it was claimed, would idle smoothly at 250 r.p.m., and turn smoothly up to 2000 r.p.m.; a really remarkable range for that year. It had mechanically operated valves. These were all on the same side; very advanced practice. It had other advanced features: internal expanding brakes, honeycomb radiator, governor acting on the carburettor and not the valves, and shaft drive. It had four speeds and reverse, and also a sprag to be dropped when it was required to hold the motor on a hill.

In 1906 a six-cylinder car was introduced. At first it had six separate cylinders; later they were cast in pairs (bore and stroke 4 in. × 4¼ in.). It was rated at 24/30 h.p. and had a three-speed gearbox. A 50-h.p. model was also listed.

In addition there was a 16-h.p. four-cylinder car. This model took part in the 1905 Tourist Trophy race in the Isle of Man and finished, non-stop, eleventh, at an average speed of 28 m.p.h., driven by Mr. Maudslay himself.

These models, with many variations and innumerable types of body, formed the basis of all Standard productions until the light 9·5-h.p. model of 1913 was introduced. A brief specification of this model is as follows: four cylinders, bore and stroke 62 mm. × 90 mm., ignition by high-tension magneto, three-speed gearbox, final drive by overhead worm. It had detachable steel wheels 700 mm. × 80 mm., and the wheelbase was 7 ft. 6 in.

STRAKER-SQUIRE

Sidney Straker was selling oil engines in 1898 and, by 1901, was in partnership with R. L. Squire, marketing the Straker steam lorry. They did not build these themselves but contracted out to a Bristol firm called Brazil Holborrow. In about 1906 Strakers acquired the manufacturing rights for England of the Cornilleau-Sainte-Beuve car. The first cars were assembled, but later manufactured, in the Bristol factory which, because of the good business in steam lorries, had been expanded. This Straker C.S.-B. was an extremely well-built 25/30-h.p. six-cylinder side-valve car, with low-tension ignition. It acquitted itself well in a 4000-mile trial under R.A.C. supervision,

30　A 1906 Maxwell "Doctor's" Runabout. A windscreen was an "optional extra"

31　The 90-h.p. four-cylinder Locomobile winning the 1908 Vanderbilt Cup Race, with George Robertson at the wheel

32 The triumphant arrival in Paris of Prince Borghese in his Itala, after he had won the Pekin–Paris Race of 1907

33 Edwardian hill-climb: a 35/45-h.p. Gladiator at Ballin-slaughter during the Irish A. C. Reliability Trials, 1908

34 2000 mile Reliability Trial, 1908: a Métallurgique at Aberfeldy

35 Wolverhampton A. C. hill-climb, 1910: a Star sheds a tyre
at Ironbridge

36 Daimler ditched: at Ewell water-splash en route for the Derby, 1909

37 Family "flat": one of the bugbears of early motoring – tyre changing before the advent of detachable rims

38 Famous driver: Charles Jarrott's De Dietrich at Brooklands for record-breaking, 1908

39 Famous designer: W. O. Bentley with his D.F.P. recordbreaker, 1914

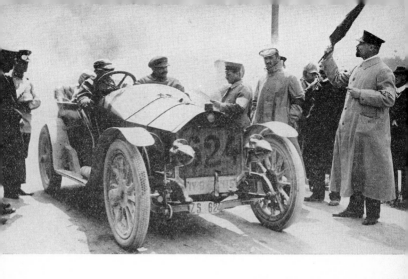

40   Fritz Erle's Benz in the 1909 Prince Henry Trials

41   Fritz von Opel in his 1908 "Gordon Bennett" Darracq

42, 43   Royal Daimlers: *above* King Edward VII's first car, 1906, and *below* Queen Alexandra's 1910 sleeve-valve limousine

but its petrol consumption was none too good, averaging 15·1 m.p.g.

The following year Straker's brought out two Bristol-built cars, a 12/14, sometimes called the "Shamrock" and 16/20-h.p. Straker-Squire. The firm weathered the recession of 1907–8 and at the Motor Show that year they announced their one-model policy, being one of the first firms in the British Isles to do so. This model was a 14/16 four-cylinder (87 mm. × 85 mm.) with cylinders cast in two blocks. The lubrication system is worthy of note. The exhaust gases blew oil out of a dashboard tank into a drip-feed lubricator! I have driven early Mercedes cars where petrol was brought from the rear tank by this method, and sooner or later a lot of carbon would clog it up, so presumably the Straker-Squire suffered the same way. There were three speeds, with direct-drive top, and a live axle. The car was reasonably priced at £315 for a very sporting two-seater, or £345 for a four-seater.

In this year Roy Fedden joined them as chief engineer. His influence was evident in the 15-h.p. (87 mm. × 100 mm.) car that replaced the 14/16 as the sole model. The monobloc engine might, except for the inspection ports in the crankcase and very curious carburettor, have been built in the early 1920s. For the next couple of years the "Fedden 15" went on, with its stroke lengthened to 120 mm.

In 1914 it was replaced by a 15/20 (20·1 R.A.C. rating) four-cylinder (90 mm. × 120 mm.) with wheelbase increased to 9 ft. 6 in. There was also a sporting edition with slightly larger bore and various other modifications. Quite a number were fitted with attractive sporting coachwork. Fedden designed a most interesting overhead-camshaft engine for the three 1914 Tourist Trophy cars of 3·26 litres which gave 83 h.p. at 3200 r.p.m. Like the Mercedes in the French Grand Prix, these engines yielded much useful data for aircraft motors in the 1914–18 war.

SUNBEAM

When the late H. Massac Buist wrote the history of the Sunbeam Company in 1924, he said that the earliest efforts

of the Sunbeam Company were "somewhat obscure" . .
"The start of the Sunbeam Company was relatively so
obscure and on so small a scale as to contain no hint of the
historic role it was destined to play." He meant modest, rather
than uncertain. But this we do know – John Marston had one
of the many japanning and tinware enterprises that flourished
in Wolverhampton in Victorian times. He entered the cycle
business, and built what were probably the first and best-
finished cycles in this country.

Marston and his co-director, Cureton, built their first car
in 1899. I can discover very little about it except that everything – casting, machinery, coachwork and even making the
sparking plug – was done in the Sunbeam bicycle works. It had
one vertical cylinder, remarkable in an age of almost universal
horizontal engines, and was never put into production.

The second Sunbeam car, of 6 h.p. with a horizontal engine,
had belt-drive, battery ignition, and solid tyres. After this they
undertook the manufacture, under licence, of a peculiar small
car designed and patented by Mr. Mabley Smith (Patent 6363,
5th April 1900). Known as the Sunbeam Mabley, it was
produced in quantity from 1901, and, as S. C. H. Davis
says, "has wheels in the most unexpected places". It was belt-
driven by a 2¾-h.p. single-cylinder air-cooled de Dion-Bouton
engine with water-cooled cylinder head, with the occupants sitting at right angles to each other as on a Victorian sofa. It
sold at £130. They also built and exhibited, at Edinburgh and
the Crystal Palace, a 6-h.p. twin-cylinder car of more conventional design.

In 1902 they were joined by Thomas Pullinger, a very
well-known motor engineer of that day who was responsible
for the 1902 four-cylinder Sunbeam based on French designs.
T. C. Pullinger had been with Darracq in 1892. In 1894 he
was building motor-cycles and a very advanced two-cylinder
light petrol car. From 1896, still in Paris, he was building the
Teste et Moret light car, famous in its day, until he went to
Sunbeam.

Next year, Brooke, Maudslay, Napier and Sunbeam were
all racing to bring out the first six-cylinder car. Napier got

theirs out first and Sunbeams had two built in time for the 1904 Motor Show. The oil-bath for the chain-cases, taken from their bicycle practice, was a great attraction. The three models, the 12-h.p. four, the Mabley, and the six, did quite well and, in 1905, Marston and Cureton launched a £40,000 company to go in for motor manufacturing in a big way. At the same time, Angus Shaw, their chief draughtsman, designed a most successful 16/20-h.p. (95 mm. × 120 mm.) side-valve, four-cylinder, chain-drive car with high-tension magneto. It had four speeds, direct-drive top, and put up some really remarkable performances to demonstrate its reliability. Amongst these perhaps the most impressive was the drive by Frederic Eastmead and Angus Shaw in June 1906, from Land's End to John o' Groats and back again. The engine ran non-stop the whole time. It sold at £480 chassis, or £530 with a standard four-seater body.

In 1907 they brought out a powerful six-cylinder which did not sell well and in 1908 this was replaced by a 35-h.p. four-cylinder.

In 1909 Louis Coatalen left the Hillman works, and went as chief engineer to Sunbeam. Although a young man in his late twenties, he had great experience, having worked for Panhard, Clément, de Dion and a German firm. He had also designed the successful 10/12-h.p. Humber car.

The first car he designed for the Sunbeam Co. was a new 16/20-h.p. four-cylinder (95 mm. × 135 mm.) car, which he proceeded to drive himself in competitions, with great success. He followed this by a 12/16-h.p. (80 mm. × 120 mm.) T-head, of which 650 were built in 1911. These were redesigned the following year as an L-head with longer stroke (80 mm. × 150 mm.), and nearly 1000 were sold in that year. In 1909 he designed and built a streamlined single-seater Sunbeam racing car, four-cylinder (92 mm. × 160 mm.) with sixteen vertical overhead valves operated by push rods, known as "Nautilus", which he ran at Brooklands. It had nickel-chrome forged-steel connecting-rods, chain-drive, and the radiator was behind the driver – which caused overheating. It lapped at 77·54 m.p.h., but was too unreliable to be successful. The lessons learnt were

151

applied, in 1911, in the design of a four-cylinder (80 mm. ×
160 mm.), eight-valve overhead-camshaft engine. Mounted on
a standard shaft-drive chassis with a very narrow single-seater
body, it lapped at 84 m.p.h. This car was named "Toodles II",
in honour of Mrs. Coatalen, and in 1911 collected twenty-two
prizes.

Up to 1911 the purchaser of a Sunbeam car was given the
option of chain- or live-axle at the same price. In that year the
immensely successful 12/16-h.p. and 16/20-h.p. cars were
supplemented by a 25/30-h.p. six-cylinder (90 mm. × 160
mm.), one of which set up seventeen records at Brooklands
from 10 laps to twelve hours, driven by L. Coatalen and
T. H. Richards. They averaged 75·66 m.p.h. for twelve hours
(907 miles), during which time the engine ran non-stop.

The firm was doing well enough to afford to race seriously.
After a promising but unsuccessful attempt in the 1911
Coupe de l'Auto race with a single car, a team of Sunbeams
scored their first notable success in international racing when
they came first, second and third and won the Coupe de l'Auto
over the Dieppe circuit in 1912. As this race was run concurrently with the Grand Prix, they also entered for that. There
they finished third, fourth and fifth, beating most of the monster
"bolides" of many times their cylinder capacity (3-litre–80 mm.
× 149 mm.). The cars used were basically standard side-valve
12/16-h.p. models, fitted with narrow streamlined racing bodies.

One of these 3-litre Coupe de l'Auto cars was later fitted
with a single-seater body, and took the twelve-hour world's
record (910 miles, 1738 yds.) beating the record set up a year
before by the big 30-h.p. six-cylinder Sunbeam of twice the
capacity. The drivers L. Coatalen, D. Resta and R. F. L. Cross-
man.

The performance of the 3-litre side-valve engines was increased in 1913 and K. Lee Guinness made the only non-
stop run in the Coupe de l'Auto to finish third to the twin
o.h.c. Peugeots of Boillot and Goux. Four six-cylinder (80 mm.
× 150 mm.) 4·5-litre side-valve 25/30-h.p. cars were built for
the 1913 Grand Prix de l'A.C.F., which was won by Boillot's
5·6-litre Peugeot. Despite their smaller capacity and their

basically standard side-valve engines, two Sunbeams finished third and sixth, driven by J. Chassagne and D. Resta. One of these G.P. cars with streamlined body later broke the world's twelve-hour record at 89·25 m.p.h. A 9-litre V-12 track racing car was also built in 1913, with which Jean Chassagne lapped at 117 m.p.h. and took the one-hour record at 107·95 m.p.h.

The three models, 12/16, 16/20 and 25/30 were continued up to the outbreak of war in 1914. They had side-valve engines, but, inspired by Peugeot's success with Ernest Henry's design, Coatalen was hard at work perfecting the 16-valve-twin overhead-camshaft engine (81·5 mm. × 156 mm.). which enabled K. Lee Guinness to win the 1914 Tourist Trophy race in the Isle of Man. A larger (4½-litre) 94 mm. × 160 mm. version of the engine was built for the 1914 Grand Prix at Lyon with which Dario Resta finished fifth.

Like many another fine old firm, Sunbeams broke themselves by building too long for the luxury-car market. But when we leave them preparing to build aero engines for the coming war in 1914 they were at the height of their glory, and even during the war they managed to design and build a 4·9-litre six-cylinder 24-valve racing engine, which was mounted in a Grand Prix chassis. It was sent to Indianapolis in 1916 in the charge of J. Christiaens who finished fourth at 79·66 m.p.h. During the 1914–18 war they built aero-engines, which embodied lessons learnt in racing, and their 12/16-h.p. car was used in such numbers by the War Office that many were made under licence by the Rover Company.

VAUXHALL

It is said, not without some truth, that Scotsmen cannot make real money out of other Scotsmen, hence the steady flow of emigrants. One of these, Alexander Wilson, set up as a maker of small marine engines and pumps on the south of the Thames under the name "Vauxhall Iron Works". Like so many of his countrymen he took an interest in heraldry, and adopted for his products the crest, a wyvern, of Fulk le Breant, a successful soldier of fortune in the time of King John, who lived close to the plot of land where Wilson had his factory. Wilson did very well for close on forty years; in fact, some Vauxhall-engined tugs are still afloat. The works employed about 150 craftsmen.

In the early 1890s the Vauxhall Iron Works became a limited company, and a couple of years later Wilson retired from it, although he still practised as a consulting engineer. Around 1896, F. W. Hodges, a marine engineer who had worked under Wilson, felt that there were great possibilities in mechanically propelled road transport. First of all he built, and tried out in his motor launch *Jabberwock*, a small single-cylinder opposed-piston engine.

Then he built, at the Vauxhall Iron Works, a complete car and a five-cylinder radial engine. Neither of these proved sufficiently successful to warrant further development. Experimental work continued, and in 1902 Hodges, who had been joined by J. H. Chambers, built a single-cylinder (4 in. × 4¾ in.) light car which was so satisfactory that it was put in production the following year.

It was, for its time, fairly conventional – tiller steering, horizontal engine with governor operating in the exhaust valve, chain-drive and two speeds. It was intended to weigh only 5 cwt., but in actual fact exceeded the designed weight by about 50 lb. The suspension was by coil-spring all round! It sold retail at £150 and was, quite fairly, I think, described by *The Autocar* as "a neat, efficient and cheap vehicle".

This little newcomer proved extremely popular and sold very well indeed. In 1904 it was endowed with a reverse gear, and the wire wheels were replaced by wooden ones. The weight went up a bit, but this was compensated by an engine yielding 6 instead of 5 h.p. Later in the year tiller steering was replaced by a wheel. The little single-cylinder did very well in trials, and in one of them averaged 38·25 m.p.g.

At the end of 1904 it was joined by its big brother, the three-cylinder water-cooled 12/14-h.p. Vauxhall. I have been told by men who have driven this car that, in a day when reliability was a new, rare virtue in motor-cars, the three-cylinder was a really excellent vehicle. By this time, the flutes

154

which were until recently the hallmark of the make, had already appeared round the stubby little bonnet. It sold at £375, including lamps and all accessories. This was rather an innovation, as these were rarely included in the price of a car.

Around this time the firm started to build motorised hansom cabs. These engaging and rather attractive vehicles were not a success. This was not because there was much wrong with them, but because the clientèle addicted to hansom cabs preferred them to be horse-drawn.

A smaller three-cylinder car was built (3 in. × 3¾ in.) but was not powerful enough to carry the coachwork of increasing weight which purchasers demanded.

At the 1905 Motor Show, Vauxhall exhibited the two three-cylinder models and a brand new 18-h.p. four-cylinder model. All cars were chain driven.

The 1905 Vauxhall Hansom Cab, with the
driving position above and behind the passengers

In 1905, also, the firm, who during the previous year had sold 76 cars, finding expansion impossible where they were, moved to Luton. Here they amalgamated with the West Hydraulic Engineering Company. By a fantastic coincidence,

Luton was the original home of Fulk le Breant, so the Vauxhall Wyvern continued to be particularly appropriate!

Another event of paramount importance to Vauxhalls in 1905 was the addition to their design staff of Laurence Pomeroy, Senior, who started off by designing a 12/16-h.p. four-cylinder (82 mm. × 95 mm.) car, the first Vauxhall to have a live axle.

In 1906 the three-cylinder cars were dropped, and a company, Vauxhall Motors Ltd., was formed solely for the manufacture of motor-cars, while the marine engines, refrigeration and hydraulic machinery continued to be made by the West Hydraulic Engineering Company.

In 1908 Pomeroy designed a 20-h.p. long-stroke four-cylinder (90 mm. × 120 mm.), which was most successful in competitions, and was kept in production till 1914.

So well did it do that the directors became very competition-minded. In fact, two of them, Kidner and Seltz, drove themselves. The two works drivers, Hancock and Watson, were equally well-known in their day.

Late Edwardian tourer: 1914 "Prince Henry"
Vauxhall four-seater

In 1909 it was found that the successful old "20" could be "souped up" to turn at 2370 r.p.m., raising the b.h.p. from 39 to 52·6. One of these, nicknamed "K.N.", had many victories at Brooklands. The 27-h.p. six-cylinder car (85 mm. × 102 mm.), and a four-cylinder car of the same bore and stroke, rated at 17·9 h.p., cannot have been so successful, for although they appeared in 1909, in 1910 they were no longer made.

In 1910 the sporting edition of the "20" did very well in the Prince Henry Reliability Trials, but failed lamentably in the speed trials; so Pomeroy designed the immortal "Prince Henry" model, easily distinguishable by its V radiator. This was based on the "20", and had the same bore and stroke. It won countless successes in the hands of amateur drivers, as well as the works team. It was popular all over the world, especially in Czarist Russia where, like the "20", it had many victories. The directors of Vauxhall Motors used also to go over and drive in Russian races. At least two of these wonderful cars are still going strong. One was presented to Laurence Pomeroy, Junior, by the original owner. The other, discovered by Tony Brooke stopping up a hole in a hedge, is now restored. It soundly trounced all the American cars in the 1954 Vintage Rally.

In 1910 and 1912 two new six-cylinder cars were produced for a short time, but the real winner to come from the stable was the 1912 four-cylinder (95 mm. × 140 mm.) "25" which was, with the Crossley, the standard staff car of the 1914—18 war, and remained in production for nearly a decade.

The "Prince Henry", its engine dimensions increased to 95 mm. × 140 mm., was made right up to the outbreak of war. Special racing cars were built for the light-car races, usually run together with the Grands Prix in France in 1911, 1912 and 1913. They went very well indeed, beating the redoubtable ultra-long-stroke Lion Peugeots.

1913 saw the first of the classic 30/98s whose glorious "turkey-gobble" sounds as satisfying today as it did to young men in the 1920s. A wealthy North Country enthusiast called Higginson asked Vauxhall to build him a lighter and more powerful car. Pomeroy designed what we know as the "E" model, L-head, side-valve 30/98. The engine was basically a "25" bored out to 98 mm., and fitted with a special crank, giving a stroke of 150 mm. Although the first 30/98s carried all before them up till the outbreak of war, they were not on

157

offer to the public until 1919.

This story starts with F. Y. Wolseley, the younger son of a
gentleman, emigrating, in the 1860s, to seek his fortune in Australia. Nobody had ever succeeded in building a mechanical
sheep-shearer, so it took a good many years of heartbreaking
experimental work before a successful model was in production.
In 1889 an English factory was established by Wolseley to
take over the patent rights, orders and goodwill of the works
he had already built up in Australia. To Australia, a year or
so earlier, there came a youth by the name of Herbert Austin.
A farmer's son, born in Buckinghamshire, he had been apprenticed, not very enthusiastically, to the Great Northern Railway
Company. He turned out to be, however, a first-class engineer and after working for various people was taken on by
F. Y. Wolseley. He did most valuable work on the machine
and took out a number of patents in his own name. In 1893
Austin returned to England and sold these patents to Wolseley
in exchange for a share in the firm.

At this time the sheep-shearing business was doing badly,
so at the instigation of Austin the firm moved to a larger works
in Alma Street, Birmingham, and built bicycles, sheep-shearing
machinery, as well as textile machines. Austin, who had followed the struggles of the horseless carriage right from the beginning, was, as was usual at this time, refused all help,
financial or otherwise, from his directors.

By 1895 he had achieved, more or less on his own, the
first Wolseley car. It was a pretty straight copy of a Léon
Bollée tricar, except that Austin had grafted a number of his
own ideas on to it. The most remarkable of these was an overhead camshaft driven by shaft and skew gears which operated
not only exhaust but inlet valves as well. It was a four-stroke,
flat-twin with electric ignition. The following year, 1896, the
second Wolseley was built, this time very much with the blessing
of Austin's directors, who had realised the fact that there was
money in building horseless carriages. It was a great improvement on the first and went into limited production, thereby

gaining the distinction of being one of the very first cars of 100 per cent British design and manufacture to be on sale to the public. Both cars, 1 and 2 , are in the Wolseley Company's museum.

In 1899–1900, the first four-wheeler appeared, described as a "Wolseley Voiturette". These cars did outstandingly well in trials, particularly in the 1000-mile trial of 1900. These successes were followed up by a spate of orders. At this time Austin helped Sir Hiram Maxim with his fantastic steam flying machine and a lot of the parts were made in the Wolseley factory. This liason with the mighty armaments firm of Vickers (Sir Hiram was a director) led to the Wolseley Company being taken over by Vickers and established in a new and larger works at Adderley Park, Birmingham. Here they went into production with quite a range of cars, from a 5-h.p. single cylinder Phaeton at £270 to a 10-h.p. horizontal side-by-side twin Tonneau at £360, with wheel steering. Delivery vans and racing cars were made to order. The following year, 1902,

The 1906 18-h.p. Wolseley-Siddeley Landaulette

Austin persuaded his directors to permit the firm to race. He designed a remarkable flat-four car with a square engine of 5 in. × 5 in., yielding an estimated 30 h.p. In the Paris–Vienna race he broke two crankshafts, too much even for those days. So the following year he had redesigned the lubrication and three racing cars, now developing 50 h.p., were bought by wealthy amateur drivers. In the "Paris–Madrid" three were entered. Austin and Foster broke down, and Porter had a terrible accident in which his mechanic was killed. They did not do much better on the "Circuit des Ardennes" but learnt valuable lessons for the next year, when they were more reliable. In 1905 the racing cars were still flat fours but quite enormous, 181 mm. bore by 152·4 mm. stroke, rated at 96 h.p. At the end of 1905, motor-racing was becoming so costly that the Wolseley Company withdrew from competitions.

The passenger cars, however, were selling well, but it was clear that horizontal engines were going out of fashion. An up-and-coming young man, J. D. Siddeley, had been importing excellent small cars with vertical engines since 1902. These were so good that the demand was greater than his resources could supply. So Vickers-Wolseley took him and his designs over, and proceeded to build the vertical-engined Wolseley-Siddeley alongside the horizontal-engined Wolseley which gradually became obsolete.

The first Wolseley-Siddeleys were 15 h.p., 18 h.p. and 32 h.p. In 1907 quite a sporting 40-h.p. was added to this range and a little later a 50-h.p.

It appears that about this time Vickers thought young Siddeley was getting too much credit and the Wolseley Company too little. Siddeley did not see why the Wolseley Company should get all the credit for his work and, in 1909, resigned. Austin had already left to start on his own. From 1909 to 1914 Wolseleys built a series of rather dull but very well-made cars, mostly 12/16, 16/20 and 24/30 models. At this time, also, the Wolseley-designed Stellite, one of the best light cars of its era, was made by one of Vickers' subsidiary companies. This was because the Wolseley Company had such a full order book that they had not the capacity.

Besides motor-cars, the Wolseley Company made all sorts of unlikely things ranging from petrol-electric rail-car engines to mobile vacuum cleaners and petrol-driven sleds for the Antarctic. They also made racing motor-boat engines and from 1906 onwards airship and aircraft engines. They even made shunting locomotives.

"PIONEER" (AUSTRALIAN)

Rather surprisingly, the Australians began motor-car manufacture very early, and about 1897 the Australian Horseless Carriage Syndicate was formed. The first "Pioneer" car, running in 1898, was much on the lines of Gottlieb Daimler's early efforts – a motorised horse vehicle. The complete carriage was built by a Melbourne coachbuilder, W. Jackson, and the engine, mounted under the seat and driving the rear wheels by chain, was built by Mr. Grayson, also of Melbourne. Details in England are scanty. It seated four, did 10 m.p.h. and ran on kerosene "of not less than 150 test". It is believed that quite a number were sold, and any information on them from Australia would be very welcome.

TARRANT (AUSTRALIAN)

The Tarrant Motor Company, which produced gas and oil engines at Melbourne, began to build motor-cars designed by the late Colonel Harley Tarrant in about 1900. By 1902 they were producing a 4-cylinder car with a bevel gear drive, fitted with solid tyres. In 1904 they decided to build a "standard" model with two alternative engines – a 10/12 two-cylinder and a 14/16 four-cylinder – and the cars were completed by the end of 1905. They remained in production until 1907 when, as the Ford Model S roadster was selling in Australia at £125 (Australian) less than the Tarrant two-cylinder car, the Company decided to acquire the Australian agency for Fords.

Details of Tarrants are as follows:

Engine: 10/12-h.p. two-cylinder and 14/16-h.p. four-cylinder. Both "T" head type with cast-iron pistons with three rings. Water cooling was by a gear pump driven by an external shaft which also acted as a drive for the h.t. magneto. The crankshaft was mounted on three bearings, and the crankcase was made of aluminium.

Lubrication: Sight feed lubricators to each engine bearing, mounted on the dashboard.

Clutch: External leather-faced cone.

161

Gear box: Three forward speeds and reverse, operating through a "gate change". Second and top gears utilised dog clutches.

Front axle: H-section steel forging.

Back axle: Straight tooth bevel drive.

8

Continental Cars

BOLLÉE

AMÉDÉE BOLLÉE had a bell foundry and engineering shop at Le Mans and, some time before the advent of the petrol car, 1873 in fact, was building steam road vehicles. His sons, Amédée, born in 1867, and Léon, born in 1871, were engineers of undoubted brilliance. There was also a third son, Camille, who raced with his brothers, but never built cars himself.

Among the steam vehicles built by Amédée Bollée père were L'Obéissante (1873, 40 k.p.h.), La Mancelle (1878, 42 k.p.h.) and the lightweight six-seater La Rapide (1881), capable of 60 k.p.h. The first-named of these can still be seen in the Musée des Arts et Metiers in Paris. A number of others were built both for Bollée's cousins and private customers, including a really magnificent mail coach for the Marquis de Broc. For this the Grand Seigneur paid what was in 1885 the really staggering sum of 35,000 francs (worth at that time about 11 to the golden sovereign).

In the same year, 1885, young Amédée Bollée junior built a lightweight (about 1430 lb.) two-seater steamer capable of 25 m.p.h. which excited the interest of Armand Peugeot. After this he took charge of the car-building section of his father's works and undertook research and development of the internal combustion engine. Both father and son believed that if their new and relatively untried motor could be made a practical proposition, it would be infinitely preferable to steam or electricity both for road locomotion and the propulsion of dirigible aircraft. Amédée the younger had already filed patents for "un nouveau moteur à gaz tonnant" in December 1894. By 1896 he had a very practical four-wheeled two-seater car in production, and in September of that year drove one in the Paris–Marseilles races. These 1896 Bollées had many advanced features including wheel steering and central grouping of grease nipples.

Shortly after this Baron Adrien de Turckheim, director of the engineering firm of De Dietrich at Lunéville, negotiated a licence to build "Dietrich cars système Amédée Bollée". The first cars to be built by this once world-famous firm appeared in July 1897.

During the first few years of motor racing, Amédée junior and Léon built, as they always did, entirely separate makes of car, but with their brother, Camille, raced as a sort of family team. Amédée Bollée junior continued to build expensive, beautifully made cars of very advanced design, up to and a few years after the Kaiser war. Production was never great, but there was a steady, if limited, demand of discriminating patrons who would have nothing else.

About 1893 Léon's doctor told him that he must no longer ride his tricycle because he had a weak heart, so he set about motorising the tricycle. Next he built a three-wheel car which had a horizontal engine and a three-speed gearbox. The drive was by means of a belt passing round a pair of pulleys.

This funny little vehicle, of which many remain today, the best-known being Sammy Davis' "Beelzebub", was a great success, and in 1896 the financier H. J. Lawson gave him no less than £20,000 in cash for the English manufacturing and patent rights. In that year, too, Léon entered several of his little three-wheelers, but with an engine each side of the back wheel, for the Paris–Marseilles race. Only one finished, and that was a single-engined tricar.

Then he built a four-wheel light car and sold the manufacturing rights to Alexandre Darracq for £10,000. In its original form the Darracq-Bollée was not good, but by the following year Darracq improved it a lot.

Bollée could now, in his early thirties, have retired very comfortably on the money he had made. But in a few years he was back again with an absolutely silent four-cylinder car. This was really silent because of its sheer mechanical perfection, not, like modern cars, because the noise is blanked off by sound-absorbent material. It was a lovely car of about 20 h.p.

although later they built a smaller 16-h.p. model. A syndicate of financiers approached him about the English rights for this and deposited £42,000, the balance to be paid on completion of the deal. The deal never was completed, and so Bollée was another £42,000 to the good. The cars were never built in England but were imported by the Connaught Motor Company, very grand coachbuilders with showrooms in Long Acre, who were to have done so.

Besides these silent cars he also built a very fine 45/50-h.p. chain-driven four-cylinder. This was more of a fast touring car than a sports car, but in spite of its weight, it had a really terrific performance. It was beautifully finished, and sold in England for a chassis price of £50 more than a "Silver Ghost" Rolls-Royce. Happy the collector who can unearth one of these. They were made from 1906 to 1911 inclusive.

In 1908 Wilbur Wright went to see Léon Bollée about an engine for his flying machine. Bollée, in his warm-hearted way, asked Wright to stay with him in his house, and the two men did a vast amount of invaluable pioneer work together. The most fantastic part about the whole story is that Bollée did not speak a word of English and Wright not a word of French. So Madame Bollée had to be available at all hours of the day and night to interpret.

Léon Bollée died in 1913. His wife, who like most French-women had a good business head, carried on the works till they were bought by W. R. Morris (now Lord Nuffield) ten years later.

BUGATTI

Ettore Bugatti left his mark on anything he touched as surely as did Benvenuto Cellini and Robert Adam. He came of an artistic family; his brother was a sculptor and his father an artist. His innate artistry coupled with his engineering genius lifted anything he designed right out of the normal. An interesting sidelight on the way his mind worked is the fact that he would never employ a man in his drawing office unless he was also a first-class freehand draughtsman. He built his first car at his home, near Milan, in 1898 and shortly afterwards he was commissioned to design a new model for the German De Dietrich Company. This was a great success, as was his next design, a 40/60-h.p. car for Deutz, which was sold in England as the "Burlington".

He designed a car to drive himself in the "Paris–Madrid" but was refused entry by the scrutineers who held that his steering column, which was well raked like a modern car, instead of projecting at 90° from the floor, was unsafe. In 1906 he and Emil Mathis, later to be a manufacturer himself, were responsible for the Kaiserpreis Hermés. This car bears a remarkable resemblance to the type 13 (the first recorded type number) Bugatti car. It was however a much larger car, made in 40-h.p., 90-h.p. and 120-h.p. models. It had low-tension ignition and mechanically operated valves one over the other. Power was transmitted through a four-speed box and chain drive. The water pump was of characteristic Bugatti design. Aided by Friderich, in later years his agent at Nice, who had joined him as a mechanic soon after the "Paris–Madrid", he built the first type 13, four-cylinder, eight-valve Bugatti in 1907.

He is responsible for one of the most astounding efforts in the history of motor engineering. His 5-litre, chain-driven car (no type number) was so far ahead of its time that it is virtually impossible to believe that it was designed in 1911. Among other features it has the first of those distinctive Bugatti radiators modelled on the plate on the hoof of a race-horse. The exact capacity is 5·027 litres, 100 mm. × 160 mm, but the car that ran at Indianapolis in 1913 was 100 mm. × 180 mm. Luckily, one of these marvellous cars is preserved in perfect and original condition in Peter Hampton's collection.

In 1909, financed by the race driver Viscaya's banker father, he set up a small works at Molsheim and went into production. He sold five cars in 1910 and his work did not prevent him from redesigning, in 1911, the famous "Baby" Peugeot (which first appeared in 1902) for that company. In 1911 he built a 2·8-litre straight eight, the first small, fast-turning, efficient motor of that type ever made. Just before the outbreak of war, 1·4-litre, sixteen-valve versions of the type 13 were built to race at Le Mans. This race was cancelled owing to the war and parts of the engines of the cars were buried. Their long interment does not seem to have done them much harm, for, as soon as racing started up again after the war, these little cars, built in 1914, carried all before them. There are large gaps missing in the early history of Ettore Bugatti and, unless some research is carried out very soon, the few old men who knew him then will be dead and the story never recorded.

CHARRON, C.G.V. AND ALDA

These names do not mean much to people now, although some people will remember the two-cylinder taxicabs, with a bonnet like a Renault, called Charron. But this dapper Frenchman has considerable claim to fame. Not only was he the champion racing cyclist of France, but he was one of the most successful racing motorists of his day, and also a car manufacturer of a considerable size. He had nearly always raced bicycles made by Albert Clément, so he was involved in the very earliest motoring. He won the "Marseilles–Nice", in March 1898, with a 6-h.p. Panhard, at an average speed of 20·4 m.p.h. He won the "Paris–Amsterdam", the Chanteloup Hill Climb, and the "Paris–Bordeaux". He also won the first Gordon Bennett race, with the great Henri Fournier, then his chauffeur, riding as mechanic. He gave up to ride, as a gentleman rider, in horse races for many years afterwards. He has another claim to fame. He and two cycle-racing friends, Girardot and Voigt, opened the first automobile agency in the world. Hitherto, customers had bought direct from the makers. Incidentally, they cleaned up a fine packet by cornering the Panhard market. From 1901 to 1905 they built C.G.V. racing cars.

The touring edition of the C.G.V. appeared about 1901; it was a 15-h.p., four-cylinder car, chain-driven and having a remarkably low centre of gravity. It had the first carburettor ever to be heated by a water jacket. The big racing cars had steel cylinders and these were later used on the touring cars. As early as 1902 they were building armoured cars for the French War Office. In about 1905 Charron sold, very profitably, the rights to manufacture C.G.V. cars in England under the name of Charron. This developed into quite a big concern, making everything from little 8-h.p. two-cylinder cabs and vans, to 75/90-h.p. sports cars, although the latter were probably C.G.V.'s imported *in toto* from France, with a British Charron name plate put on.

Charron married one of Clément's two extremely pretty daughters, sold out his interest in C.G.V. and took over the management of his father-in-law's huge Clément-Bayard factory. He found, however, that old Adolphe Clément was impossible to get on with, and went back to his Champs-Elysées showrooms, in which he had retained a controlling interest. About 1913 he bought a factory at Courbevoie and built the little known "Alda" car, a 15-h.p. four-cylinder 85 mm. × 140 mm.).

CHENARD ET WALCKER

Monsieur Chenard was, in the early nineties, a prosperous bicycle maker. Very early on he was anxious to take advantage of the coming demand for motor-cycles. At that time almost the only proprietary engines that could be bought were De Dion-Bouton, and M. Chenard decided that, as these were in somewhat short supply, he would build his own. With this end in view he took into partnership a very able engineer, Monsieur Walcker. The partners figured that the greater part of their customers would be completely inexperienced and that the main policy would be to build a vehicle as near foolproof and as free from trouble as possible. As a result their motor-tricycles were successful and sold well. Even more successful was their quadricycle with a fore-car for passengers, patented by Chenard. A car was, of course, the logical conclusion, and in 1900 they had one of 6 h.p. running. Owing to its belt drive, they met considerable sales resistance, but next year they built a similar one with final chain-drive, which was most popular because of its outstanding economy.

The demand was brisk and the two partners took in a third, Monsieur Leger, and expanded their works at Asnières very considerably. The policy of the company in its early days was to participate in reliability trials rather than in racing. This arrangement seems to have paid dividends as sales were good enough for further expansion and, by 1903, they were turning out an 18-h.p. car which was selling well in France and England. From about this time onwards they wore the Eagle of Napoleon on their very distinctive radiators. The following year, 1907, a larger model, a four-cylinder (120 mm. × 130 mm.) 30/40 was added to the range. Between then and 1914 no less than a dozen different models were built including an 8-h.p. single-cylinder (100 mm. × 120 mm.) runabout. Some of these pre-1914 Chenards are remarkable for reduction gearing mounted in the rear hubs.

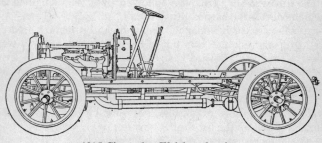

1905 Chenard et Walcker chassis

No pre-1914 Chenards are known to exist in England, but judging from one built immediately after the Kaiser war, in my possession, their standard of workmanship must have been extremely high.

CLÉMENT, CLÉMENT-BAYARD AND CLÉMENT-TALBOT

Young Adolphe Clément, born in 1855, studied engineering. His guardian, for he had been orphaned at an early age, had, however, other plans for his career: that he should become a grocer. The young man flatly refused and got work with a local blacksmith. Here he built himself a wooden bicycle and, on this, set out to make his fortune. He worked his way around France earning his living in various engineering shops and gaining valuable experience, and also taking part in bicycle races. In 1878 he set up in a tiny workshop in the Rue Brunel in Paris building bicycles. He also made money out of a "riding school" for teaching people to ride them! Five years later he had several workmen in his employ and was making some of the best racing bicycles in France. He also acquired the French patent rights for the newly invented Dunlop pneumatic tyre, which brought him in a small fortune. In the cycle boom of 1894 the small fortune became quite a large one. In the nineties, one of his cycle firms, Clément-Gladiator, built a number of motor-cycles and rear-engined cyclecars. But he did not go in seriously for motor-car production till 1901. His first car was designed by Commandant Krebs, a director of Panhard-Levassor. This was followed by a front-engined car which Marius Barbaroux drove in the "Paris–Berlin".

During one of his financial coups he had somehow sold the right to manufacture cars under his own name, so they were now known as "Bayard" or Clément-Bayard. At Mézières, where he had a factory, there is a statue of the Chevalier Bayard and from this the name was taken.

In 1903 he handed the racing over to his sons. They raced with some measure of success, not winning many events but finishing well up the list for the next five or six years.

His concessionaire in England was D. M. Weigel, who prevailed on the wealthy Lord Shrewbury and Talbot, in 1903, to finance a large and very well-equipped works at Ladbroke Grove to built the Clément-Talbot in England. In 1910 he built an immense dirigible airship powered by two 220-h.p. Clément engines. This he sold to the English War Office who, rather surprisingly, never used it. He retired from the motor business before 1914. He obtained permission from the French Government to change his name to Clément-Bayard. It seems rather odd that a man who, by all accounts, was utterly ruthless in business and would stick at nothing to attain his ends, should want to adopt the name of the *Chevalier sans peur et sans reproche*.

DARRACQ

Alexandre Darracq started life as a draughtsman in the arsenal at Tarbes, and then went to the firm of Hurtu, which at that time made sewing machines but later made cars. In 1891, in partnership with a Monsieur Aucoc, he started to build "Gladiator" bicycles, just in nice time to profit from the cycling boom. By 1896 the business had grown huge, and was sold to an English combine. In the agreement Darracq undertook not to start up again in the bicycle business. It did not say that he should not make *parts* for bicycles. This is exactly what Darracq now did. He equipped a large works at Suresnes with the latest American machine tools and proceeded to undercut everybody else on component parts for bicycles. It was here that the first Darracq cars were born. Since 1894 he had been building the "Millett" motor-cycles. This was more or less an ordinary push-bike with a five-cylinder rotary engine mounted directly *in* the back wheel!

Darracq's extremely astute mind was very busy with the idea of self-propelled vehicles. He exhibited light cars at the Paris Salon of 1895, but it is thought that nobody bought one. He experimented with an electric car, but nobody seemed to want that, either. When you consider what batteries were like in 1896 it is not surprising. In 1897, as well as bicycle parts, he was building motor-cycles, tricycles and quadricycles. He also built a 70-h.p. racing car, a veritable monster for its day, which was sold but never raced.

Alexandre Darracq was not interested in the luxury-car market – he wanted to build cheap cars in large quantities. In 1898 he started to build a light car under licence from Léon Bollée. It was not too good, but he improved it the next year. In 1900 he brought out a 6½-h.p. car and built 1200 of them.

He was keenly aware of the publicity value of racing, and although he did not drive himself, he always entered a strong team in every race. He realised, too, the importance of drivers and founded a small school for them, from which several famous drivers of the early 1900s graduated.

Darracq was among the earliest manufacturers to establish representation in this country and he was advertised widely in the English motor journals of that time. Probably the two most popular models were the 12-h.p. two-cylinder, immortalized by the film "Genevieve", which, selling at under £200 deliv-

ered in England, was outstandingly good value, and the
"Flying Fifteen". Bob Gregory's car, which I used to drive in
the early 1930s, is a fine example of the latter classic model.
The car which cost, when new, well under £500 complete,
would show a clean pair of heels to almost anything except a
sports car in 1932, when it was already twenty-eight years old!
My only criticism was that it had very heavy steering. Undoubtedly pre-1914 Darracqs were uncommonly good value
for money and deserved the success they enjoyed.

A very large number of models were, as was customary,
available, and in 1912, 15-, 16- and 20-h.p. valveless cars were
made under Henriod's patents.

In 1912 Alexandre Darracq, now a millionaire, retired.
One night, someone abandoned a baby girl on the Darracq
doorstep. So Monsieur and Madame, who were childless,
adopted her and brought her up as their own daughter.

The Talbot-Darracq merger, although the two firms enjoyed
close relations, did not take place till 1919.

DECAUVILLE

The Decauville was a sporting little light car, built in Paris,
whose origin is rather obscure. The firm had acquired the
Guedon design.

It was racing in 1898, possibly even earlier, and there does
not seem to be much evidence as to when the first one was
built. As the firm went out of business about 1909, the trail
has got somewhat cold. The earliest known examples were
tubular-framed, rear vertical-engined four-wheelers. The power
unit consisted of two 1¾-h.p. engines coupled at 180.° Ignition
was electric and there was a surface carburettor. It had a two-
speed box and differential gear, all mounted direct on the back
axle. The following year they made a four-seater car with a
5-h.p. vertical engine mounted for'ard. By 1900 they were
entering in most of the principal races, but do not appear to
have had much success. In 1903 they were making an extremely smart motorised hansom cab and a conventional 10-h.p.
touring car. A 30-h.p. Decauville did well in the "Paris—Madrid", averaging 53·9 m.p.h. and coming third in its class. *The*

Autocar, of 23rd June 1906, carries drawings and a full description of the 12/16-h.p. Decauville chassis; a straightforward and apparently excellent job. They were, with landaulette bodies, quite popular in England. It is a little difficult to understand why they went out of production.

DE DION-BOUTON

It would be hard to find a more odd combination than the gay, duelling, aristocratic Marquis de Dion, a good six feet in his socks, and the tiny, apologetic, thoroughly plebeian figure of Monsieur Bouton.

The de Dions were originally a Belgian family who had been settled near Nantes for several centuries. Marquis Henri de Dion was a celebrated engineer, and his grandson, Albert, took after him, even if he did so in a slightly more dilettante manner. At the house of the Duc de Morny, Albert de Dion saw a really outstandingly ingenious toy steam-engine and ran to earth the makers, Georges Bouton and his brother-in-law, Trépardoux. Delighted with the quality of their work, de Dion took them into permanent employ at ten francs a day each.

In 1883 they built their first steam-propelled vehicle. In this quadricycle, which steered with its rear wheels, "Le Comte Mécanicien", as his friends called him, used to trundle slowly round the Port Maillot area belching clouds of black smoke, due to not very efficient combustion of solid fuel. His next achievement was to convert an English Rudge tandem tricycle with a 1-h.p. steam-engine weighing only 100 lb. It did 18 m.p.h. Other vehicles followed, all steam-driven, and the Count established a small works at Puteaux. His family were upset by this. It was right and proper for a young nobleman of rank and wealth to maintain racehorses, a ballet dancer or a steam yacht. But to pay from his own pocket all the expenses of a rapidly growing engineering works making completely unsaleable nonsense; that was sheer insanity. In fact, so strongly did the Marquis de Dion feel about it that he brought an action in the courts to restrain his son from his extravagant folly. Of this, Count Albert de Dion took not the slightest notice and went on building steam carriages. It is, however, pleasant to

173

recall that before his father's death in 1901 they had become reconciled, and the old man thoroughly enjoyed trips in his son's horseless carriages.

In the meantime the Count (he did not become a Marquis till his father's death) was increasingly turning his mind towards the internal combustion engine. Monsieur Bouton was in entire agreement with him, but Trépardoux was stubbornly in opposition. They were, he claimed, doing extremely well with their steam carriages, so why should they forsake the substance of steam for the shadow of an unproved motive power that was probably no good anyway? Finally, Trépardoux withdrew from the firm and, by all accounts, no longer prospered. In the meantime the Count had built himself a steam motor-boat that went so fast on the Seine that he had his nautical licence taken away! However, he won most of the very early races and competitions for cars. In 1889 he took out his first patents for "detonating motors cooled by water". Some of the first of his engines were four- and twelve-cylinder rotary, but the fortunes of the firm were founded on the little single-cylinder engines which they not only fitted to their own motor-cycles and voiturettes but sold to anyone who wanted them. In 1895 they had a motor-tricycle in production and in the ensuing five years sold many hundreds of them. Motor-tricycle racing became very much the vogue and by the turn of the century the racing models were being powered by 8- and 10-h.p. engines.

The original small car, with a water-cooled single-cylinder engine (80 mm. × 80 mm.), which appeared at the Paris Salon of 1899 was an instantaneous success. This was rated $3\frac{1}{2}$ h.p. but, by 1902, it had been increased to 6 h.p. (90 mm. × 110 mm.).

In the early years of the century these proprietary single-cylinder engines went all over the world to be fitted in cars and motor-cycles. They even went as far as America for Pierce-Arrow and Peerless. De Dion, together with Baron van Zuylen de Nyfeldt de Haar and Paul Meyan, started the Automobile Club de France, but it was originally his idea. The club was once raided and temporarily closed in its early days. De Dion was very much a stormy petrel of politics, and the police thought the newly founded club was a cloak for a Royalist coup!

In spite of this the firm of de Dion, Bouton et Cie, went from strength to strength. Although they were always prepared to build engines for anyone who wanted to race, they raced very little themselves. Most of the De Dions that raced pre-1914 were privately prepared by amateurs. Their success lay in producing reliable little cars that were within the reach of the humbler pockets. Almost up to the outbreak of the Kaiser war they were still turning out the immensely popular 6-h.p. single-cylinder light car, which sold in England for £157. About thirty various models of De Dion-Bouton were available at different times ranging from this to the 50-h.p. eight-cylinder, introduced in 1910, which, I am told, was not a very good car. When the Marquis de Dion died recently at a great age the newspapers gave him the most fitting epitaph, "Father of the French Motor Industry".

DELAGE

Louis Delage came up the hard way. He was born in the brandy town of Cognac of far from wealthy parents, worked hard for his diploma and got a job in the engineering section of Public Works. Soon he was able to realise his ambition to get into the motor industry, and was employed as a draughtsman at the Turgan Foy works, where he rose rapidly to head of the department. From here he moved to Peugeot where he gained valuable experience.

In 1905 he managed to scrape up £1400 and established, on his own, a small machine shop in Levallois-Perret, a Parisian suburb, even then the hub of the motor industry for the city. He and two other workmen started off by making parts for the long defunct motor-car "Helbe". Other contracts followed and soon they were doing well in bigger premises. In 1906 he was able to build a car on his own. This was a single-cylinder De Dion proprietary engine in a Delage chassis. There was a choice of 4½-h.p. and 9-h.p. engines, both singles. At the Paris Show this excellent little car was very well received, and the following year the works had eighty-five men on the payroll.

In 1908 Delage set the seal on his success by winning, with Guyot at the wheel, the Grand Prix des Voiturettes. That year he sold over 300 chassis and cars. In 1909 the single-cylinder cars were dropped in favour of four-cylinder cars. First of all the engines were of De Dion-Bouton and Ballot make, but soon he was building his own. His racing successes are recorded elsewhere in this book. Delage himself does not seem to have driven in races.

In 1912 he was employing 350 men and turning out well over 1000 cars a year. In 1913 René Thomas won at Indianapolis with a Delage. A very fine specimen of the 1911 Coupe de L'Auto racing car was recently in the possession of the late Lord Charnwood.

Between 1909 and 1914 they built 11 models, all with four cylinders except for a 15-h.p. six, introduced in 1911. These small Delage cars, with elegant coupé coachwork, were very popular with lady drivers in Edwardian times.

DELAHAYE

Delahaye were an old-established firm of agricultural-machinery makers who were making an occasional experimental motor-car in the very earliest days. The first one of which I have record was a 6-h.p. single-cylinder which Monsieur Delahaye drove in the "Paris–Marseilles–Paris" of 1896. Rather surprisingly it was fitted with pneumatic tyres. It acquitted itself very well. There may well have been earlier cars built by Delahaye.

The single-cylinder cars – 4½ h.p., belt drive, three speeds and reverse – continued for some years, but in about 1900 they were supplemented by a two-cylinder 9½-h.p. model. Two salient features of these rugged, popular little cars were the facts that they had far more of their mechanism enclosed than was customary at that date and cooling was effected by horizontal water tubes running the length of the chassis, which was tubular. Ignition was by trembler coil and battery.

In 1902 the company, which had moved its motor division to

Paris, had joined the pioneers of forward-mounted vertical engines. The cars so engined were a 15-h.p. two-cylinder and an 8-h.p. single, but for a few years longer they retained the horizontal engines in their commercial vehicles. In 1903 came a 12-h.p. two-cylinder and a 24-h.p. four-cylinder. These had detachable cylinder-heads and transmitted their power through a gearbox and final chain-drive. The gear lever was, as in many cars of its day, in a position recently rediscovered by the modern designer – horizontally under the steering wheel.

Delahaye were never short of ideas: their 1904 16/20-h.p. had a water-cooled silencer – the idea being that the rapidly contracting cooled gases would escape with less noise. Perhaps one day in the future some "bright boy" in Detroit or Coventry will "discover" that one too. In that year, also, they already had magneto ignition. Delahaye also designed the first of the American White petrol-driven cars.

In 1905, all the four-cylinder models had separate cylinders.

By 1907 they were producing three models of four cylinders and one 10-h.p. two-cylinder. The largest was 45 h.p. These good, sturdy Delahayes had attracted the attention of the French Government and in 1907 the first of a series of contracts for delivery vans, light cars and trucks was placed with them. But it was not till 1909 that they came on to the English market, handled by H. M. Hobson, who later founded the carburettor factory. In 1911 the first Delahaye six appeared. The block of the six, consisting of two sets of three cylinders, set at a 30° angle, was also cast in one. The next year there was another innovation, many years ahead of its time. The shackles were pressure-lubricated instead of by the dreary old Stauffer cap routine. In 1913 they pioneered hand adjustment for the brakes, and a year or two earlier they had begun to mount rubber under the leather clutch cone to make for sweeter engagement. In 1914 seven models were available, from the little 8-h.p. twin-cylinder runabout, selling in England at £210, to the 20/30 which sold for a very modest chassis price of £460. There is not space here to go into all the ideas, far ahead of their time, pioneered by Delahaye, but the next time anyone says, as so many people do, that every new development began at Cannstatt or Stuttgart-Untertürkheim, tell them to go and look up the specification of pre-1914 Delahaye cars.

F.I.A.T.

This story starts like a musical comedy, with two lighthearted young cavalry officers not taking life too seriously in the eighties of the last century. But the interest in engineering of Lieutenants Agnelli and Gropello was probably nowhere near as dilettante as they would have led you to believe. Aided by their faithful batman Scotto, a smith in civilian life, they were forever trying fresh experiments.

One of these was the resuscitation of a scrap Daimler stationary engine which they bought from a junk man. They got it going, but a home-made pulley flew to bits and knocked poor Scotto for six. So, for a time, further research into the mysteries of the internal combustion engine was suspended.

Italy came into the motor business rather late, but in about 1898 quite a few people, including Lanza, the Ceirano brothers, Storeo and a very young boy called Ettore Bugatti, were all building "one off" motor-cars. Agnelli bought a motor-tricycle from Storeo and later a cycle-car with which he won a race at Verona in 1899. Cavaliere Agnelli, Count Biscaretti di Ruffia and others met up with Count di Brichesario, who was backed by the Turin banker Deslix, and drew up an agreement in 1899 to start a motor works. Their signatures look like a page from the Almanac de Gotha. They started by taking over the Ceirano business which had been making "Welleyes" bicycles and a few "Welleyes" cycle-cars. This provided a nucleus of fifty skilled workmen, also the extremely useful Faccioli patents, and, indeed, Signor Faccioli himself, about the one engineer in Turin capable of designing a car in its entirety. Faccioli was also a pioneer of heavier-than-air flying machines. F.I.A.T. stands for "Fabrica Italiana Automobili Torino". I believe it was Faccioli who thought of this.

The first production car had a two-cylinder horizontal engine mounted at the back, and this, in 1900, won the Padua circuit race at an average speed of nearly 30 m.p.h.

Agnelli wanted a vertical engine in front but Facciolo vio-

178

lently opposed the idea, and eventually resigned rather than design a car of this nature. Luckily they got a brilliant engineer called Enrico to replace him, who in 1901 produced a car with a vertical four-cylinder engine in front, which the following year, had pressure lubrication. 1903 saw a carburettor on modern lines and irreversible steering gear. In 1904 they had friction-type shock absorbers and a multi-plate clutch. A 75-h.p. F.I.A.T. did well over 100 m.p.h. 1905 saw overhead valves and completely automatic carburation, and in 1906 came fully enclosed cardan-shaft transmission and compressed-air starting. In 1907 separate cylinders were replaced by monobloc; and the clutch and gearbox built integral with the engine. And so it went on, every year there were improvements, often well ahead of their time. Much of the credit for this must go to Enrico who was in charge of design till his health broke down from overwork. He was succeeded by Guido Fornaca who became General Manager and who was still in the same post in 1914.

All through this period the policy of the F.I.A.T. Company was to race whenever and wherever possible.

Among the assets that F.I.A.T. took over with the Ceirano "Welleyes" works were two boys, Vincenzo Lancia and Felice Nazarro, who were to lay down the fine tradition of F.I.A.T. racing drivers. Lancia was the son of a wealthy maker of tinned soup and Nazarro was the son of a small coal merchant. In spite of the difference in their upbringing and background both were superb mechanics and drivers.

Pre-1914, about eighteen models of touring F.I.A.T. were built. As far as England went, the little 12-h.p. cars were popular as runabouts, but the 20-h.p. models were even more so, for carrying landaulette or touring coachwork. A few wealthy sportsmen acquired the magnificent 70-h.p. car of 1907–8 and the even more magnificent "90" of 1909, 1910 and 1911. The engines of these, filling every scrap of the bonnet, with their beautiful finish and shaft-driven overhead camshaft, are a joy to behold. In fact, if you look at any F.I.A.T built in the golden age before the Kaiser war, you cannot help but agree that "Every Italian engineer is an artist at heart".

179

Quite one of the most remarkable motor engines ever produced was the opposed-piston Brillié, which continued, modified only in detail, from the late 1890s till the slump of 1929 caused the firm to close. Two cylinders had two pistons in each of them. The two bottom pistons were coupled by connecting-rods in the ordinary way to the crank-shaft. The upper pistons were joined by a crosshead and this, in turn, drove long connecting-rods coupled to the crank at 180° to that of the lower pistons. To quote their catalogue – "As the pistons draw apart, a charge of gas is drawn into the cylinder through the inlet valve. This charge is compressed by the pistons coming together again

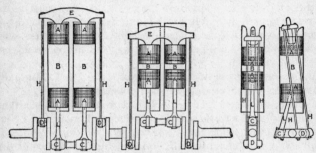

SECTION OF GOBRON-BRILLIE ENGINE, 1911

A–pistons; B–cylinders; C–bearing of lower connecting rods; D–bearings of return connecting rods; E–cross heads; H–return or long connecting rods; L–lower connecting rods

and then fired (electrically), the impulse being transmitted to the crankshaft by the lower and upper connecting rods. On the next upward stroke the exhaust gases are disposed of through the exhaust valve in the ordinary way". The four-cylinder Gobrons from 1903 had two of these two-cylinder blocks.

The first record I have of a Gobron-Brillié is the appearance of a beautifully finished wagonette with the engine mounted vertically, but at right angles to the chassis, under the driver's seat, at the Richmond Show of 1899. Worby Beaumont[1] de-

[1] *Motor Vehicles and Motors* by W. Worby Beaumont, Constable, 1902.

votes a whole chapter to its fascinating technicalities. It may well have been in production in France a year or two prior to this. In 1900 they brought out a 35-h.p. edition, and by 1902 the engine was in its normal position. One of these cars did well, both in the "Paris–Vienna", and Circuit des Ardennes, also winning prizes in major hill-climbs. Next year, 1903, they brought out their classic 110-h.p. car, which raced quite successfully in the hands of Rigolly in almost every race up to the Targa Florio and Kaiserpreis of 1907. Then the formula of 1908 excluded it, otherwise it might have gone on even longer.

They made all sorts of sizes of this opposed-piston engine, ranging from the little two-cylinder (90 mm. × 180 mm.) which was in production right up to 1913, to a six-cylinder 70/90, which was dropped in 1911 in favour of a four-cylinder 40/50, which sold in England in 1914 for £960 the chassis. The cars were handled over here by Turner of Piccadilly, and enjoyed limited popularity. Turner's catalogue shows the full range of cars. The open-bodied ones, especially the very sporting open-sided 40/60, are attractive, but those with closed coachwork are mostly very cumbersome. D. B. Tubbs of Crouch, Kent, has a very fine 30-h.p. touring car which goes splendidly.

Gobron-Brillié cars were not offered with Chapuis-Dornier engines as an alternative until after the 1914–18 war. Up to 1914 only the opposed-piston model was available. Apart from this remarkable principle, the design of the Gobron-Brillié car, both generally and in detail, could not have been more conventional.

HISPANO-SUIZA

In 1904 a brilliant young Swiss engineer, Marc Birkigt, backed by Spanish capital, set up a factory to build motor-cars in Barcelona. By 1906 they were making two hefty four-cylinder models, 100 mm. × 120 mm. and 130 mm. × 140 mm. To the best of my belief Birkigt never built a chain-drive car. The engines were conventional T-head design with their cylinder blocks cast in pairs. The next year, 1907, he added two six-cylinder cars to the two fours which continued in production.

Both sixes were "square" engines. One had bore and stroke 115 mm. × 115 mm., the other 130 mm. × 130 mm. In 1908 these were replaced by sixes, 100 mm. × 120 mm. and 130 mm. × 140 mm. The firm made its racing début in May 1909 in the Catalan Cup, a road race run near Barcelona. These cars were very long-stroked, 65 mm. × 140 mm., and though they still had T-heads, the engines were now monobloc. In this race they were well beaten by the big single-cylinder cars. In the Coupe des Voiturettes they did a little better, finishing fourth and fifth.

For the next year Birkigt increased the stroke to 200 mm. which gave him a capacity of 2½-litres. The team consisted of the veterans Zucarelli and Pilliverde, with a promising French youngster, Jean Chassagne. The cars were now fitted with Rudge Whitworth patent detachable wheels. With this type they won the Coupe des Voiturettes and it is this car, its bore increased to 80 mm., which was to be the prototype of the immortal "Alfonso" model. Built originally as a sports car for the young king, it sold in England for the very modest price of £400 for the chassis. From 1913 onwards they were very popular in this country. Lord Exmouth raced one of the first ones at Brooklands. They were good for over 70 m.p.h. and over 22 m.p.g.

In 1912 the Hispano-Suiza wore, for a very short time only, a rather smart V radiator. About this time Marc Birkigt was experimenting with superchargers, but it is believed that he never achieved sufficient success either to race with them or put them into production.

Hispano-Suiza as a firm did little racing after this, although a new overhead-valve racing engine was reputed to have been built but never used. A curious, narrow tandem-seated Hispano was raced in France in 1913, but the pictures of it look as if it was a private effort rather than a works-built car.

The Barcelona works built well over a dozen different model touring and sports cars between 1908 and 1914. These ranged between a 12-h.p. four-cylinder and a 60/75-h.p. six. Very few, if any, seem to have found their way to England, except for the "Alfonso XIII", of which quite a number were sold.

Several of these still exist in good condition.

In 1914 Birkigt was still building in Barcelona only and had not yet started the works at Bois Colombes, Paris.

HOTCHKISS

The origin of the Société Hotchkiss dates from the Franco-Prussian War of 1871. As ever, there were plenty of Americans in Paris, among them one extremely able engineer called Hotchkiss. He had a knowledge of the mass production of firearms and offered his services to Napoleon III. He was immediately given facilities and started to produce a light, quick-firing gun that was of invaluable service to the French. After the war was over, the Hotchkiss works at St. Denis continued to make artillery. It was only natural that, from the earliest days of the industry, their works, with capacity for machining in quantity to fine limits, was in great demand to make specific parts for motor manufacturers. About 1902 they built a complete prototype 50-h.p. car. This so impressed the great Henri Fournier – who, as well as being a leading race driver of his day, also conducted an automobile business – that he undertook, like Jellinek, to take the whole production for one year.

Thus encouraged, the Hotchkiss Company put in production a series of 18-h.p. and 35-h.p. cars. They also built a few 100-h.p. racing cars. Their racing cars were not a spectacular success. Even that great ace of the early days, Henri Fournier, could not do much with them. In fact, by 1907 they had virtually abandoned racing for it was not necessary to stimulate the sale of their cars which, on account of their sound design and really superb workmanship, were selling extremely well. Private entrants did, however, run mildly "souped up" Hotchkiss touring cars at Brooklands almost till the outbreak of the Kaiser war. They were also pioneers of the form of transmission where the torque of the driving shaft is taken by a stout tube surrounding it and anchored to the back axle. Further, it was a policy of their designer, from the very earliest models, to use ball bearings wherever possible.

As was customary, the number of models was increased and by 1912 five cars were available, ranging from a 12/16 to a

40/50 priced, extremely moderately for such a fine car, at £800. This range continued till 1914 with the exception of the 40/50 which was dropped in 1913 in favour of a 25/35 six-cylinder, priced at £650.

For any collector wishing to acquire a pre-1914 Hotchkiss, may I commend the country districts of France. These old cars virtually cannot be worn out, and only the fairly high petrol consumption keeps them off the road. But they can still be seen, buried under piles of odds and ends at the back of small country garages, for the Frenchman is far too frugal to throw such a useful tool away. One old man bricked up a 1912 Hotchkiss, belonging to him, in 1939. Not, he said, to keep it from the Germans, but from the French Army authorities who had attempted to seize it in 1914. He was going to make sure that they did not get it this time.

MERCEDES

Gottlieb Daimler and his close collaborator Wilhelm Maybach pooled their ideas and patents. So closely were they integrated

22/50-h.p., four-cylinder Mercedes Sport-Phaeton
with chain-drive, 1910

that even the late Dr. Siebertz, official historian of Mercedes-Benz, was unable to say who thought of what. But it does seem as if the credit for the first Mercedes car should go to Maybach, for when it was being developed from the original 24-h.p. "Phoenix Daimler", a rather heavy and dangerous car,

Daimler was a dying man. Emil Jellinek, banker/consul for Austria-Hungary, an immensely wealthy but not very successful amateur racing motorist, ordered the entire production for a year on condition that the new model was called after his daughter "Mercedes". He was an excitable little man who usually wore a panama hat and pince-nez, but he was also capable of a gesture in the grand manner. He enquired how many could be built in the first year and, on being told approximately thirty-five, wrote out one cheque to pay for the lot. He then proceeded to sell them all to his wealthy friends at a fine profit which showed that it was not entirely by luck that he was a successful banker.

It is not generally known that, before their historic appearance at Nice Motor Week, where they swept the board, the new Mercedes cars were entered for the Pau races and were a dismal failure. They broke almost everything it was possible to break.

From the Nice Motor Week of 1901 this firm never looked back, but one thing is manifest from their records. Whenever they ceased to race officially, as a firm, their sales and profits declined in no uncertain manner. Their highlights as far as racing and prestige were concerned were victories in the 1903 Gordon Bennett, the 1908 Grand Prix at Dieppe, and, of course, the dramatic line-ahead win in the 1914 French Grand Prix. They were one of the earliest makers to standardise high-tension magnetos as opposed to the earlier "low-tension" system where the make and break actually occurred inside the cylinder. They made an immense variety of models, ranging from the early "forties" and "sixties" to the *beau ideal* of Edwardian youth, the great "ninety" which remained in production right up to the Kaiser war. As well as the sports and racing cars, they made large quantities of touring cars, most beautifully built but, especially the small ones, not very inspiring performers. Just as the first Mercedes pioneered almost every feature that was to become standard practice for upwards of twenty years, so many innovations which we regard as the very latest practice appeared on pre-1914 Mercedes cars.

185

It is interesting to note that Mercedes took out a licence to manufacture Knight sleeve-valve engines about the same time as the Daimler Company in England. They built Knight-engined Mercedes cars up to 1914 and after the first war, and very good they were, even to the extent of having a limited success in racing.

It is a curious and fascinating sensation to drive a big sporting Edwardian Mercedes. Sitting high up, the wind whistles past your ears, all but drowning the deep slow beat of the engine and the rhythmic rattle of the driving chains. The heavy direct steering and board-hard springs give wonderful control. You step back for a moment into the heroic age when men raced from one European city to another and washed the thick grey dust out of their mouths with red champagne. For a brief moment, you are de Caters, you are Jenatzy, you are Eliot Zborowski.

MÉTALLURGIQUE

In 1898, the old-established locomotive and rolling-stock building firm of S. A. la Métallurgique started to build motorcars at their La Sambre works. In 1900 they opened a special automobile factory at Marchienne au Pont, and built twenty-five chassis in this year. There were two models – a two-cylinder, and a four-cylinder – both 76 mm. × 80 mm., both chain-drive and low-tension ignition. In 1902, shaft-drive took the place of chain. In 1903, Ernst Lehman took over the technical direction, and the cars were materially improved. In 1905 they brought out two new four-cylinder cars, 90 mm. × 140 mm. and 100 mm. × 150 mm. These cars were among the first to be fitted with high-tension magnetos. These cannot have been very reliable, as for several years afterwards buyers were given the choice of high- or low-tension ignition, and some cars had both.

About this time, Warwick Wright and Lord Brabazon established an agency to handle these cars in England. The great Bergmann Electric Works in Berlin took out a licence to build Métallurgique cars in Germany. They built quite a large quantity. In 1906 the flat radiator was replaced by a V-radiator.

Curiously enough, Bergmann engaged an Englishman, Sidney Smith, who had worked with S. F. Edge, as Chief Engineer on this project.

From 1907 to 1914 the parent company at Marchienne au Pont in Belgium produced a very wide variety of models, from a small two-cylinder to a big 80-h.p. four-cylinder car. They never made one with more than four cylinders. Electric lighting was available from 1913 onwards. The Métallurgique competed successfully in races, both in England and on the Continent, and was well-liked for its outstandingly fine workmanship, freedom from trouble and, with the larger models, its very sporting performance.

During the 1914—18 war, the Belgian Métallurgique works were stripped by the Germans of all machine tools, and though they were in production for some years after the war, they never regained the position of very considerable eminence which they held during the decade prior to 1914.

Such records as exist in this country are in the possession of the son of one of the concessionaires, Mr. Raymond K. Wright, 110 Park Hill, Clapham Park, London, S. W. 4. He is always very pleased to give all the help he can. He also knows where one or two of the old Métallurgique mechanics are working.

PANHARD ET LEVASSOR

This firm shares with Mercedes-Benz the honour of being the only two of the original competitors in the early motor races to be still racing, although of course Panhard no longer does it in a big way. That this firm built motor cars at all is largely due to the fact that Frenchwomen, however beautiful, are extremely practical and businesslike.

Daimler entrusted the handling of his French patent rights to an old friend, from gas-engine days, named Sarazin. A friend of Sarazin's, Emile Levassor, was making woodworking machinery in partnership with René Panhard at Ivry on the outskirts of Paris. Levassor was making, for Sarazin, a petrol engine under Daimler patents. Before it was finished, Sarazin died. Daimler, most impressed by the business ability of

Sarazin's widow, gave her the French rights together with a new Daimler engine as a prototype. Levassor married Madame Sarazin and went into the automobile business. In the year 1890 it was customary to put an engine into a horse-drawn carriage, or something very similar, usually over the rear-axle. Levassor designed the whole car as an automotive vehicle and, after two experimental vehicles, put the engine in front.

The story of how Levassor won the first motor race ever held, the "Paris–Bordeaux–Paris" of 1895, is an epic. The "Paris–Rouen", which took place a few months earlier, was a trial, not a race. Levassor was at the tiller of his solid-tyred car for forty-eight hours, forty-seven minutes. His relief driver overslept and failed to show up, so he drove right through himself, surely one of the greatest feats of endurance in the history of motoring. The engine of this car was a 4-h.p. narrow V-twin (80 mm. × 120 mm.) with automatic inlet valves and hot-tube ignition. Power was transmitted to the iron-shod wooden wheels by a double leather cone clutch and chains.

The "Paris–Marseilles–Paris" of the following year was won by a four-cylinder, 8-h.p. Panhard driven by Monsieur Mayade, but Levassor crashed. He did not appear hurt, and felt none the worse for his spill. But a year later he collapsed and died at his drawing-board from, it transpired, internal injuries he had received. The firm, however, continued to race and won a vast amount of major victories.

Shortly after Levassor's death, the company was re-formed with a capital of 5,000,000 francs, a very considerable sum in those days. The Chevalier Réné de Knyff became a director. From the dawn of motoring history the Panhard et Levassor was always extremely popular and well thought of among the better-class cars. The number of veteran motorists who started on Panhards must be legion. And, right up to 1939, I can remember elderly people who had started motoring at the turn of the century, on a Panhard, and who would not dream of having any other car. Unfortunately, there is not space here to describe the thirty or forty different models turned out before 1914. I can only generalise and say that as the popularity of their touring cars increased and also the cost of racing, Panhard et Levassor gradually stopped entering for competitions. But in spite of this they continued, almost up to the outbreak of the Kaiser war, to build 40-, 50-, and 60-h.p. touring cars, race-bred, with a very sporting performance, which were much sought after by wealthy young sportsmen. In 1911 they started to build 15-h.p. and 25-h.p. sleeve-valve cars under Knight patents.

PEUGEOT

Peugeot Frères were an old-established firm of manufacturing ironmongers. In fact, even today half the pepper and coffee mills you see in France have "Peugeot" written on them. Armand Peugeot was sent to England for his engineering and commercial training. In 1885 he started to make bicycles and as he already had established agents all over France selling his ironmongery, his bicycle venture soon proved a great success.

8-h.p. Peugeot, 1902

He had for some time been doing business with Panhard over woodworking machinery, and Levassor found it very easy to convince him that there was a future in self-propelled vehicles. Peugeot, however, did not agree with Levassor that an internal combustion engine was a suitable motive power, and reached an agreement with Léon Serpollet.

However, the first experimental Peugeot-Serpollet was not

good, and Armand Peugeot returned to Levassor, from whom he ordered engines. In 1890 he had a Peugeot-Levassor running quite satisfactorily, and soon afterwards they were in production with the narrow V-twin engine, but it was mounted horizontally instead of vertically as in the Panhard. Monsieur Peugeot then had the bright idea of entering his car in the "Paris–Brest" bicycle race. Needless to say, much trouble was encountered en route, but they arrived at their destination at an average speed of about 9½ m.p.h., so of course were beaten by all the cyclists!

From 1896 they built their own engines.

Armand Peugeot did not have, I suspect, any great love of racing, but he was an extremely shrewd man, and realised its commercial importance, so they raced steadily up to 1902. From 1906 onwards they raced with the immortal long-stroke voiturettes and later with the Henry-designed Grand Prix cars. Of the fifty-odd models which they turned out pre-1914 there is only space to mention that the famous Baby Peugeot was born as early as 1902, although it was not re-designed by Ettore Bugatti till nearly a decade later. In 1913 they brought out a 40/50-h.p. four-cylinder sleeve-valve car, selling at over a thousand pounds for the chassis. They never made a three-cylinder or an eight-cylinder car; only one-, two-, four- and six-cylinders.

Armand Peugeot himself died early in the 1914–18 war, having created a vast automobile firm which had, at a very early date, been separated from the manufacturing ironmongery business.

RENAULT

Louis Renault, the son of well-to-do Parisian business people was, by way of a hobby, a bit of a mechanic. On 1898, when he was twenty years old, he bought, for fun, a 1¾-h.p. De Dion tricycle. He did not like the tricycle, so he took the engine out and built a small car, with pneumatic tyres and wheel-steering, to put it in. The motor was in front, and the rear-axle had a differential and was driven by a cardan shaft. On this extremely up-to-date vehicle he had taken out a number of patents. He

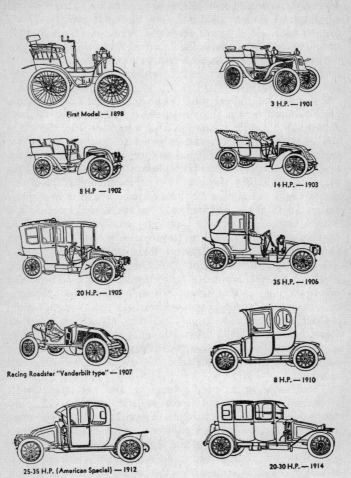

First Model — 1898

3 H.P — 1901

8 H.P — 1902

14 H.P. — 1903

20 H.P. — 1905

35 H.P. — 1906

Racing Roadster "Vanderbilt type" — 1907

8 H.P. — 1910

25-35 H.P. (American Special) — 1912

20-30 H.P. — 1914

Some representative Veteran and Edwardian Renaults

seriously considered selling both car and patents to one of the several firms already manufacturing, but his friends persuaded him to build a few like it for them. More and more friends of friends fell in love with the charming little car of advanced design, and soon it was obvious that it would be hopeless to attempt to supply the demand from his little amateur workshop at Billancourt.

So promising, indeed, were the prospects that Louis took his elder brother, Marcel, into partnership and started a factory. A third brother, Fernand, was also a partner. In 1899, they started to race. The Renault cars were small, light and reliable, so they often won races from the larger, more cumbersome and complex cars which went faster for a short time. As early as 1899 they made a $3\frac{1}{2}$-h.p. water-cooled De Dion-engined light car at least a couple of years ahead of its time in design. In 1900 the brothers built for the army manœuvres a mobile searchlight run off a dynamo worked by the engine, which also moved the car. In that year they sold 350 cars and had to double the capacity of their workshops.

Up to 1902 they used only De Dion engines. The brothers, go-ahead as ever, wanted a four-cylinder, and De Dions did not make one, at that time, with more than two cylinders. Georges Bouton's brother-in-law, Monsieur Viet, was, however, building four-cylinder engines, so they ordered a batch of these. Marcel won the "Paris–Vienna" in 1902 with a Viet-engined Renault, which resulted in far more orders than the Renaults could cope with, and the works were once more enlarged.

There were further racing successes until the tragic death of Marcel Renault in the "Paris–Madrid", after which, only naturally, the surviving brothers temporarily withdrew from racing. The following year only one racing car was built, to special order, for an American, Gould Brokaw. It was of 60 h.p. (160 mm. × 150 mm.) and ran in the Vanderbilt Cup of that year, but it went out on the second lap. The following year, 1905, the firm was racing once more in the Circuit D'Auvergne. Louis himself never drove again in a race.

In the meantime, touring-car production was increasing

rapidly and, because Louis Renault had, in 1899, patented direct-drive top gear, all French manufacturers had, for some time, to pay him a royalty!

Although the main production line of Renault handled light cars of 8- and 12-h.p., they were soon making a range of larger models. One in particular, the 20/30 four-cylinder (100 mm. × 140 mm.) found considerable favour in England.

These old pre-1914 Renaults have little to commend them in the way of silence, refinement or speed, but they were reliable and utterly incapable of wearing out. This probably accounts for the fact that, as late as 1914, the two-cylinder 9-h.p. Renault was selling for a chassis price of £234, when there were plenty of complete four-seater, four-cylinder cars selling at under £400.

In March, 1909, Fernand Renault died at the early age of forty-four. From then on, the huge works were run by Louis Renault and his widowed mother.

SERPOLLET OR GARDNER-SERPOLLET

Somebody ought to write a book about Léon Serpollet. As a person he is fascinating, and so are his motor-cars. If he had not died, quite young, in 1907, steam cars might have developed in a way that the conservative Stanley brothers never dreamed of.

As a boy, the son of a poor workman, he dreamed dreams and saw visions and, by the time he was only twenty-three, he had himself built, from bits of scrap metal and wood, a single-cylinder tricycle, coke-fired, with a "flash" boiler. This means that the water, passing through a heated "flash-coil", is instantaneously vaporised into steam.

It went very well indeed, but the only snag was that every time he took it out he had to go to the police station and obtain written permission. So he applied for, and was granted in 1889, the first driving licence ever issued in France. He had a tremendous sense of humour and was a most lively raconteur of the incredible troubles that beset him in his early efforts. He did the first really long journey ever accomplished, 461 kilometres, in fifteen days!

He made quite a number more solid-fuel vehicles and took part in many of the motor races. Constantly making improvements, he turned very early to paraffin burners. He was lucky enough to acquire an immensely wealthy American partner, Frank Gardner, who ungrudgingly financed his experimental work and introduced him to a number of wealthy clients, including the Prince of Wales, later King Edward VII. He also sold a couple of steamers to the Shah of Persia.

Continental Steamer: the 1902 P.T.L. Serpollet Double Phaeton

Long before other people had realised their importance, he was a pioneer of streamlining and lightness (his 1904 two-seater only weighed 17¼ cwt., full of water and paraffin.) By 1904 he was building a steam car that was as good as, or better than, most petrol-driven vehicles. He also built steam omnibuses. There are a number of obviously unsolicited testimonials in contemporary journals testifying to the beautiful workmanship and reliability of the Serpollet. By the time of his death, from consumption, his cars had only one draw-back – the difficulty of starting up the burner. And judging from contemporary accounts the experiments he was making would, had they been continued, have enabled the Serpollet steamer to start from cold as quickly as any petrol car.

At the end of the nineteenth century a Swiss hydro-electric engineer called Züst settled by the lakeside at Intra in Northern Italy. Here he built hydro-electric machinery and machine tools. He also had a works at Milan and a subsidiary works at Brescia. He was in production of cars in 1907. There seem to have been official agents in England, Züst Motors Ltd., and quite a number of these reputedly excellent cars came into this country up to 1914. They also figured in competitions in Europe, and in the Pekin–Paris race. Six models were made, from the 10/15 three-cylinder, some of which came to England as taxicabs, to the powerful 50/70 four-cylinder, costing £1000 for the chassis. Each cylinder was separately cast and the gearbox had its own oil pump.

The cars were made at the Brescia factory which was specially laid out for the job. Hence the name of Brixia-Züst. There is a description with photographs of the 24·8-h.p. model in *The Motor Car Journal* of 1st May 1909 (Number 434).

9

American Cars

I MUST beg the indulgence of my American friends for this chapter. I am afraid that some of it will be "old stuff" to them. However, so little is known in England about Veteran and Edwardian American cars, a fascinating subject, that I think a chapter should be included. I must apologise also for some large omissions. In a book of this kind meticulous accuracy is essential and I have, therefore, included nothing for which I do not have documentary evidence. So, of necessity, this chapter is in many ways incomplete.

I do not propose to attempt to say which was the first American car to be built, but assuming that, as I believe has been established in a court of law, the Selden was a fake, built many years after its reputed date of 1877, the position appears to be as follows. Taking petrol automobiles, not steam, it seems that, in 1892, Olds, Ford, Haynes and Duryea had all built cars that ran. Who was actually first is a matter of conjecture and it is impossible to hazard an opinion from the evidence available in this country. In America, however, the acrimonious controversy between Charles Duryea's relatives has brought to light a great deal of information which points to his being the first. But, in any case, any claim could be easily nullified by the discovery of fresh authentic documents – which is well within the bounds of possibility.

BUICK

Of all the advertising slogans coined by motor manufacturers in the last half-century probably the neatest is "When better cars are built, Buick will build them". This gigantic organisation grew from a very small firm that came into the market at a relatively late date, for it was not in production till late 1903, with a capital of less than $40,000.

David Buick was born in Scotland, where his rather unusual

196

44   A 1912 50-h.p. Simplex at the Smithsonian Institution,Washington, U.S.A.

45   Cadillac were still in production with the rear-engined, single-cylinder
       Runabout as late as 1908. Note the dummy bonnet

46 A relay race at Brooklands Track, Weybridge, Surrey, in 1909

47 The type 13, 1.3-litre Bugatti, driven by Ernest Friderich, finished second to a 10-litre F.I.A.T. in the 1911 Grand Prix

48 A fine sporting 60-h.p. Napier which, in 1912, travelled from London to John o'Groats and back, via Land's End, all in top gear

49 J. Higginson driving the first 30/98 Vauxhall, at Beacon hill-climb in July, 1914

50 Kenelm Lee Guinness, at Quarter Bridge, winning the 1914 Tourist Trophy Race on Sunbeam I

51 "K.L.G.", 1908

52   Opulence: 1910 "Silver Ghost" Rolls-Royce

53   Performance: 1914 Grand Prix Mercedes; Christian Lautenschlager
at the wheel

54, 55 Free-thought: *above* a 40-h.p. Lanchester touring car which had the engine alongside the driver's feet and *below* the 2-wheel, single track, 3-ton, 20-h.p. "gyroscopic car" built by Wolseley for Dr. Pierre Schilowsky in 1914. The inventor is sitting beside the driver

56 French Grand Prix, 1913: Champoiseau (5½-litre, four-cylinder Th. Schneider) sliding the right-angle corner at Moreuil. He finished seventh at 65.1 m.p.h.

name is quite common, in 1854. His parents emigrated to America while he was still an infant in arms. He started work, when he was fifteen years old, in the employ of a building supplies merchant. He eventually gained control of the business in which he was employed at the turn of the century. In 1903 he built a two-cylinder 22-h.p. car, a good, powerful slogger with overhead valves. The following year William Durant, a wealthy coachbuilder, financed the firm to the tune of $1,500,000, but in that year and the next, only two-cylinder 22-h.p. cars were built. In 1906 the Model D, a 30-h.p. four-cylinder, was made. It had a bore of 4¼ in. and a stroke of 4½ in. It sold for $2500.

In 1906 David Buick left the firm he had founded and was involved in a number of commercial enterprises, but he had no luck at all and died in a poorly paid and obscure clerical job.

The two-cylinder car continued to be built right up to 1911, but in 1908 a range of four-cylinder cars of various horse-powers and wheel-bases were on offer. The following year this range was somewhat reduced but the famous Model F, a 45-h.p. four-cylinder (5 in. × 5 in.) with a 122 in. wheelbase, was introduced. This fine car is much sought after by American collectors, but it does not appear to have found favour with the buying public – perhaps because of its price, $2750 – for its manufacture was not continued in 1910. From 1909 onward a very sporty 30-h.p. four-cylinder two-seater with a bolster tank was made. There were also cars with custom-built coachwork priced up to $4000.

A choice of four models, of four cylinders and two cylinders, continued until 1914 when the first of the famous six-cylinder cars was made. This was named "B 55" and rated at 48 h.p. with cylinders of 3¾-in. bore and 5-in. stroke and a wheelbase of 130 in. It sold well in spite of its rather high price of $3360.

Towards the end of the year 1908, the Buick Company had become part of "General Motors", a combine started by William Durant.

CADILLAC

I mean nothing irreverent when I say that the traditional

197

excellence of Cadillac cars bay be attributed to Henry M. Lelands's high Christian principles. A deeply devout man, he believed that in his work, as well as in his life, the very best was only just good enough.

"Uncle Henry" as he was always known to his friends and employees, started as a toolmaker with Brown and Sharpe. At the turn of the century the firm of machinists Leland and Falconer were making engines and other proprietary parts for Ransom Olds' curved-dash, tiller-steering Oldsmobile. Their engines were considered far superior to any others fitted by Olds. In 1902 Leland started the firm of Cadillac to make complete cars. Not many were turned out till 1903. One of the very first was the first Cadillac in England imported by the late F. S. Bennett. In 1953, this wonderful old single-cylinder Cadillac repeated the 1903 R.A.C. 1000-mile Trial under Veteran Car Club observation with Fred Bennett again at the wheel.

1912 American tourer: the four-cylinder Cadillac
fitted with an electric starter

This little 6½-h.p. car made a most successful début at Sun-rising Hill, ran well in the R.A.C. 1000-mile Trial and stole the thunder from the great Charles Jarrott by ascending Arthur's Seat, near Edinburgh – a feat accomplished by Jarrott's big Crossley.

It was three Cadillac cars which were dismantled, had all their parts "scrambled" and re-assembled, all under R.A.C. observation. A standardisation test of this type had never been seen before, or since, in England or America and Cadillacs were awarded the Dewar Trophy by the R.A.C. in 1908.

Cadillac were well-established by 1908 when they brought out their four-cylinder car. This had four separate cylinders, water-jacketed in copper.

General Motors, suffering at that time from acute financial growing pains, bought a majority holding in Cadillac. In fact, at the time of this, their latest purchase, it was touch and go whether they would make the grade. However, by a combination of the high standard of engineering laid down by "Uncle Henry" and his son, Wilfred Leland, and first-class commercial management by William Metzger, they were more than successful. It is interesting to record that the net profit to the makers on each Cadillac as it stood waiting to be collected by the agent was no more than $20!

Up to 1908 Cadillacs were ignited by wipe contact and trembler coil, then they changed to the Delco system. Closely associated with them was "Ket" Kettering, who was both an electrical genius and a brilliant fuel chemist, and who later became head of the General Motors Research Department.

He is responsible for the Delco electrical system fitted to the four-cylinder Cadillac in 1912, which was to be the first production car to be fitted with a self-starter as standard, and the starting handle removed. As a publicity stunt to popularise this novel feature, a wonderful little scale model car, equipped with electric lighting and starting, was built and shown all over Europe. It was bought by Queen Alexandra for the young Prince Olaf of Norway.

In 1913 Cadillac brought out the first V-8. This was the first of a long line of V-8 cars, built to the highest standards America knows. Anyone connected with Cadillac in those days will tell you that this accent on quality was always inspired by that lovable old engineer, "Uncle Henry", who was never seen without a micrometer in his hand.

CHADWICK

Most enthusiasts in Europe would like to know more about that fascinating car, the Chadwick. Certainly, little is known of it in this country, apart from the fact that it was the first car to use a supercharger. The firm was not represented in Europe, and there is no evidence that any Chadwick cars ever crossed the Atlantic.

In 1903, Lee Chadwick, then trading as the Searchmount Motor Company, built a four-cylinder car. At least we know he built the engine (4½-in. bore, 5-in. stroke); whether he built the rest of it is obscure. He sold the complete car to a steel tycoon for $4000, and on the proceeds started the Fairmount Engineering Company in Philadelphia, to build Chadwick cars. He began in quite a modest way in an old stable. They made four-cylinder cars of 24 h.p. and 40 h.p. A distinguishing and attractive feature of these engines was the spun copper water jacket. Another amusing but hardly necessary feature was a gauge glass, like that on a boiler, mounted on the extremely efficient Chadwick-built carburettor to show the level of the petrol therein!

Chadwick built about 40 four-cylinder cars and then in 1906 superseded them with the "Great Chadwick Six" which seems to have been about the best-finished car ever built in the U.S.A. Even at the high price of $5500 upwards, there was sufficient demand for these cars for Chadwick to remove to a larger factory at Pottstown, Pennsylvania. Certainly neither attention to detail nor expense were spared. Both the lubrication system and the cooling were probably better than anything else of that day, but production costs of these must have been very high. It also had dual ignition and everything necessary for silent running was ground to fine tolerances. The "Great Chadwick Six" had four speeds, and the most expensive nickel-chrome steel was used throughout on the transmission. The final chain-drive was encased in greasetight dustproof cases and tension could be adjusted from the outside.

Chadwick, ever in search of perfection, found coachbuilding firms so unsatisfactory that he started his own, the Fleetwood Body Company. This firm was later taken over by General Motors for its magnificent reputation for fine coachwork.

From 1908 onwards they turned out a six-cylinder sports car reputedly capable of 100 m.p.h. in standard trim and priced at $6500. These have a fine racing record over the ensuing three or four years.

About 1910 the firm ran into financial difficulties. Chadwick, like Bugatti and Royce, thought, with good reason, that if you want a job done absolutely to perfection, you must do it yourself. About this time, Chadwick built a lot of new machine shops to do more of his own machining. Prices were very high; a limousine sold at about $8000. Sales were not all satisfactory, largely, I suspect, because the sort of Americans who could afford a Chadwick bought European cars for their "snob-value".

This combination of overspent capital and wilting sales caused the firm to go into liquidation about 1914, just in time for someone else to make a fortune out of the manufacture of war material in the beautifully equipped Chadwick machine shops.

In all, about 235 of these splendid Chadwick cars were built. I think one may safely say that they rank with Stutz, Mercer and Simplex as the "dream car" of the American collector.

CUNNINGHAM

It is of interest that this legendary millionaire's car of the twenties was beginning to get under way in Edwardian times. Cunningham and Son of Rochester, New York, had been coachbuilders for a century or more. They had built automobile bodies and a few electric vehicles in the very early days but were all tooled up to produce a four-cylinder car in 1910. None of these are known to exist, and information about them is very scarce. All I can gather is that they were beautifully built and most surprisingly fast. Volney Lacey, designer of the "Great 8" went to Cunningham in 1910, so although this car was not in production till after 1914 it may well have existed in prototype form.

CROW-ELKHART AND ELCAR

I am dealing with these two cars together, because they were both made together in Elkhart, Indiana, not far from Indianapolis. Fred Pratt, owner of the local hardware store, went into production, in 1910, with the Elcar.

Martin Crow, at the age of twenty-four, went into business building automobiles in 1909. The Crow-Elkhart was quite successful, and by 1914 was keeping 500 men employed. When the Speedway opened, the Crow-Elkharts raced there. They never won anything, but nearly always finished well. Crow sold his factory just after the Kaiser war, because, the story goes, he had gotten bored with making automobiles and wanted to do something else.

DURYEA

Charles Duryea, like so many other American pioneers, was in the bicycle business. He built a gas buggy which was running in 1892. A number of these were built, and by 1895 production was of the order of about a dozen a year. In 1898 he brought out a very practical three-cylinder car which remained in production for about a decade. It had low-tension ignition, a planetary two-speed gear, and, fairly early on, acquired a carburettor with float chamber. The inlet valves were of the automatic type. It was rated at 10-h.p. and was available with four or three wheels, although not many in the latter category were built. Final drive was by chain. In its earlier days it did quite well in competitions, and gained considerable popularity in America. In fact, so considerable was the demand, that in 1904 the makers sought to popularise it in England. So, in conjuction with Henry Sturmey, a factory was established at Coventry to build Duryea cars under licence. These are believed to have been the first American cars to be built in England. This venture does not seem to have been a success, for after building three-cylinder cars, now increased in power to 15 h.p., and four-cylinder 18 h.p. cars till 1908, the Coventry factory closed down.

E.M.F., FLANDERS, MAXWELL AND CHALMERS

Walter Flanders is first heard of as head of a firm of precision machinists in Ohio. Ford ordered from him, in 1907, 1000 crankshafts. Flanders was ahead of scheduled delivery time, Ford himself was well behind, so Ford cabled Flanders offering him the job of Production Manager.

Flanders worked out his contract with Ford, and did not renew it. Instead, he started up the E.M.F. Company, building a four-cylinder light car with quite a hefty engine (102 mm. × 115 mm.), rated at 20/25-h.p. and selling at about $750. This was a successful venture, and he sold out to Studebaker.

Next, he started the Flanders Company. This was a not dissimilar car, tough, powerful, light and reasonably priced. It had a four-cylinder engine, 92-mm. bore, 96-mm. stroke, dual ignition, only two forward speeds (this was quite common in American cars of this date) and a leather-covered cone clutch. It was priced just under £200 for the complete car, and sold quite well in England. This company was rather under-capitalised and about 1912 was absorbed by Studebaker.

1912 also saw the big combine "United States Motors" crash in ruins. It was much on the lines of General Motors, and was founded by Benjamin Briscoe. It included Maxwell, Winton, Brush, Stoddard-Dayton and Thomas Flyer cars, also the Alden Samson truck and Gray marine-motors.

Flanders swept up the pieces of this ambitious but unsuccessful combine, and quite ruthlessly killed off every model in favour of a one-model Maxwell car, though Gray Marine carried on as a separate firm. The Maxwell was a typical Flanders job. A rugged 25-h.p. (21-h.p., R.A.C. rating) 92 mm. × 114 mm. monobloc side-valve engine was mounted on a typical high, light American chassis with a pressed-steel four-seater body. The complete car sold at £185 in England. In 1913 Maxwell cars raced at Indianapolis. About 1914 Flanders acquired the Chalmers Motor Company and added it to Maxwell. I shall always remember the later slogan of this company as a masterpiece of neat under-statement. "The Maxwell is a good car", even better perhaps is their earliest slogan "Perfectly Simple and Simply Perfect".

FORD

As surely as Daimler and Benz were the first men to make the automobile a practical proposition, so Ford was the first to bring it within the reach of the lower-income groups. Born in 1863 into the large family of a well-to-do farmer near Detroit, from the earliest days he had a passion for all things mechanical. On leaving school in 1879, in spite of his father's efforts to keep him on the land, he served an apprenticeship with the Michigan Railway Car Company, some six miles away from his home, earning $2.50 a week. Like Benz, he repaired watches to bring himself in a little of extra money. For some years he worked as a machinist and later as chief engineer of several firms and during 1891–3, reputedly, built a gas-buggy which ran. In this year he was building small, experimental engines in the kitchen while working as chief engineer of the Edison Company.

He then started to build a car, concentrating on lightness (it was supposed to weigh 500 lb. dry). The design for the engine, curiously, came out of a magazine, and was considerably modified by him and a helper called Cato. He had now transferred his activities from the kitchen to a small brick shed at the back of his house. When the car was finished, one wall, as in the case of Richard Shuttleworth's aeroplane, had to be knocked down to get it out. His landlord, instead of being furious about the damaged brickwork, was most intrigued with the light car, and became thoroughly co-operative. The car itself ran for quite a distance at the end of May 1896. Quite soon it was running a dozen miles or more at a time. Two years later a syndicate of friends advanced him $2000 to further his experimental work and with a view to putting the results into production. He worked at night, keeping on his job with Edison by day. By midsummer 1899 he had produced a perfectly practical vehicle weighing 875 lbs., far lighter than most other cars of its day. At this point his employers offered him a better job on condition that he gave up his experiments with motor-cars. Ford's answer was to resign and take over the job of superintendent of the newly formed Detroit Automobile Company. Ford was already campaigning to build cars down to a new price level. His directors disagreed and they built twenty or thirty rather undistinguished flat-twin automobiles with governed engines, and then, through lack of sales, the company went out of business.

Ford now turned his attention to racing. He did not take

another job but he and his wife, Clara, lived frugally so that he could devote his whole time to building a racing car. To the great surprise of the crowd, this completely unknown car and driver beat, in their very first race, the redoubtable 70-h.p. Winton, driven by the great Winton himself, then at the top of his form. Nothing succeeds like success and a number of backers, some of them from the defunct Detroit Automobile Company, were only too anxious to establish the Ford Motor Company in November 1901. Ford, who never liked driving racing cars, was glad to get back to production. But he was still very keen to build racing cars for other people to drive. He and a wealthy racing cyclist, Tom Cooper, built two, "The Arrow" and "999", the latter being called after a famous American express. A youthful racing cyclist, Barney Oldfield, even then chewing the inevitable black cigar, was enlisted as a driver. The fact that he had never driven a car before did not prevent him from winning his first race.

This racing success brought in more moneyed backers and soon Ford was able to realise his dream of attacking the cheap market. It was a cut-throat business. Winton and Haynes-Apperson were selling models at $1000 and Pope and Olds marketed small cars as cheap as $650. Ford started off with a small shop and contracted out a good deal of work. Dodge Brothers, who had very large and well-equipped machine shops, did the lion's share of the work. In spite of the additional capital that had been put up, Ford was still terribly short of money for an enterprise of such magnitude. Net cost was $384 for parts, assembly $20, incidentals $150. Total net cost $554, so it could be sold retail at only a slightly higher cost than the Olds.

The first model to go into production was the Model A, a flat-twin 8-h.p., capable of about 30 m.p.h. In the first nine and a half months he sold 650 of them. As early as 1903 Ford was sending round mechanics to instruct the dealers, most of whom were completely ignorant, in the service of these cars.

Such was the motoring boom in 1904 that the Ford Company started to build more elaborate and costly cars. There was a heavier, faster four-cylinder touring car, the Model B, selling at $2000. In January a Ford, basically a Model B, driven by Huff on cinders thrown on a rough ice track, took the world's record over the flying mile in 39 seconds.

The Model A was superseded by a much-improved version, Model C, selling at $800, and a de luxe version, called Model F, also a flat twin, sold at $1000. Ford was not pleased at his co-directors' decision to go into a higher price-range, but it paid immediate dividends. In the first year they sold 1700 cars.

In 1905 came the historic Selden case. It will be remembered that Selden had, in the very earliest days of motoring, taken out patents which he claimed precluded anyone from building a motor-car without a licence from, and royalties to, him. He cunningly held his hand for many years till the automobile industry was well under way. *Prima facie,* he had a very good case, but through the stubborn obstinacy of Ford, his partner Couzens and others who fought back, he was beaten in the end. In that year, also, they moved into a new factory ten times as large as the earlier one, and Ford, who was in charge of production, laid down what was to be the forerunner of the modern assembly line.

Here they started to build the Model N, planned as an improvement on the Models C and F. They also jumped with both feet into the luxury market, constructing the magnificent and costly Model K, Ford, who was much more interested in outselling the $650 Olds model, had furious rows with his co-directors. Very soon he proved to be right. The Model N, a front-engined, vertical four-cylinder sold in astronomical numbers. The Model K, a luxurious six-cylinder whose transmission was nowhere near up to the power of the engine, could not have sold much worse. They had to bribe the agents with 20 per cent discount instead of 10 per cent on the Model N, and force them to take into stock one K for a given number of Ns. It weighed a ton and retailed at $2800. Built by the Dodge Brothers, it was only assembled in the Ford works. Five of these cars are in existence. Elmer Bemis, of Vermont, has two, and the Ford Company one.

The Model N was supplemented by de luxe versions of the

same car: Models R and S. It was impossible to keep the price of the Models Ns down to the initial $500 which had caused such a stir, and in 1907 they had risen to $600, but were selling like hot cakes at that price. They appeared in England in that year, selling at the competitive price of £125 for the complete car. At least one of these is preserved in England in the Science Museum in South Kensington. The costlier models soon faded out, but the Model N had put Ford right on top of the world and already, in 1907, Henry Ford was thinking up the historic Model T.

When, in 1908, the first Model T appeared it was priced relatively high at $825 upwards. But the orders poured in so fast that they could not be dealt with and Ford had hurriedly to make plans for a yearly output of not less than 25,000. The early Model T was full of teething troubles and there was plenty of competition (e.g. the 14-h.p. Maxwell at $825). In spite of this they went on selling faster than they could be built. All Models S, R and K remaining in stock were knocked out for what they would fetch. In 1911 a factory was established at Trafford Park in England. This was the first foreign assembly plant. To cope with the demand a huge new plant was built at Highland Park, where most parts for car and body could be made. What was then probably the most modern assembly line in the world was in action by 1911.

As efficiency in production increased, costs came down. The standard Model T cost at first, in 1908, $850 ($25 more than the roadster), but its price had dropped to $490 by 1914 and sold in England at £135. Henry Ford had proved himself as a master of mass production, and then, on New Year's Day, 1914, he introduced a minimum daily wage of $5 for all employees. He was beginning to try his hand as a social reformer.

MERCER

American readers need not bother with this little bit. They know it all already. Just as the faithful Bugattisti bind their children's feet so that they may not grow too big for the pedals Ettore designed, so each New England child is taught to lisp the type numbers and other Mercer data, almost before he can say "Ma-Ma".

The Mercer car was built by Mr. C. G. Roebling, of the firm John A. Roebling Sons Co. from 1911 onwards in Trenton, New Jersey. They were designed prior to 1914 by Finley R. Potter. At the period with which we are concerned, although the company never grew very big, a small specialised labour force was turning out about two or three cars a week, all of the type 35 – that is to say, with the T-headed engine. There were alternative engines, basically the same, but one had a slightly larger bore than the other, and they yielded 58 h.p. and 32·4 h.p. respectively at 1700 r.p.m. The cylinders were cast in pairs. Very curiously, the early "Raceabouts" and "Runabouts" had only three speeds, while the touring cars had four. A few were equipped with electro-magnetic transmissions. All

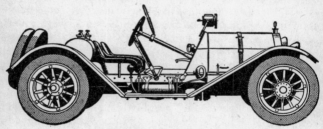

Type 35J Mercer "Raceabout", 1914

cars made prior to 1914 are of the basic "type 35" except for one or two of a special racing model, like the one driven by Caleb Bragg in the 1913 Indianapolis race. The "Runabout" was what we would call a roadster, with a windscreen and excellent weather equipment. The "Raceabout" is too well known to need detailed description – just two bucket seats, no screen or scuttle (some had a monocle screen fitted as extra), a big bolster tank and several spare wheels.

A Mercer, like a Rolls-Royce, is quite easily dated. The type numbers are shown on page 209.

At a time when most American manufacturers were cutting each other's throats to build down to a price, Mercers were

1911	R	Runabout	1913	E	Limousine
	R	Raceabout		G	4-seater tourer
1912	A	4-seater tourer		H	5-seater tourer
	B	5-seater tourer		J	Raceabout
	C	Raceabout		K	Runabout
	D	Runabout	1914	H	4-seater tourer
	E	Limousine		M	5-pass. tourer
	F	Special racing model, first to fit detachable wire wheels		J	(above 1590) Raceabout
				O	Runabout

much more interested in turning out a first-class engineering job. They had forty-four steel-to-steel clutch-plates running in oil, and the road springs were best quality chrome vanadium. Each car was sent out with a guarantee that it would cover a mile in 51 seconds, and it was the proud boast of the company that no customer ever brought one back complaining that it did not. Under these circumstances it is not surprising that prices were relatively high. The cheapest Mercer ever sold was the 1911 "Runabout" at $2250, and prices rose to $4000 for the Limousine. The factory offered delivery in the following standard colours – azure blue, white stripe, black upholstery; canary-yellow, black stripe, black upholstery; battleship grey, grey stripe, black upholstery; Mercer red, English vermilion striping, black upholstery.

From the moment the "Raceabout" appeared, amateurs were winning races everywhere, just as they did with the Bugatti with the same type number, "35", a couple of decades later. There was always a long waiting list for the "Raceabout", but it was nothing like the waiting list there will be if ever one more type 35 "Raceabout" is unearthed, however poor its condition may be. Their slogan, coined over thirty years ago, is just as true today, "The most talked-of car in America", for the fortunate owner of a "Raceabout" rarely talks about anything else.

PACKARD

There is a certain similarity between Henry Royce and the Packard brothers, William D. and S. W. Packard were also manufacturers of electrical equipment. They also bought a car and felt that, from an engineering point of view, it could be immeasurably improved upon. In 1898 they called upon Mr. Winton, who had built their car, and made, in the friendliest spirit, helpful and constructive suggestions. Winton was not impressed and told them that if they thought they could build a better car, they could try. Within a year, on the 19th November 1899, the first Packard car drove up to Mr. Winton's workshop. It was infinitely better than anything he had ever built and even, *mirabile dictu,* had automatic advance and retard! This first Packard was called the "Ohio" car.

Like Royce, the brothers were perfectionists; only the very best was good enough for them. For several years they built excellent automobiles of the tiller-steered buckboard type. In 1902 Henry B. Joy, wealthy socialite, bought a controlling interest in the company. Then they were joined by Charles Schmidt, an engineer from the Mors factory, at that time one of the leading firms in Europe. From then on, until 1914 and even later, all their cars had sporting tendencies and showed definite signs of the best European influnces. In 1909 they were building a 30-h.p. four-cylinder car, with honeycomb radiator, which looked more European than American. Packard originated the clip-secured "quick lift" radiator cap, with which they replaced the conventional screw-on cap in 1912.

By 1912 they were turning out a fine range of four cars. There were two "fours" of 25 and 40 h.p. and two "sixes" of 38 and 48 h.p. The last was a magnificent sporting motor-car fitted with acetylene lighting, and was well into the Rolls-Royce price range. It cost over £1000 in this country.

A little later they dropped the four-cylinder cars and concentrated on the two six-cylinder models. I don't think that the famous twin-six quite comes within the compass of this book as, although it may have been under development in 1914, it did not appear till the following year.

PEERLESS

Packard, Pierce-Arrow, and Peerless were the famous "Three Ps" of the American motoring world in the days before World War I. The order in which the names were stated depend ed upon the allegiance of the person speaking, but there was no question but that here were three of the most honoured names in the great luxury cars, and each had a life-span of thirty years or more. The make about which the least is known, of these three, is the Peerless.

Late in 1900, the Peerless Manufacturing Company of Cleveland, Ohio, introduced a line of "motorettes" built under the De Dion patents. These were built with the engine mounted on a rigid tubular frame, in the rear, as with most "motorettes". The De Dion 2¾-h.p. engine was used with air-cooled head. A French-type cork-float vaporiser and jump-spark ignition, with batteries and coil, were used. Two main body styles were provided, the two-passenger version being called type B and weighing only 460 lb. Type C carried two extra passengers in a front seat that folded into a box dash when not in use. The Peerless "motorettes" were spoken of in the contemporary press as having excellent appearance and finish.

For the 1902 season the "motorettes" were dropped and three sizes of conventional touring cars were offered, with vertical engines of Peerless' own make, under a sloping bonnet in the front of the car. These cars had a number of very advanced features, and some peculiarities, most worthy of note. One single-cylinder, and two sizes of double-cylinder, engines were offered with horsepowers of 8, 12 and 16 respectively.

Since these cars set the Peerless pattern in many ways, it is interesting to go over them in detail. The engine fed power to the wheels through a three-speed and reverse transmission (planetary in the 8-h.p. and progressive in the others), down a drive shaft to a bevel-gear rear-axle. The axle was so constructed with block-type universals that the rear wheels were pitched in the same manner as the front, giving the car an interesting appearance from behind. This feature was continued until the end of the 1915 Peerless 48-Six. The frame was made of channel iron, the first American car so constructed, although Autocar was just a bit earlier with shaft-drive. Steering was non-reversible (honestly) and the wheel had a fat-man feature in the form of a sleeve which could be pushed down so that the

211

wheel might hinge out of the way for easy entrance and exit from the driver's seat. Two braking systems were provided; foot-brake on shaft and hand on rear-wheels, as per European practice. Ignition was by jump spark with a patented mechanical vibrator as well as the conventional buzzer coils and dry batteries. The 8-h.p. model would do 32 m.p.h., it was claimed.

The next year, the two-cylinder model remained with improvements. The tubular radiator was replaced by a cross-flow model peculiar to Peerless, with brass tanks above and below. Circulation was still by water pump, positively driven instead of by friction from the flywheel. The standard body was a rear-entrance tonneau with 32-in. wheels, but a racer was offered with 36-in. wheels. This racer had some little success at meets at Narraganset and other places, because the car was really fairly fast and could approach 45 or 50 m.p.h. (the touring version could reach about 42 m.p.h.). Probably the main complaint was vibration. When idling, the front wheels of the car could actually leave the ground at times. This vibration was due largely to the fact that the crankshaft was so designed that both pistons always travelled in the same direction simultaneously, thereby receiving no counterbalancing effect as with the more conventional type in which one piston is on the up-stroke while the other is on the down. As always, the finish and good looks of the cars were among the selling points of the Peerless.

The company was not, however, content to make the smaller cars only, and during 1903 they introduced three separate series of four-cylinder cars in 24-, 35- and even 60-h.p. sizes. These engines were T-head in design with cylinders cast individually, or in pairs. The 24-h.p. was the most popular model, the "60" being very rare indeed, and frequently not mentioned in circulars and descriptions.

With these four-cylinder models, the company advanced rapidly, introducing a number of other innovations to the American market. They claimed to be the first to offer side-entrance tonneau bodies, the time being in 1904. Peerless was also the first car to provide closed formal bodies, although these were on special order. It is a fact that a Peerless limousine completed the 1904 A.A.A. Tour to St. Louis – one of the most arduous of all cross-country events, since the roads were pre-historic.

The 1904 engines were T-head with the cylinders cast singly on the "24" and in pairs on the "35". The next year, all engines were overhead-valve types, cast in pairs, similar to the "Green Dragon" racer which had become quite famous. The 60-h.p. car was advertised as having an exactly similar engine to the racer, even to dimensions. Barney Oldfield had made 9 miles in 8 minutes 04 seconds to break all closed track records for that time in October of 1904 at Los Angeles, along with a number of other exhibition runs.

By 1906, however, the "Green Dragon" was forgotten and Peerless settled down to making T-head engines cast in pairs, a practice they continued through to the end of the famous model "48-Six" in 1915. Oddly enough, they returned also to the cross-flow radiator, which, as any Peerless owner can testify, it is impossible to keep from clogging up. The radiator was a continuous tube, winding back and forth, with tanks on the top and bottom. The strange camber of the rear wheels was continued also, as was the governor which started with the little two-cylinder car. Both hand- and foot-brakes worked on the rear drums, and the frame was given a drop to lower the car.

The next four years saw only gradual improvement on this fundamentally sound design. In 1907, French storage batteries supplemented the dry cells for ignition, and the following year an Eismann low-tension magneto was provided to operate through the coils as well. In 1910, the more reliable Bosch dual system was employed instead. This system remained until the end of the "48-Six". Other minor developments were a new and quieter herringbone water pump in 1909, along with improved universal, joints in the clutch and rear axles. These latter were now like an internal and external gear just fitting over each other.

The four-cylinder Peerless cars performed well in the Glidden Tours of 1906, 1907 and 1908. One-, two- and three-car entries, respectively, won a medal and certificate, two certificates and three certificates for perfect scores in the three years. Other competitive efforts were a 1000-mile non-stop record of twenty-five hours plus at Brighton Beach in May of 1905 with the 24-h.p. car, and a climb up Mt. Washington in 29 mins. 6·8 secs. in a 60-h.p. car in July 1904, defeating all American petrol-driven cars.

A six-cylinder car, of the same bore and stroke as the four, was added in 1908 and the success of this car indicated the direction of progress. By 1912, three sixes headed the Peerless line, although two fours had been retained. The original "50" had become the "60" and with the "48" and a "38", produced a situation remarkably like Pierce-Arrow, their closest competitor. These cars were powerful and were kept up to date with electric lighting in 1912 and electric starting by 1913, the system used being the Gray & Davis six-volt, two-unit arrangement. This system was less complicated and more reliable than the much-vaunted Kettering-Delco technique. These cars were, as with all Peerless cars, well built and superbly finished. They represented the best type of heavy American motor car.

Unfortunately, Peerless had a change of heart in 1915, bringing out a cheap "four" and "six", unworthy of the name. The year after, both of these and the old reliable "48-Six" were killed off and a 33·8-h.p. V-8 was produced. This marked the end of an era as far as Peerless was concerned, although they struggled along until the depression in 1932. It is rumoured that the factory now produces a rather superior variety of ale.

PIERCE-ARROW

In America motoring circles over a considerable span of years the name Pierce-Arrow meant approximately what Rolls-Royce means in England. True, there was much greater competiton in the fine-car field in the United States, but the Pierce was definitely recognised as the number one car of those who held appearance, quality and dignity to be the most-sought-after attributes in a motor-car. Other fine cars had more distinguished racing records, were more expensive, and were less common, but none surpassed the Pierce in quiet elegance and good manners on the road.

214

As with many makers, the George N. Pierce Company drifted into the manufacture of automobiles from making other metal products. Since its founding in 1883, it had made hardware speciality items such as bird cages. When the bicycle became popular, in the last part of the century, Pierce entered that field with success. From there to the automobile was an easy step, especially since the first car was almost a quadricycle, called the "Motorette", patterned after the French practice. The first of these, which appeared in 1901, carried a 2¾-h.p. De Dion single-cylinder engine on the rear axle. The power was increased very shortly to 3½ h.p. for 1902, and finally to 5 h.p. in 1903. Pierce tooled up to produce its own engines, and replaced the De Dions with an exactly similar motor with the name Pierce on the crankcase of the last two sizes mentioned.

The "Motorette" was not unlike other machines of the same type in that it was underpowered, awkward to drive had no reverse and was hardly a good touring car. However, it prospered, and Pierce sent two of the first models on an endurance run from New York to Buffalo, a most difficult trip of 391 miles, in September of 1911. Both cars completed the ordeal with almost perfect scores, defeating many larger machines – an amazing performance considering the very bad roads and the fact that theirs was the lowest-powered model.

Success with the "Motorette" led to the introduction of the larger Stanhope model with a 6-h.p. motor, later increased to 8 h.p. This machine was built in the same plan, but with an extra seat in the sloping front which could be opened for carrying two additional people. This model won a Gold Medal on the New York to Pittsburg Endurance Test in October 1903.

The real need was for a conventional car, of course, and in the latter part of 1903 Pierce introduced a car that was to give its name to the entire line – the "Arrow" Motor Car. This car was powered by a two-cylinder De Dion engine mounted upright behind a radiator under a bonnet at the front of the car. In 1903, the model had a sloping bonnet with a coil-type radiator hung low in front, while, in 1904, the model had a ceilular radiator and straight bonnet. The body was a rear-entrance tonneau with divided front seat. The only remnant of the bicycle days was the tubular frame. Steering was by wheel, with the lever for the progressive transmission on the steering column.

This gear-change position was one of the key features of the "Great Arrow" car, which appeared in 1904 and which made Pierce famous. The first "Great Arrow" was a 24-28-h.p. four-cylinder car on the same plan as the "Arrow". Incidentally, those names were the *makes* of the cars; the name Pierce-Arrow was not used officially until 1909, although it gradually came into common usage. In 1904, the Stanhope model "Motorette", the "Arrow", and the "Great Arrow" comprised the entire line.

The next year, Pierce concentrated on the "Great Arrow" offering three engine sizes: 24–28, 28–32 and 40 h.p. Side-entrance bodies were standard and, later in the year, a line of three closed styles by J. M. Quinby became available. Still available into 1906, however, was the Stanhope with only minor changes, to supply the old light-car market which was being abandoned.

In 1906 the smallest "Great Arrow" was dropped and the other cars refined, in line with experience gained as the result of the 1905 Glidden Tour through New England. This 1000-mile run from New York to Mount Washington in New Hampshire and back, was won by the Pierce "Great Arrow" car with 996 points out of a possible 1000. Pierce never entered their cars in races, concentrating on reliability runs as the best test for a reliable touring car. In this programme they were eminently successful, winning more Glidden Tours than all other makes combined.

1907 saw the continuation of the two four-cylinder cars, now called the "30" and "45", with the addition of a six-cylinder car with a bore of 5 in. similar to that of the "45". This model was first called the "65" then "60", and finally the "66", which continued with changes to 1918. In 1908, a 40-h.p. six was produced for that year only. This engine had separately cast cylinders. Also in 1908, the 28–32 h.p. four-cylinder car was dropped, thus leaving three models to end the "Great Arrow" era; the first great period in Pierce history.

The year 1909 was a major turning point in the company's ideas and organisation. The name Pierce "Great Arrow" was simplified to Pierce-Arrow, and later on the company name was changed to the Pierce-Arrow Motor Co. Three new models were introduced with cylinders cast in pairs: the "24", the "36", and the "48". The first two, a four and a six respectively, had the same bore and stroke; the last was to become the most popular Pierce-Arrow car. The four-cylinder 45-h.p., now called the "40", and the 60-h.p. models were continued, giving a total of five models; more than they offered in any other year.

The two-cylinder per block design proved superior and was incorporated in the "66" the following year, when the "40" was dropped. Also abandoned at this time was the little "24", one of the nicest of all Pierce cars, which had only been built in runabout and town-car types. This left three basic models which were maintained through 1918: the "36" (later "38") the "48", and the lordly "66", giving Pierce a medium-sized car, a large car, and an enormous one.

The success of these three models was such that they were only changed in minor respects from time to time. In 1912, they began to be identified as Series I and so on through to Series 4, instead of yearly changes. Since these series changed at odd times, it is sometimes difficult to spot the exact year of a given car, even with the aid of the Pierce "Rescension Table".

Important developments by year would be: Oil tank in engine with gravity feed to bearings, 1903 to 1911; front doors, optional in 1911, standard thereafter; electric headlight in the bumpers, the famous Pierce-Arrow hallmark, started with Series 2 in 1913; right-hand drive retained longer than any American car except the Springfield Rolls-Royce until 1920; steering wheel gear-change until 1908, after which a selective transmission replaced the progressive and was operated by a conventional gear lever.

The six-cylinder Pierce-Arrow cars from 1909 onwards distinguished themselves as delightful cars to drive. Steering was

217

finger-light, even with the "66"; gear-changing was slow but very easy, even if double de-clutching was required; but the main feature was the smoothness and quiet of the engine. All these features were in contrast with some competing cars like the "Locomobile", which were hard to drive. All in all, the Pierce-Arrow was probably the most pleasing American touring- or town-car of its time.

POPE

Colonel Pope built up one of the very earliest and largest cycle businesses in the U.S.A. By 1894 he had built an experimental horseless carriage. Soon afterwards he was in production. There were a vast number of varieties: Pope-Hartford, Pope-Toledo, Pope-Tribune and Pope-Waverley, which was electrically propelled. These were built at different Pope bicycle factories. Like Winton, although not as early, these cars appeared in European competitions. A Pope-Toledo driven by Lytle ran third in the 1904 Vanderbilt Cup, but they were not so well placed in 1905. The cheapest car they ever built was a 6-h.p. runabout in 1904, costing $650. They were mostly good-quality cars in the medium-to-high price-range. A very few may have come to England and one, a Pope-Tribune, beautifully preserved, competed in 1954 for the first time in the London – Brighton run. The Pope Tribune was designed by Gilbert Loomis, who used to make the Loomis car.

There was also the Pope-Robinson, built at Hyde Park, Massachusetts from 1902 to 1904, which was already in production as the Robinson car before the Pope empire took it over. Rather unusually, for an American maker, instead of contracting-out they made practically every component of the cars themselves.

Quite a number of Popes, especially the rugged four-cylinder Pope-Hartford, still exist in America, and are highly prized by collectors. It is a little difficult to see why such an apparently flourishing motor firm stopped manufacturing in 1907.

STUDEBAKER

Over a hundred years ago, young Studebaker joined the gold

rush. Like so many others, he lost what little money he had, and got no gold. So he came home to South Bend, Indiana, and started up a smithy and wheelbarrow-building shop with his brother. Henry and Clem Studebaker prospered and soon they were making wagons as well. What really put them on their feet was the American Civil War, for the Northern Army ordered 100 wagons from them. Two more brothers, Peter and Jacob, joined the firm. Soon they were making buggies as well as wagons, so they were well aware of the possibilities of horseless buggies when they arrived. They did not cautiously market one till 1902, although experimental models may have been built. This was an electrically propelled light car, of very conservative lines. It was virtually a buggy without the shafts. It gave 40 miles on one battery charge, and the advertisements laid great stress on the efficiency of its brakes, together with strength of its construction. They continued to build electric runabouts for another six or seven years alongside the petrol cars. Their first internal-combustion-engined car was built in 1904. It was a sturdy, conventional two-cylinder 16-h.p. four-wheeler with tonneau, selling at the rather high price of $1600. There is little doubt that agencies, built up all over the country for Studebaker wagons and horse-drawn vehicles, coupled with their excellent reputation in that field, were responsible for their initial prosperity. In 1906 they brought out a four-cylinder 28-h.p. car, priced at $3000 with, as would be expected, fine quality coachwork.

Coachwork was, indeed, always their strong suit and, in 1908, they came out with the Studebaker "Suburban".

This was not dissimilar to the coachwork patented in England, a few years earlier, by Commander Windham. The two front seats were a fixture with, behind them, a flat platform equipped with fixing devices. On to this a variety of half-bodies could be lowered, transforming it at will. Alternatively, it could be left absolutely bare and used as a two-seater with luggage platform.

A couple of years later the firm of Studebaker, who were growing fast, took over the distribution of the 40-h.p. Garford, a very good car indeed, made in Elyria, Ohio. This they marketed as the Studebaker-Garford. Soon they absorbed the Garford firm, founded in 1907, and the car became the highly successful Studebaker "40" which remained in production for a number of years. They also bought, from William Flanders, the E.M.F. Company and, in 1912, came out with the Studebaker E.M.F. "30" which they marketed at $1190, not an unreasonable price for this car. In 1913 a 27·2-h.p. car was offered, priced at $1290 for a seven-seater tourer.

Studebaker, like most American makers, were early in the field with electric starters and lights. The headlights gave a wretchedly poor light and I was always told that this was because of bye-laws in certain states of the U.S.A., severely limiting the candle-power.

By 1914, the Studebaker Company had grown up into a vast concern, occupying many acres of ground, with their own railway sidings. Up to this time, too, subsidiary companies within the organisation continued to make horse-drawn vehicles, harness and saddlery.

STUTZ

It was the practice among the majority of American manufacturers to "contract out" the greater part of their components. Harry Stutz supplied ready-built back axles, and, in fact, I believe one could buy complete transmission units from him. He made them for Lennox, Henderson, Marion, American Undersling and others. I have been told that he had some interest in the last two of these firms.

In 1911, he built a racing car purely to test his back axles under more gruelling conditions than normal.

This test car put up the most astonishing performance. In its very first race, the Indianapolis "500", it averaged nearly 70 m.p.h. and gave no trouble at all. It was second at Fairmont Park and second in the Santa Monica road race, averaging 72·5 m.p.h. over the 150-mile course. No wonder Stutz adopted the slogan. "The car that made good in a day".

So Stutz took over the Ideal Motor Company (founded 1903), and went into production. The first cars, and very successful they were, used a four-cylinder Wisconsin engine (4¼-in. bore,

220

5¼-in. stroke). By 1913 Stutz was building his own four- and six-cylinder engines. The first six-cylinder engines were also Wisconsin.

In 1913 and 1914 both "fours" and "sixes" could be had with 120-in. wheelbase and "Bearcat" or "Roadster" bodies, or 130 in. with touring or closed coachwork. The cheapest model was the four-cylinder "Bearcat" at $2000 and the most expensive was a very curvaceous coupé on the six-cylinder long chassis at nearly $3000.

In 1914 they built six special racing cars, with a four-cylinder overhead-camshaft engine, ball-bearing crankshaft, turning at up to 2950 r.p.m. They gave the Peugeots a very good run for their money. One of these is still owned by its original driver, Earl Cooper.

The duels between Stutz and Mercer were heroic spectacles that no one who witnessed them ever forgot.

WINTON

Alexander Winton, of Cleveland, Ohio, developed a practical petrol-driven motor vehicle in his bicycle factory, and considered it saleable in 1896.

A second car was started, but Winton then decided that financial assistance would be necessary for suitably establishing a business. He accordingly drove his first car from Cleveland to New York, a distance of 800 miles, where aid was obtained from Irving D. Metcalf, of Oberlin College, and the carriage was soon ready for the market. The first production car was sold to Robert Allison, of Port Carbon, Pennsylvania, on 24th March 1898, and this is claimed to be the first "over-the-counter" sale on record by an American manufacturer. The price was $1000, and by the end of the year twenty-five cars had been built and sold.

Winton made nearly all the parts for his early vehicles, and for these he obtained many patents, although he collected no royalties. These patents included a steering gear with wheel control, and a braking system having internal and external bands operating on the same drum.

An early buyer was J. W. Packard, of Warren, Ohio, and

221

Jesse L. French, who later, with George P. Dorris, also built his own motor-car.

The earlier cars built by Mr. Winton utilized a single-cylinder engine under the seat, controlled by regulating the inlet valve, speed varying from 200 to 700 r.p.m. In 1898, the cars incorporated a wick drip oiling system, a laminated wood frame, and "the largest flywheel ever built into an automobile".

Sales made direct from the factory, without agents, were Winton's practice at this time, and Charles B. Shanks, prominent in newspaper work, was engaged as advertising manager. A spectacular endurance run of sixty-four days, from New York to San Fransisco, here contributed to the Winton prestige, and perusal of early motor magazines leaves one with the impression that the firm's advertising space exceeded by far the volume of all contemporaries combined. Production, too, was organised along modern lines, with large and economical manufacturing of lots of identical machines.

The employment of air-actuated mechanisms was a fetish with Alexander Winton. Air was utilised to limit inlet valve travel by means of a pneumatic piston under a foot pedal. The Winton air starter made an early appearance and, *circa* 1911, a delegation of Winton salesmen journeyed to Cleveland to dissuade Winton from continuing it, but without success.

Early in 1900, the Winton Motor Carriage Co. was sued by the Electric Vehicle Co., controllers of the Selden Patent, with the result that Winton ultimately took out a licence under this well-known patent.

The 1900 Winton "Special", forerunner of several hundred other "Specials" to be lanched by the motor industry, was powered by a 9-h.p. engine, had 4-in. tyres on the driving wheels and, for a consideration of $1000, endowed the buyer with a "French" body which included a tool box in place of the conventional dash-board of the buggy era. The Surrey, at $1500, had a top speed of 15 m.p.h. Winton was, at this time, producing two cars per day.

As a result of wagers made with James Gordon Bennett and others, Winton built a racing car for the classic contest bearing the publisher's name. The choice of improperly devel-

222

oped tyres and rims for this car resulted in an ignominious failure, which brought undeserved aspersion upon an otherwise reliable mechanism. Winton derived satisfaction from driving his early racing creations himself, and competed in the first years of the new century with Henry Ford, Barney Oldfield, and other worthy opponents. The first edition of the famed Winton "Bullet" was constructed in 1901, with four vertical cylinders, Bullet No. 2 following with eight in a row, and No. 3 with four horizontal cylinders. The two latter went to Ireland for the Gordon Bennett race, with results mentioned above. It is worth recording that a two-cylinder Winton racer of 1901 achieved 40 m.p.h. with a modest rated power output.

The "tonneau" arrived in 1902, employing the motor of the two-cylinder racer, which boasted 15 h.p., jump-spark ignition, with generator and storage battery, steel-girder-type frame, semi-elliptic springs, and wooden wheels, which combined to lend a progressive appearance to the company's design for this period.

For 1903, power was increased to 20 h.p., and the price to $2500. Listed as extra equipment were headlamps, canopy "top" and glass windscreen, but these items were made standard for the next year without an increase in price. This was typical of Winton the salesman, who took care to manufacture a more attractive product each year, to lure the buyer on.

The Winton line for 1905 continued this practice, offering three four-cylinder cars with side-entrance bodies. Limousine coachwork was optional on the two larger chassis. Clutch and throttle were combined in one pedal, and vertical-tandem springs provided reserve leaves to supplement the normal springing under heavy load conditions.

One chassis only, the Model K, was offered for 1906. Features included plywood bodies and fenders, raw-hide timing gears, a vertically split crankcase, and air control for engine speed and fuel feed. A maximum pressure of 200 lb. per square inch could be built up in the event of obstruction in the air lines, which again marked the designer's pneumatic obsession, and even the Hill lubricator was air-operated. The two-speed transmission employed individual clutches, and the trend toward high-powered roadsters was economically met by mounting a two-seater body on the standard chassis.

Model XIV succeeded Model K in 1907, and a new Model M had a four-speed transmission with direct drive in third speed, and an overdrive fourth. A reserve petrol supply was introduced for this year, and pressed-steel bumpers, presumably employing advanced die practice, were also adopted. In July of this year, the first of the famous Winton "sixes" appeared and, with this Model XVI, the company staked its entire future on the "six", withdrawing its four-cylinder models. Pair-cast cylinders were continued, with the vertically parted crankcase with hand holes for bearing adjustment. A clutch with 65 steel discs ran in oil, and drove a gearbox of three ratios, 3·7, 3·2 and 2·6 to 1. An Eismann magneto and Winton's own carburettor, with a Hancock oiler, served the new engine.

The 48-h.p. Model XVI grew up to 60-h.p. in 1909, but employed a four-speed drive. This was a $4500 car, with 130-in. wheelbase and a bore and stroke of 5 in.

For 1910 a return was made to 48-h.p. and the wheelbase was lengthened, with a frame narrowed forward to reduce turning radius. Air starting was continued, with four speeds, while "Torpedo" and "Gunboat" bodies abetted weather protection and sales talk.

Honeycomb radiators, I-beam front axles, and electric side-lights marked Winton progress for 1911, and ¾ elliptic springs made for softer riding in 1912. In 1914, left-hand drive and electric headlights were added, with a Kellogg four-cylinder air-pump for starting and tyre inflation. In this year, a prize for economy of maintenance was offered by Winton. The winner drove 24,362 miles without repair expense.

The stubborn exponent of air-for-everything reluctantly bowed to public indignation in 1915, when Winton belatedly offered his customers their choice of air- or electric-starting. The company advertised that the buyer could write his own guarantee, but history does not record the result of this novel policy on customer relations.

224

10

Motoring Clothing

IN the very earliest days of motoring, people just put on anything old and warm that could be easily shed when pushing the car home or trotting alongside it as, relieved of the passenger's weight, it chugged uphill. Motoring dress, as such, does not really start till the late 1890s when cars were able to maintain a steady 20 m.p.h. or an even greater speed.

This is more or less the critical speed when the wind, unbroken of course by any windscreen, began to pierce in grim earnest the thickest of normal clothes. The first period of motoring dress can be said, roughly, to run from about 1896 for a decade, and its form was determined largely by the need to keep out the weather. My mother's Vulcan car, bought new in 1906, had a windscreen fitted as an extra at the cost of £6 or £7. Her dashing, chain-driven Mors, purchased a little over a year later, had a windscreen as a standard fitting. It is a little obscure why the industry was so long in adopting this very necessary fitment. One can only suppose that automobilists took some time to overcome their natural dread of flying plate-glass, razor sharp and heavy, in the event of a screen being shattered by a sideslip or collision.

In France, during the last five years of the century, a goatskin coat with the fur outside became almost a standard uniform. This garment, loose and roomy but buttoning up tight at the neck, had the advantage that the rain did not cling to it and it dried very quickly. It also kept out the coldest winds. Old timers, who have tried both, claim that the racoon skin coats so popular in America and Canada, and in use for many years previously in open sleighs, did the same job even better than the goatskin. The English, however, with their inherent dislike of anything that made them at all conspicuous, never took kindly to these practical garments, although, in any case, the really keen automobilist was hardened to the ribald chaff of butcher boys and horsebus conductors. My father's motoring coat of thick dark-blue melton cloth lined with fur – an incredibly heavy garment – is much more typical of what was generally worn in England.

For the same reason the hard peaked cap, *de rigueur* on the Continent, never became popular in England. The Englishman, feeling this form of headgear made him conspicuous, preferred to motor in a cloth cap or a bowler hat. The latter, as many of us have found, makes an excellent impromptu crash helmet. The peaked cap is not, as might well appear, a development of the yachting cap, but the German Korps cap. Germans did and still do wear their caps as badges of their various University Societies. That embattled old diehard Karl Benz was still motoring in his in the 1930s. In England, from about 1902 onwards, the peaked cap became rapidly the badge of office of the motor servant, as the chauffeur was often called at that time. Justices of the Peace and army officers of high rank soon transferred the traditional eighteenth-century cockades from the top hats of their coachmen to the peaked caps of their chauffeurs.

Englishmen in pre-windscreen days had frequent recourse to suits, usually of the Norfolk variety, lined with leather. These proved uncomfortable, so a perforated chamois lining was adapted, which by all accounts was a great success. The "Poncho", which was nothing more or less than the cyclist's cape of today made of much heavier real rubber, enjoyed a considerable vogue for wet-weather driving. Keeping the legs warm was a great problem, for there was little dashboard protection, and front doors, if any, were merely token ones 8 or 10 in. high. Old timers say that the only possible solution was a heavy fur-lined rug wrapped tightly round the legs. This was, of course, perfectly adequate for the passenger, who could even use a foot muff, but the unfortunate driver had either to brave an icy draught on his feet and ankles or risk an accident by a rug getting entangled in the pedals. During the opening years of the twentieth century a variety of curiously devised garments were marketed to attempt to solve this problem. By 1904 motoring was beginning to be recognised as, if not a logical means of transport, an amusing if slightly lunatic sport. Early in February a correspondent in *The Queen*, writes:

"A very slight experience of motoring bears the fact forcibly home that the primary aim is to exclude every draught, which becomes, travelling at even the prescribed rate (20 m.p.h.), a veritable hurricane. This is met by such details as shields, cuffs, adjustable collars, pockets deftly disposed to preclude the entrance of both rain and air, and lastly a generosity of skirt."

1904 was an interesting year sartorially for women motorists, because, although windscreens were still a rarity, the dress houses were beginning to vie with each other to make women look as attractive as possible under the circumstances. Now fashion began to take a hand. Such reigning beauties as Lily Langtry, Mrs. Cornwallis-West, her sister the Princess of Pless, and Lady Randolph Churchill began to be seen in motor-cars. Notes were taken, lightning sketches made and such houses as Derry and Toms, Peter Robinson and even the exclusive Worth each produced their version based on what was worn in the *haute monde*. Most particularly the veil, which had replaced the hideous mackintosh hoods of the very early women motorists, now ceased to be something merely to hold the hat on. It became a form of *haute couture*.

As far as I can make out the "steel bound and whalebone lined" corsetry, so necessary to produce the Edwardian tight waist, was not worn in the motor-car until a good deal later. It is a little hard to realise that Edwardian women not only went as well as men in the hunting field but indulged in tough sports like ice hockey and ski-racing. For these they were excused the fantastic carapaces demanded by fashion, and also for motoring, though doubtless at journey's end the lady's maid, sent ahead by train, was waiting to lace them tightly in again.

Long hair, universally worn, was quite a problem. A few of the very earliest lady motorists, like the redoubtable Madame du Gast, who so chivalrously threw away her chances in the

Paris–Madrid race to render first aid to an injured rival, favoured the Korps cap. But all women who have written about this form of headgear claim that it was both heavy and uncomfortable. A few wore something like a French Kepi, popular for cycling in the early nineties. My mother in 1896 frankly and unashamedly went to her brother's hatter in Jermyn Street and bought a man's cap. This was secured by the most murderous hatpins and was in use for almost a decade till the advent of windscreens. As soon as these arrived fashion started to take a hand. In 1905 the fashion plates show hats like monstrous straw muffins adorned with a chiffon scarf. In the following year they become like plates of exotic flowers and by 1907 they have become aviaries, peopled by stuffed birds, their wings beautifully arranged in crescent formation. These, of course, had to be kept in place by a veil and pins. The tam-o'-shanter, which had first appeared for motoring wear about 1904, was extremely popular for open cars. Indeed it continued to be so until it was ousted by the beret in the twenties.

All this called for much greater protection, and the landaulette was beginning to enjoy its long vogue. In an era of rigid class distinction, this form of coachwork was not without its drawbacks, for we read in a fashion journal of 1906:

"It cannot be called graceful, the abrupt square form that rises suddenly behind the front seats being decidedly ugly. Nor can the owner of such a vehicle take the wheel himself without looking as if he were a coachman."

But as another fashion writer recorded in the same year:

"The motoring woman is becoming daily more fastidious and exacting."

This may well be far more than a contributory cause to the terrific improvement in weather protection that took place between the years 1906 and 1908. Lovely Princess Ena of Battenberg married young King Alfonso of Spain and the interest in what she wore for motoring, of which needless to say

228

the young couple did a great deal, was no less than that in the clothes of a film star of today. Daimler, Lanchester and Rolls-Royce led the way, for their customers, many of whom were wealthy women, had coachwork built to their own requirements. Some of these may seem heavy and cumbersome to us today, but they were designed for hats bearing great erections of feathers and stuffed birds. These were followed by "toques" which, no less curious to our eyes, took up just as much headroom. And, of course, it must be remembered that up till 1914 any occasion of the slightest social importance, even leaving a visiting card, called for a tall silk hat. I can remember one *grande dame* saying, "Young man, as far as I am concerned a sports car is any car which you cannot *walk through* with your hat on."

Soon the less expensive builders were all making high roomy closed coachwork and by 1910 even touring cars had little worse weather protection than they have today. So the manufacture of special motoring clothes was on the wane, and though, even in 1914, we see all sorts of specialities in the way of motoring garments offered to the public, the need for them had really begun to decline some five of six years earlier.

Index

The numerals in **heavy type** refer to the *Plate Numbers* of illustrations

230

232

234

237

238

239

241

242